CHARLOTTESVILLE
UNTOLD

CHARLOTTESVILLE UNTOLD

INSIDE UNITE THE RIGHT

ANNE WILSON SMITH

SHOTWELL PUBLISHING
COLUMBIA · So. CAR.
EST. 2015

For rights and permissions, please contact:

SHOTWELL PUBLISHING, LLC

PO Box 2592

Columbia, SC 29202

www.shotwellpublishing.com | info@shotwellpublishing.com

ISBN: 9781947660588

FIRST EDITION

1 2 3 4 5 6 7 8 9 10

For nothing is hidden that will not be made manifest, nor is anything secret that will not be known and come to light.

Luke 8:17

CONTENTS

INTRODUCTION

THOUGH BORN IN CHAPEL HILL, N.C., most of my life has been lived in Columbia, the capital of South Carolina. The history is a palpable part of the city. I walked the statehouse grounds many, many times while working downtown during my twenties. There is a marker indicating where the original statehouse stood before it was burned by Sherman's Army, and six bronze stars mark the location of the indentations left by his cannonballs. Statues of George Washington, Wade Hampton, Strom Thurmond, and a bevy of other memorials for events and people from the Revolutionary War to the present decorate the grounds.

For most of my memory, the Confederate Flag had a presence on the state house grounds. For many years it flew atop the bronze dome. Placed in 1962, it was a subject of never--ending controversy, sparking debate in the legislature, demonstrations both for and against on the grounds, and continuous coverage on the local news. In 2000, the flag was moved from its position atop the statehouse to a memorial display on the grounds. An African-American History Monument was erected on a different part of the grounds. Many residents hoped the construction of these memorials would be a permanent compromise, ending the debate once and for all. Afterwards, the controversy was largely quelled, and though some dissatisfied parties still complained about the presence of the flag, it became mostly a back-burner issue for many years.

On June 17, 2015, everything changed. Dylann Roof shot 9 people attending a Bible study at Emanuel African Methodist

Episcopal Church in Charleston, S.C., reportedly with the hopes of beginning a race war. Shortly thereafter, pictures of Roof holding a Confederate flag began to circulate on the internet. Instantly, without apparent reflection or explanation, the flag itself became the center of the national firestorm of outrage. Nonsensically, because of the Confederate Memorial at the Statehouse, the national media placed collective blame on the residents of South Carolina for the shocking and unprovoked murders for which one man alone was responsible.

Then-Governor Nikki Haley at first made some meek, perfunctory remarks attempting to distance the flag from the controversy. After, one suspects, direction from Republican Party Headquarters, Haley pivoted to the need to remove the flag to promote "healing." Haley, born to immigrant parents as Nimrata Rhandawa, had risen to power as part of the "Tea Party" wave of Republican populism, becoming Governor in 2011. South Carolinians had embraced her as one of their own, and elevated her, twice, to the highest office in the state. In an almost unfathomable act of betrayal, Haley turned on the people who had elected her by allowing their cherished and honorable past to be defined by a deranged mass murderer.

That Haley believed that "healing" could be accomplished by purging the historical symbols of the founding population of her state is wildly misguided at best. Haley could have shown courage, statesmanship, and gravitas, promoting the healing she claimed to value using honest leadership to build bridges and foster understanding amongst Black and White South Carolinians, all of whom were grieving the murder of innocent churchgoers. Instead, she chose a path of short-sighted, self-serving opportunism, paving the way for what was to become a nationwide cultural purge that left a wake of destruction from which the country will never recover. She remains seemingly oblivious to the gravity of her transgression or the immensity of its impact.

The flag came down from the Confederate monument on the statehouse grounds on July 10, 2015.

The "healing" which Haley had opportunistically promoted in the form of cultural genocide against her supporters was the first of many dominoes to fall in the following months and years. Emboldened, the enemies of American history and culture began seeking to destroy all emblems of Western heritage throughout the nation. Though the march of destruction began by targeting Confederate history, it predictably continued to encompass every symbol of Western culture within reach.

Though survey after survey showed that the majority of the public favored retaining historic monuments, there was little practical resistance to the destruction. Some small groups meekly protested that historical preservation was "heritage not hate," and some injunctions against removal were quietly filed with mixed success. For a while, there seemed to be nobody willing to provide bold and effective resistance.

In 2017, the continuing tide of destruction threatened another historic city: Charlottesville, Virginia. When local officials moved to have the state of Robert E Lee removed from Lee Park, Jason Kessler took decisive action by planning a large rally in protest. He explained his reason for making a stand about the statue and the rally in support of White civil rights. "We have a serious double-standard in this community and across this country where people who are White are not allowed to advocate for their own interests. . .this is a country that was founded by European Americans. It's absolutely unacceptable for these liberals to have displacement-level policies which are removing indigenous people from the country."

I learned that the rally in support of the statue of Robert E. Lee, perhaps the most admirable man our country has ever produced, was planned for August 12th in Charlottesville Virginia. I knew nobody in Charlottesville, and had not been to Virginia since a childhood trip to Monticello and Colonial Williamsburg. However, I resolved to go - in fact, felt I must - as a show of support for the first real demonstration of resistance to the cultural cleansing of the symbols of my forebears.

The massive rally was to feature a large number of "Alt-Right" speakers and groups. I had been following some of these "new right" personalities online in the season preceding the upset election of Donald Trump. This was an invigorating time for political junkies such as myself. For the first time in my lifetime, there seemed to be real promise of a breakup of the calcified political system held in gridlock by two parties, neither of which had any real interest in protecting the welfare of the average American voter. The flurry of new upstart movements and personalities made for an exciting time in politics - ideas outside the usual realm of discourse were being seriously volleyed around in the public square. New pundits and potential movement leaders were emerging. Early in the new movement, most of us following these "Alt-Right" personalities were still sifting through a hodge-podge of new ideas and waking up to potential new methods of activism. I relished the opportunity to hear from some of these people first hand, though there were many with whom I expected to disagree. As a free-speech enthusiast, I enjoy challenging myself by hearing differing points of view. Like the Founding Fathers, I believe that there is no need for anyone who loves the truth to fear a hearty, free exchange of ideas.

I made the trek from Columbia to Charlottesville alone, planning to meet up with some online acquaintances to attend the Unite the Right rally. I was expecting something not unlike the many flag rallies I had witnessed over the years in Columbia, though on a larger scale. I did not anticipate that I would watch events unfold which would have a lasting national impact. I could not have known how catastrophically misrepresented this event would be to the American public. I was appalled as I watched the day's events solidified into a tragic and utterly false narrative that was to become cemented into the national psyche. I did not anticipate that I would be present at a defining event in modern American history, so noteworthy that from that time forward, every utterance of the city name will evoke its memory. "Charlottesville."

In the years since "Charlottesville" changed the life of thousands of people including myself, I have concluded that I have a duty to put forth the truth as I know it to be. I do not relish controversy or the spotlight. But if I am to honor the forebears I claim to revere, I can do no less.

AUTHOR'S NOTES

ONE OF THE MOST POWERFUL and insidious techniques used by leftists is the weaponization of language: the subversion of the true meaning of words and the application of false descriptions to things or people. These manipulation tactics are meant to convey counter-factual ideas and create a distortion of reality in the public mind.

A common example today is the application of the usually inaccurate and emotionally loaded, inflammatory terms like "White Nationalist," "White Supremacist," or, the new n-word, "Nazi" to anyone who opposes leftist extremism - including non-White conservatives, run-of-the-mill Republicans, or sometimes even moderate Democrats. These words are meant to smear, marginalize and dehumanize their subjects while instilling revulsion and fear towards them in society at large. Being designated as a "Nazi" in the modern age can make a person ostracized, unemployable, and even place them in physical danger. From the day of August 12, 2017, the smear of Unite the Right attendees as "Nazis" and "White Supremacists" by virtually every major media outlet planted a lie firmly in the public mind which has made it almost impossible for the attendees to receive a fair hearing of their side of the story, or, in most cases, any kind of hearing at all.

There were a wide variety of groups and individuals attending Unite the Right, and people who may accurately be described as Nazis, White Nationalists, and White Supremacists were indeed among them. However, in most cases those terms are used with no regard for accuracy, but as a political weapon. I will not apply ideological labels to anyone except those they have used to describe themselves. Furthermore, I am not going to tiptoe around the idiosyncratic "gender identity" preferences of individuals who refuse to honor the much more reasonable and factually sound preference of others to be referred to as "not Nazis."

Similarly, I am aware that the cultural cleansers who seized the Charlottesville government have renamed the park that was the location of Unite the Right. At the time of the Unite the Right rally, it was known as "Emancipation Park." (It has since been renamed to "Market Street Park"). However, the place has historically been known as Lee Park. It was built on land donated in 1917 by Charlottesville financier Paul Goodloe McIntire, who also commissioned the statue of Robert E. Lee which was presented to the city in 1924. Since the park is thought of by defenders of American history, including the Unite the Right attendees, as Lee Park, that is how I am going to refer to it.

There were numerous groups and political ideologies represented by attendees of Unite the Right. My particular interest, and my focus for this book, will be on Southern heritage supporters and Southern Nationalists. Though briefly addressed by President Trump in his remarks on the day of the rally, then quickly dismissed by almost everyone, there were quite a few people, "very fine people," who showed up to oppose removal of the Robert E. Lee statue. These people have been accused by the most powerful voices in the nation of being "Nazis" and every other despicable name imaginable. None of them have ever been offered a platform to refute these accusations and tell their own version of the story. Not only are these individuals personally harmed by being prevented from addressing the accusations against them, but the nation as a whole has suffered under a tragic false impression of the events of August 12, 2017.

The claims of the unheard Unite the Right organizers and attendees have been largely vindicated by the Heaphy Report, an extensive independent government review commissioned by the City of Charlottesville and performed by Hunton & Williams, the law firm of former Federal Prosecutor Timothy Heaphy. In a healthy media environment, the results of this review would have been headline news all over the country. However, in service of the preferred narrative of powerful political actors, the important information documented by Heaphy has also been ignored. I hope to make a small contribution to correcting the tragically erroneous record and vindicating the unjustly maligned attendees in this book.

Throughout the text, the term "counter-protesters" is used as a generic term for left-wing demonstrators and groups, while "protesters" is used to describe rally attendees and right-wing groups.

Part One:

Before Unite The Right:
The Players and the Stage

CHAPTER 1

INCEPTION

"We're not gonna live in intimidation and fear."

BORN IN CHARLOTTESVILLE, VIRGINIA in 1983, Jason Kessler was raised in a Republican, centrist home. Though his family moved to New Mexico when he was a child, he maintained a connection to Charlottesville through regular visits with his grandparents for Christmas, where the family would attend church and the occasional UVA game. He returned to the city as a young adult where he graduated from the University of Virginia in 2009. By then, it was clear that the city of his childhood had changed dramatically, with pronounced leftward shift in the culture.

A writer by vocation, by 2016 Kessler had penned two novels, a screenplay, and a collection of poetry. He was beginning to get his footing writing as a reporter for some right-leaning news outlets like GotNews.com and the Daily Caller. Meanwhile, he was paying the bills by working at a variety of odd jobs, sometimes scouring Craigslist for whatever opportunities he could find. Talking to a client at one of these Craigslist jobs, he learned about the antics of Charlottesville City Council Vice Mayor Wes Bellamy. Bellamy presented himself as a champion of equality and anti-racism, but his social media posts revealed an open hatred of White people.

The following are a sample of his tweets. (Misspellings in original).

"Lol funniest thing about being down south is seeing little White men and the look on their faces when they have to look up to you." @ViceMayorWesB Tweet 10/13/2012

"So sad seeing these beanpole body White women in these sundresses smh..." @ViceMayorWesB 10/18/2012

"This nigga just said he don't have 2work as long as its White women walkin the Earth. Lmaaaaaaaoooooooo. That's some VA shit." @ViceMayorWesB 6/27/2010

"lol people in here calling Thomas Jefferson a White Supremacist.... making a lot of valid points proving the accusation. Interesting..." @ViceMayorWesB 5/14/2014

"I really #hate how almost 80% of the Black people in here talk White...#petpeeve. #itstheniggainme. #dontjudgeme" @ViceMayorWesB 3/30/2010

"I DON'T LIKE WHIT PEOPLE SO I HATE WHITE SNOW!!!!! FML!!!!" @ViceMayorWesB 12/20/2009

"White women=Devil" @ViceMayorWesB 3/3/2011

"I HATE BLACK PEOPLE who ACT WHITE!!! (B U NIGGA) – Jeezy Voice! @ViceMayorWesB 11/17/2009

The distasteful social media posts are just the tip of the iceberg. Bellamy's committee appointments were almost all Black. He used his bully pulpit to voice support for a boycott of a local restaurant whose owner had criticized Black Lives Matter. He later justified this in his book, explaining "I felt obligated in my soul to use [my platform] to speak up and speak out against oppressive microaggressions."[1] He has also described himself as being "infatuated with the [Black] Panthers."[2]

---

1   Dr. Wes Bellamy, *Monumental: It Was Never About a Statue* (Black Gold Publishing, 2018), p. 64.

2   Hunter Wallace, "Wes Bellamy: Charlottesville Backs 'Reparations Fund'," Occidental Dissent.com. Aug. 9, 2017.

When Wes Bellamy began the push to remove the Robert E. Lee statue and rename Lee Park,[3] Kessler saw it as a racist attack on his heritage. Though he had grown up with a stepfather that was interested in the Civil War and participated in re-enactments, Kessler himself didn't really think too much about his Southern heritage until it came under attack. It wasn't until the things that he had always taken for granted began to be purged from the public sphere that he began to embrace his Southern identity.

Kessler explained in a 2016 article on his own website that Bellamy "has created deep divisions within the Charlottesville community by taking a largely administrative position and turning it into a bully pulpit to attack White culture and history." He became concerned about the open hatred towards Whites displayed by city government, and the potential slippery slope that might result from this open anti-White racism. He saw that American history was being attacked and White people were being scapegoated, and it didn't seem that anyone was standing up to it.

He decided to take action.

On November 24, 2016, Kessler broke the story of Bellamy's offensive tweets on his website, drawing a great deal of local attention and even some mentions in national news outlets. After the unearthed tweets were made public, enough public pressure was created that Bellamy was placed on administrative leave from his job as a teacher at Albemarle High and he was forced to resign from his appointment to the state Board of Education. On November 27, 2016, Bellamy took to Facebook to apologize, calling his own prior comments (including additional ones Kessler uncovered that were homophobic and seemingly pro-rape) "disrespectful, and quite frankly, ignorant... I sincerely apologize for the inappropriate things I posted to social media many years ago."[4] Though Bellamy

---

3   At the time of the Unite the Right rally, the park where the event was held was known as "Emancipation Park." It has since been renamed to "Market Street Park". However, it was historically known as Lee Park. It was built on land donated in 1917 by Charlottesville financier Paul Goodloe McIntire. McIntire also commissioned the statue of Robert E. Lee which is the central focus of Unite the Right, presenting it to the city in 1924.

4   Lisa Provence, "UPDATE: Bellamy takes leave from teaching position," C-ville.com, Nov. 29, 2016.

implied to the public that the tweets were posted when he was much younger, the time stamp proved some of them were more recent. For example, the tweet "Lol funniest thing about being down south is seeing little White men and the look on their faces when they have to look up to you." was dated October 2012, which was only three years before he was elected to City Council.

Mayor Signer offered support of Bellamy, stating that while he was "shaken" by the contents of the tweets, "I believe in second chances."[5]

Councilor Kristin Szakos expressed a similar sentiment. "Charlottesville is a city of second chances, and if anyone deserves one, it is Wes Bellamy."

Similarly, Councilor Kathy Gavlin signaled support for Bellamy. "Those past tweets were troubling, but they do not match my experience of the man today."

Councilor Bob Fenwick went on the offense against Kessler, decrying the "...shame that people who seem to want to find fault with someone keep digging until they find something," and praised Bellamy as "a smart, energetic young man, and I'm glad I'm working with him on the council."[6]

Not satisfied with a perfunctory apology, Kessler took to the streets to gather signatures for a petition to have Bellamy removed from City Council. On December 5, 2016, Kessler appeared at a meeting of City Council to present the petition which by then had 527 signatures. The meeting hall was full of interested citizens, including many sign-carrying Bellamy supporters. Wearing a gray blazer over a Black t-shirt, Kessler appeared confident, even cocky, about taking the council to task, at one point facetiously grinning for the camera of a left-leaning local news outlet, giving them a big thumbs up.

He began his statement by playing part of a recording of Tom Petty's song "I Won't Back Down," then began to speak. "I am here to demand Wes Bellamy be removed from office... Any one

---

5   Lisa Provence, "Who's a racist? Wes Bellamy and Jason Kessler speak out at City Council," C-ville.com, Dec. 6, 2016.

6   Bellamy, *Monumental*, p. 77.

of Bellamy's tweets would have forced a resignation a week ago if he were a White man," he argued, evoking a chorus of boos from the audience.[7]

When Kessler started gaining attention for the dispute with Bellamy, local left-wing activists were galvanized. One described it this way, "A group of us decided that we wanted to stop any movement from him before he gathered more steam as a clearly fascist organizer... So a lot of this work was led by the local Anarchist People of Color Collective and we have been working very much on a platform of direct action, and a strategy of no-platform for White supremacy. Around that time was also the growth of the local chapter of SURJ [Showing up for Racial Justice], and that collective started working along those lines."[8]

Kessler continued to promote the petition over the coming months. In January 2017, an altercation occurred while he was at the Charlottesville Downtown Mall attempting to gather additional signatures. Jay Taylor approached Kessler, and after reading the petition called him a "fucking asshole." Kessler reports that he found Taylor's demeanor threatening, and punched him in what he viewed as an act of self-defense. On April 6, 2017, Kessler pled guilty to misdemeanor assault, testifying, "Yeah, I was having a bad day, clearly...I try to be [a nice guy], [but] I don't always succeed."[9]

(The incident was later parlayed by Commonwealth Attorney Robert Tracci into a perjury charge based upon Kessler's sincere but perhaps inapt description of the altercation. Kessler described Tracci's pursuit of the perjury charge as "a political hit job," explaining, "This was an attempt to undermine my credibility so I can't testify about the city of Charlottesville and their sabotage of that rally that got people hurt. And no one on any side should have gotten hurt."[10] The perjury charge was dismissed on March 20, 2018.)

---

7   Lisa Provence, "Who's a racist?" C-ville.com.

8   Jason Kessler, "Antifa Comms Director Luis Oyola on Charlottesville Conspiracy," BitChute.com, video, posted June 19, 2020.

9   Samantha Baars, "'Unfortunate outcome:' Kessler perjury charge tossed," C-ville.com, Mar. 21, 2018.

10   *Ibid.*

The petition to have Bellamy removed from City Council was dismissed in March, 2017 when a judge ruled the number of signatures collected did not meet the necessary threshold. Bellamy poised himself as noble, demurring when asked to speculate about Kessler's motivations for submitting the petition. Meanwhile, his attorney Pam Starsia, who along with her husband was a leader of SURJ, described the effort to oust Bellamy as "a modern-day lynching,"[11] portraying her client, who had gloated about using his position of authority to humiliate men of another race, as the victim.

On April 8, 2017, Kessler, in the capacity of a reporter, attended the Alt-Right protest in Washington, D.C. against the bombing of Syria early in Trump's presidency. It was there that he met Richard Spencer, a man who would play a major role in the events of Charlottesville over the next year, including Unite the Right. Though the two had some common goals and worked together on occasion, Kessler explains that the relationship between them was never good. He recalls that from the beginning Spencer seemed "cold", "not genuine," and at times treated him with disrespect.

"I wish I had listened to my gut about him."

Spencer had a connection to Charlottesville as well, having attended college at the University of Virginia. Spencer had organized a torchlight march in support of the Robert E. Lee monument in the city which took place on May 13, 2017. Kessler reported on this event for the Daily Caller. Local news reported that marchers gathered around the monument, chanting things like, "You will not replace us," and "Blood and soil."

The next night, a group of "anti-racist" counter-protesters gathered at the Lee statue in response to the torchlight march. [NOTE: Throughout the text, the term "counter-protesters" is used as a generic term for left-wing demonstrators and groups, while "protesters" is used to describe rally attendees and right-wing groups.] Kessler's appearance at that gathering resulted in his arrest. On his website, he explained what happened from his own perspective.

---

11   Lisa Provence, "'Insufficient': Kessler petition to oust Bellamy thrown out," C-ville.com, Mar. 8, 2017.

I was charged with 'disorderly conduct' for appearing at an Antifa rally the other night. I want to get my side of the story out there. I used my megaphone to communicate with my friend and make sure he got his phone back. This is important because the police said I was using my megaphone 'to get in peoples face'. I was just using it to communicate with my friend.

Hundreds of Antifa were there harassing my friend doing a livestream. I showed up to make sure he was okay and tear down the 'Black Lives Matter' sign defacing the monument. When I tried to leave the park, a woman who had been smacking at my megaphone told other Antifa to "link arms" and they trapped me in a circle in the middle of the road. When I tried to duck and run under their arms, they squeezed in together and I had to push them off me to escape. Then a policeman arrested me for "shoving" the woman, and another Antifa spit in my face.

The prosecutor assigned the case against Kessler declined to prosecute, stating that his actions constituted free speech and "cannot support a conviction." The man accused of spitting, Jordan McNeish, pled not guilty, and the city agreed that the charge would be dismissed pending six months of good behavior.[12]

Kessler reports that after the first torchlight march, Charlottesville social justice warriors started following and harassing rally attendees, himself included. One local left-wing organizer explained on a podcast, "The APOC [Anarchist People of Color] organizers in particular made an effort to confront Jason Kessler after these rallies everywhere he went, whether it was a smoothie shop, whether it was hanging with his buddies at a downtown bar, we would call on the community to show up and confront him. It was met with a lot of resistance from locals who had this idea that if you just ignore the fascists, they will go away.

---

12   Lisa Provence, "Kessler dodges disorderly conduct charge, man who spit on him pleads not guilty," C-ville.com, Aug. 21, 2017.

However, particularly the organizers with APOC knew that ignorant attitude is exactly what helps them rise to power."[13]

Activists put up "Know your Nazi" flyers and encouraged businesses to deny Kessler and other "Nazis" service. Charlottesville resident Hannah Zarski was one of the people actively supporting Kessler in his opposition to the goals of City Council. She was targeted by these activists and remembers, "It was a terrible experience." They posted pictures online of her and her infant daughter. She was part of a group that was with Kessler when a mob swarmed them at a restaurant. "One guy spotted us, then all of a sudden there were thirty people." They were live-streaming their flash mob, refusing to stop even when Kessler asked them to give privacy to Zarski, who was breastfeeding her baby. "It got to be pretty volatile when Jason started live streaming back," she recalls. Activists repeated events like that throughout the summer. Zarski says some statue advocates abandoned the cause because of these tactics. "Some people couldn't handle it."

The efforts by Charlottesville social justice warriors to deny their political opponents' rights to freedom of commerce, speech, and assembly reflected a growing trend at the national level. Rather than being dissuaded by the harassment campaign, Kessler became determined to respond with an even stronger showing in support of the Robert E. Lee statue.

Thereby, the idea for Unite the Right was born.

Local news blogger and podcast host Rob Schilling, who had lived in Charlottesville for about twenty years and served on the city council, describes the mood in the city at the time as "more tense than I've ever seen. Frankly it was disturbing to see what was going on." He attributes the tension to "a polarizing cause and polarizing personalities," explaining that lot of people who were born and raised in the area were very resentful of Vice Mayor Bellamy and Councilwoman Szakos' attempt to remove markers of their culture.

The tensions in the city were apparent when Kessler attended a public meeting of the Charlottesville City Council on June 5, 2017.

---

13   Jason Kessler, "Antifa Comms Director Luis Oyola on Charlottesville Conspiracy," BitChute.com video, posted June 19, 2020.

He patiently waited, hands in pockets, for several minutes for his allotted three-minute time period to speak, as Mayor Mike Signer explained the principles of free speech to noisy protesters in the crowd and issued warnings that people speaking out of order would be removed.

He began:

> My name is Jason Kessler. I've lived in the city of Charlottesville over ten years. I was born here. My family are from here. My ancestors are Confederate veterans. I believe in the First Amendment. I believe in the right for people to peaceably assemble and speak their minds. Everyone else in the city of Charlottesville except for right-wing people, White people, and Confederate supporters, are allowed these rights. We do not go to any Black people or brown people and tell them where they can eat at night. We do not harass them where they live. We do not post their addresses where they have young children living. We don't post the names of their businesses to try to get them fired. This is ridiculous behaviour. It's hyperbolic. It's out of control. And these people are talking about a peaceful rally that happened on May 13th which was protected by the First Amendment... and they talk about the KKK? Excuse me? When I think of the KKK, I think of people who are harassing people where they have young children, who are telling people...

At this point, protesters in the crowd began chanting in a childlike, sing-songy tune, "Fuck White supremacy." Some of the protesters were dramatically flipping the bird with both hands.

An exasperated Signer reacted. "Call to order. Okay, we're gonna have to remove everybody here who's doing this. So this meeting is going to take a lot longer because of these tactics, and I'd like to move us along, but... We're gonna take a five-minute break."

Bailiffs moved in to eject the disruptors, who continued to sing and flip the bird until they were removed.

Eventually, Kessler was able to resume speaking.

> As I was saying, every day you guys come up here and talk about Black people, about gay people, you don't give a damn about White people. And White people have a right to organize and advocate for our rights as well. You people are implementing policies which are displacing us in our home countries and we will not be allowed to survive. You don't even recognize our right to exist. And people like Councilors Szakos and Bellamy have directly worked with Antifa who are groups who have advocated violence against police officers, who have advocated overthrowing the government, who have advocated violence, and none of you have condemned that activity. The Alt-Right did not harass or attack anybody on May 13th... Your people, Mr. Bellamy, were attacking my friend, who is not even White, and I had to go there and support him because... any of my friends who are not White who come out to support me you call them Uncle Toms, and other stuff, so who are the racists here? Okay? I support White people but I don't have anything against anybody else. And you guys can't get that through your heads. I have a right to organize. I have a right to have friends. I have a right for them to gather in peace and use their First Amendment rights. And your supporters, your Antifa supporters, do not agree with that.
>
> We're gonna have a rally on August 12th. It's gonna be open to anybody who wants to come and support right-wing policies. We're not gonna live in intimidation and fear from these people who are the anti-White KKK. SURJ is the anti-White KKK. Antifa is the anti-White KKK.

I'll see you guys August 12th."

Signer concluded. "You're done. Thanks."[14]

---

14   The Schilling Show, "CHAOS at Charlottesville City Council Meeting, Episode 1: Jason Kessler 060517" YouTube video, posted June 7, 2017.

The "Quick Links" section that appears at the end of most chapters provides the reader with quick access by QR code or easy to copy URLs to take them quickly and directly to videos and/or documents of importance to the narrative of the preceding chapter. Some codes/links appear at the end of more than one chapter so that the reader does not have to flip back to previous chapters. If you find that a QR code or link no longer works, please contact the publisher at bit.ly/CUcodes.

CHAPTER 1 QUICK LINKS:

 Jason Kessler, "Antifa Comms Director Luis Oyola on Charlottesville Conspiracy," video, June 19, 2020. URL: qrs.ly/4acvtbm

The Schilling Show, "CHAOS at Charlottesville City Council Meeting, Episode 1: Jason Kessler 060517," video, June 7, 2017. URL: qrs.ly/d7cvtbr

THE KLAN RALLY
– TENSION BUILDS

"Cops and Klan go hand in hand."

ON MAY 30, 2017, Kessler applied for a permit for a "free speech rally in support of the Lee monument" to be held on August 12th from 12:00pm to 5:00pm, for an estimated crowd of about 400 people. Between the date of the application and the date of the rally, the stage was being set in Charlottesville for Unite the Right.

Around the same time that Kessler submitted his permit application, Amanda Barker, Imperial Kommander of the women's division of a North Carolina based Ku Klux Klan group, filed a permit to hold a rally for their group on July 8th in Charlottesville. Though entirely unrelated, the Klan event was to have an impact on Unite the Right nonetheless.

Unhappy about the Klan rally being held so close to the one he was organizing, Kessler contacted the Barkers and asked them to reconsider whether to even hold their event, trying to persuade them that their planned demonstration would be unhelpful to the interests of White people. Local news reported "Kessler has distanced himself from the KKK rally, saying that the leader of the Klan chapter that filed for the city permit is an FBI informant and was paid by left-wing groups to discredit legitimate conservatives."[1] (Having the two events so close together has indeed caused them to be somewhat conflated. Some news stories about Unite the Right contained photos and videos from the Klan rally.)

The independent investigation commissioned by the city of Charlottesville after Unite the Right, the Heaphy Report, found numerous problems with the law enforcement management of the Klan event which foreshadowed the problems that would plague Unite the Right. For example, they concluded that the "[Charlottesville Police Department's] training efforts to prepare for the Klan event were fragmented, unfocused, and inadequate..." and that "[t]hese fractured efforts left CPD officers feeling ill-prepared."[2] As they would later do for Unite the Right, the Virginia State Police partnered with the City of Charlottesville for the Klan rally. Heaphy concluded that "...successful coordination between CPD and VSP was critical. Unfortunately, that coordination was erratic and produced inconsistent approaches to the event."[3]

As city officials worked together on plans to manage the upcoming Klan rally, they simultaneously performed public outreach meant to discourage citizens from "taking the bait" by attending the rally in protest. The city coordinated with local business and non-profit groups to offer alternative activities for people to attend that day, and even helped fund some of these alternative events. Some members of left-wing activist groups, such as the Reverend Seth Wispelwey, did not welcome the alternative options, but rather found them patronizing, arguing that the Klan should be confronted.[4]

On the day of the rally, the Klan contingent of about 50 people was met by about 1,500 to 2,000 counter-protesters, including members of SURJ, Antifa, Black Lives Matter, and clergy groups.

---

1   "Kessler discusses KKK, Unite the Right rallies and his political beliefs," *Charlottesville Daily Progress*, July 11, 2017.

2   Timothy J. Heaphy of Hunton & Williams LLP, Final Report: Independent Review of the 2017 Protest Events in Charlottesville, Virginia, pp. 35.

3   Heaphy Report, p. 38.

4   Heaphy Report, p. 47.

Some of the counter-protester groups were extremely well-prepared and organized, having brought their own medics, gas masks, helmets and body armor, and walkie talkies.

The counter-protesters identified where the Klan was planning to enter Justice Park. They locked arms to block their entry, and refused to disperse when ordered to do so by the police. One high-profile local activist, Emily Gorcenski, who was live-streaming the event, complained that police were being too aggressive in arresting people who were blocking the path of the Klan members. The counter-protesters attempted to create noise to drown out the rally, and threw things like food and bottles at the Klan members.

When the event ended, the Klan members, separated from the crowd by a wall of police, left Justice Park and headed towards the parking garage which held their vehicles. Hundreds of counter-protesters followed. The Klan members reached their cars in the parking garage, but were unable to exit the building due to the huge swarm of people surrounding it. Police became increasingly concerned as the mob of counter-protesters continued to swell. The CPD issued an all-hands call to bring more officers to the garage, and Chief Thomas gave permission for an unlawful assembly declaration. The police finally managed to part the sea of protesters enough for the Klan members to exit the garage. As they drove away, some of their vehicles were hit with weapons or blocked by counter-protesters in the road, but they were all eventually able to exit the city.

With the Klan out of sight, counter-protesters, under the impression that the police had been primarily concerned with protecting the Klan members, turned hostile towards the law enforcement officers present. Chants of "Cops and Klan go hand in hand" erupted in the crowd. Police vehicles were crowded. One officer was assaulted, and pepper spray was deployed against counter-protesters who attempted to shield the officer's attacker from being arrested.

The police used a bullhorn to call an unlawful assembly and repeatedly ordered the crowd to disperse. The crowd failed to do so, and the police struggled to maintain control of the situation. Despite repeated warnings that tear gas was going to be deployed, many counter-protesters (and, as a result of confusion about chain of command and poor communication, some police) were caught off-guard when the three canisters were shot off. Antifa medics tried to help members of the crowd who were exposed to the tear gas. When police officers tried to assist, they were told to go away - one was even spat upon. The events of the day resulted in 22 arrests, all of counter-protesters.

Zarski believes that the Klan rally was used to "prime the crowds" for Unite the Right, noting that Antifa took the opportunity to "bait" Black participants by distributing fliers implying that their community would be under attack by Unite the Right attendees.

Impact On Unite The Right

After the Klan rally, there was considerable outcry about the police response to the event from both citizens and more formal groups, as summarized in the Heaphy Report:

> On July 17, the Legal Aid Justice Center, National Lawyers Guild, ACLU, and the Rutherford Institute sent a letter to Governor McAuliffe, Charlottesville City Councilors, City Manager Jones, and Chief Thomas which criticized the "outsized and militaristic governmental response" to counter-protesters on July 8. The letter asserted that counter-protesters "were met with a highly militarized law enforcement presence who, prior to any clear and present danger of violence, descended on the scene dressed in riot gear, driving armored vehicles, and carrying weapons typically used only in war zones." The July 17 letter also criticized the use of tear gas: "[w]e are highly concerned about the use of chemical agents to facilitate the dispersal of demonstrators. The letter alleged that counter-protesters were "standing a good distance away from the line of riot police" yet "three gas grenades were deployed" in front of the JDR Court.

Reverend Seth Wispelwey explained that community progressives and faith leaders had an extremely strong reaction to the tear gas after July 8. To many, "it seemed like [the police] had no plan, other than protecting White supremacy."[5]

The Heaphy Report also faults the City for failure to communicate with the public in the wake of this event, allowing confusion and resentments to fester among Charlottesville residents. "The failure to provide information to the public or give people an opportunity to express concerns had direct consequences on the preparations for August 12... If the City had undertaken a conscientious effort to facilitate understanding of those complex issues, our community would have been more prepared for August 12. The City should have responded to July 8 with more speech, not less—particularly in anticipation of the larger Unite the Right event on the horizon."[6]

Governor Terry McAuliffe wrote that the effect of the public backlash was that "[t]he mindset for the Charlottesville City Council was to be wary of any strong law enforcement presence," and noted that the ACLU letter "really had city officials nervous."[7]

Furthermore, the Klan rally incident exacerbated distrust between law enforcement and left-wing groups in Charlottesville. It also led to finger-pointing, blame, and residual hostilities between members of the Charlottesville city government and law enforcement officials. All this served to increase tensions in the weeks leading up to Unite the Right, which was already expected to be a volatile event.

---

5   Heaphy Report, pp. 62-63.

6   Heaphy Report, pp. 68-69.

7   Governor Terry McAuliffe, *Beyond Charlottesville: Taking a Stand Against White Nationalism* (New York: Thomas Dunne Books, St. Martin's Press, 2019), pp. 61-62.

CHAPTER 2 QUICK LINKS:

 Timothy J. Heaphy of Hunton & Williams LLP, Final Report: Independent Review of the 2017 Protest Events in Charlottesville, Virginia (Hereafter, "Heaphy Report"). URL: qrs.ly/dpcvtcb

CHAPTER 3

GOVERNMENT PREPARATIONS

*"More like a concert than a
potentially violent confrontation."*

The Charlottesville Police Department

THE KEY PLANNERS FOR LAW ENFORCEMENT for Unite the Right were Captain Victor Mitchell, Captain David Shifflett, and Captain Wendy Lewis. Though Chief Al Thomas was involved in the planning as well, his leadership was lacking. For example, even when they were unable to reach consensus about some matters, Chief Thomas "suggested that he deferred entirely to his captains when it came to tactical decisions for August 12th" [1]

Clashes between right and left-wing groups had been occurring all over the country over the previous year, so the Charlottesville Police Department was able to draw from the knowledge and experience of other jurisdictions for information about what to expect. *"Those contacts suggested that the Alt-Right groups were generally cooperative with law enforcement, but also that the opposing groups needed to be physically separated."* [2] (My emphasis).

---

1   Heaphy Report, p. 89.

2   Heaphy Report, p. 87.

A Virginia State Police officer (note, not the CPD) reached out to law enforcement in Portland, Oregon, where there had recently been an event at which members of the Alt-Right and Antifa were present. The Oregon officer "emphasized the importance of keeping protesters and counter-protesters separated and recommended the use of barricades as 'force multipliers.'"[3]

The ADL warned the CPD that Unite the Right "will likely result in an extremely boisterous counter-protest from militant anti-fascist groups."[4]

An FBI agent who had knowledge of a protest in Pikeville, Kentucky earlier in the year informed the CPD that the Traditionalist Workers' Party "was not likely to cause problems, though groups that might show up to oppose them could."[5]

Other law enforcement intelligence gathering entities reported what weapons each group was likely to bring. "Unite the Right supporters would bring bats, batons, flag sticks, knives, and firearms to confront their political opponents [and] left-wing counter-protesters, such as Antifa, would attempt to disrupt the event using soda cans filled with cement and balloons or water bottles filled with paint, urine, or fuel."[6]

Officials from Charlotte, North Carolina, who had recently dealt with civic unrest after the shooting of an unarmed civilian, were interested in speaking with Chief Thomas, but he declined to connect with them, saying he "did not have time."[7]

Despite the willingness of law enforcement entities from other parts of the country to share what they had learned from their experiences with similar rallies and protests, Captain Mitchell admitted to Heaphy Report investigators that "the input from outside jurisdictions was not a factor in planning for August

---

3   Heaphy Report, p. 88.

4   Heaphy Report, p. 70.

5   Ibid.

6   Ibid.

7   Heaphy Report, p. 88.

12th." Some police officers reported their impression that the CPD leadership was preparing for the rally as though it was a concert and not a potentially violent confrontation. [8]

The Heaphy Report states: "Efforts to train police officers ahead of August 12th were meager if nonexistent... There was no field training of any kind in advance of August 12th." Seventy-five pages of training documents were emailed to all CPD officers with the request that they review them.[9]

Some officers wanted to start the day wearing riot gear, but because of concerns that would send a message that violence was expected (and perhaps because of the recent criticism for appearing over-militarized during the KKK rally) leadership decided against it. Instead they opted to place the gear in a number of nearby locations for retrieval in case it was needed during the day. This lack of readily available equipment contributed to police hesitancy to intervene on the day of Unite the Right.

Additionally, the anemic strategy for the management of traffic in the downtown area would prove to have calamitous consequences. "A traffic plan was in place that called for a combination of manned and unmanned barriers... police personnel were not staged at every altered intersection due to a perceived lack of resources. Moreover, many of the manned traffic posts were occupied by unsworn personnel like forensic technicians, animal control officers, and school resource officers."[10]

The aforementioned errors were but a few of the shortcomings that would negatively impact Unite the Right. Event staging, communications between different public safety entities, and officer training were all lacking. After all was said and done, the independent investigation commissioned by the city would attribute a lengthy catalogue of failures to the Charlottesville Police Department.

---

8   *Ibid.*

9   Heaphy Report, pp. 85-86.

10   Heaphy Report, p. 90.

The Virginia State Police

Virginia State Police made themselves available to assist with law enforcement needs to the CPD, who had ultimate responsibility for the local event. Efforts were made to coordinate between the CPD and the VSP. Captains Mitchell and Lewis met with VSP representatives several times to work on operational plans, but communication between the agencies was in some ways inadequate.

Plans for radio communications within the VSP did not include any mention of including the CPD. Unbelievably, it was not until after the CPD and VSP had arrived downtown on the morning of Unite the Right that they discovered that they were not even communicating on the same radio channels. They spent the day communicating either face-to-face, or indirectly through the Command Center. Chief Thomas later reported to investigators that by the time he became aware of the radio communication problem, he was too immersed in other matters to rectify the situation.

The VSP had created a detailed plan of over 100 pages for August 12th which called for about 600 officers to be present in various places, and two aviation teams to provide helicopter surveillance, but the CPD was unaware of the existence of the plan until an officer happened upon a copy of it on the day of Unite the Right. In the weeks before Unite the Right, the CPD had cycled through a number of different plans for staging officers, protest and counter-protest groups in the downtown area. VSP officers seemed surprised when they arrived to find that the final plan provided for five instead of four zones as they expected. Some last-minute changes to the zoning plan were not conveyed to counter-protest groups either.

Remarkably, the Heaphy Report concludes that as a result of the last-minute changes that were made, *"no officers were assigned to open areas in which protesters and counter-protesters would interact."* Furthermore, when discussions were being held about whether law enforcement officers might be posted between Unite the Right attendee shuttle drop-off locations and the park, Chief

Thomas said *"I'm not going to get them in and out."* [11] (Both my emphasis.) Medical personnel would later report that most of the injuries that occurred that day happened along the entrance and exit routes to and from the park.

Leadership with both the Virginia State Police and the Albemarle County Police Department said that CPD Chief Thomas seemed to be dismissive of their expressed concerns, and disinterested in their offers of helpful resources. The Director of Emergency Management at the University of Virginia Health Systems expressed frustration about how difficult it was for him to obtain information for planning purposes from the CPD.

Some instructions were provided to officers regarding arrest procedures for August 12th. However, findings within the Heaphy Report help explain the passivity of law enforcement the day of Unite the Right, and create doubt about whether they had any meaningful intention to keep the peace at the rally and protect the free speech of the participants:

> Despite these written instructions, officers had a very different understanding of the expectations for arrests on August 12. We spoke to multiple officers at all levels who expressed concern that normal arrest procedures would put officers in harm's way. In the week before August 12, the Virginia Fusion Center shared credible threats that members of Antifa would bring soda cans filled with cement and might attack police. Then, on the morning of August 12, rumors circulated among CPD that Antifa might attack officers with fentanyl.
>
> Out of concern for officer safety, Lieutenant Brian O'Donnell, commander of Zone 3 (1st Street) instructed his officers to avoid engaging attendees over "every little thing." Officer Lisa Best was assigned to Lieutenant O'Donnell's zone. She told us that officers "were not going to go in and break up fights" or enter

---

11   Heaphy Report, pp. 96-97.

the crowd to make arrests "unless it was something so serious that someone will get killed." Sergeant Robert Haney described the instructions he received as "do not interrupt mutual combat" unless someone is seriously injured. Lieutenant McKean commanded Zone 1. He told us that he was "not sending guys out there and getting them hurt." This concern is reflected in our review of body camera footage, which reflects multiple instances of officer uncertainty about potential engagement with the crowd.

Rather than engage the crowd and prevent fights, the CPD plan was to declare the event unlawful and disperse the crowd.[12] (My emphasis.)

Further confirmation that the CPD did not intend to protect the right of Unite the Right participants to peacefully rally is the fact that there were hundreds of VSP officers stationed in various buildings in the downtown area, but the CPD decided that they would only be called out in the event of an unlawful assembly declaration.[13]

Albemarle County Police Department And University Police Department

CPD Captain Mitchell reported that his requests for assistance from the Albemarle County Police Department were rebuffed. It was agreed that the ACPD would assist by answering priority calls for service within the city that were not related to the protest. However, ACPD Chief Rick Lantz states that he repeatedly offered resources and information to Chief Thomas and the CPD, and that Thomas did not accept the help. Lantz informed Thomas that the ACPD SWAT team would be available to assist with protest-related issues, and later reported that he did not understand why Thomas did not call them into service or even acknowledge their availability.

---

12   Heaphy Report, p. 98.

13   Heaphy Report, p. 100.

ACPD Captain Sean Reeves reported that during interagency planning meetings, Chief Thomas was dismissive of concerns that were raised. Specifically, he recalled a discussion about the dangers of dispersing Unite the Right attendees in the direction of the Downtown Mall in the event of an unlawful assembly - concerns Thomas minimized or ignored.

The University Police Department agreed to answer emergency calls on August 12th but did not want to be involved with crowd control for the event.

City Government

Since attempts to counter-program the previous months' Klan rally had been poorly received by the public, the city did not plan alternative events for Unite the Right. However, at Mayor Signer's urging, some public programs were offered at UVA on the same day. Signer considered inviting a national figure to the city before the rally, ostensibly to "calm nerves," though it is difficult to imagine that the figures considered, such as Michelle Obama, John Lewis, and Jesse Jackson, would have helped to alleviate racial tensions. There was also discussion amongst city officials about holding a town hall meeting to address public concerns about the event, but as officials were already spread thin and overwhelmed, this event never occurred.[14]

Concerned about the city's preparations for Unite the Right, Virginia Secretary of Public Safety Brian Moran recommended that Governor McAuliffe call Mayor Signer. Moran provided a list of suggested ideas that he thought would make the rally safer, such as limiting its duration and prohibiting backpacks and certain items that could be used as weapons. Signer recalls the conversation as "odd" in that McAuliffe made suggestions about prohibiting weapons which he must have known were not legally feasible, and that the call should have properly been directed to City Manager Jones rather than himself. In retrospect, Signer believes that the call was an attempt to pre-emptively deflect blame, that is, "... not actually to effect any change, but instead to create a narrative

---

14   Heaphy Report, pp. 79-80.

that the Governor's Office – by demanding changes ahead of an impending disaster, whether they were achievable or not – had been in the right, while the city was, by default, in the wrong."[15]

The Fire Department

The Heaphy Report states that Deputy Fire Chief Mike Rogers worked closely with the CPD and other agencies, and that "the department had a comprehensive plan for organizing both fire and EMS resources for August 12th." To mitigate potential hostility from anti-government leftist protesters towards emergency staff, Rogers ordered CFD and EMS responders to wear specific-colored t-shirts rather than uniforms for the event. Heaphy investigators learned that Rogers had particular concerns about Zone 5, the Market Street area. He believed it was too close to the Command Center and a likely spot for conflicts between protesters and counter-protesters. Because of these concerns, he decided not to place CFD or EMS personnel there. This meant that CPD would be required to extract injured individuals who were in need of treatment.[16]

Medical Services

Tom Berry, The Director of Emergency Management at UVA Health Systems, recognized that Unite the Right had the potential to be a mass casualty event. He held meetings that included staff members from a bevy of medical facilities and emergency service providers to share information and make plans. He arranged for UVA to cancel all elective surgeries, and created contingency plans for potential security threats, mass casualty intake procedures, and decontamination for victims of possible chemical attacks. Berry expressed frustration that he was unable to get useful information from the CPD and was not invited to any briefing meetings despite repeatedly requesting to attend.

---

15   Michael Signer, *Cry Havoc: Charlottesville and American Democracy Under Siege* (New York: Public Affairs, 2020), p. 186.

16   Heaphy Report, p. 104.

The Virginia National Guard

Though the National Guard began preparing to mobilize in the weeks leading up to Unite the Right, Heaphy investigators had difficulty learning any specifics about their plans, objectives, or mission. Even Captain Wendy Lewis who was the exterior commander for the event reported that she was given no information about the National Guard's mission or role.

Governor McAuliffe wrote that on Friday, August 11th, he ordered the National Guard activated and relocated from Manassas to Charlottesville, making it the first time in 85 years a Virginia Governor had called out the Guard for a domestic situation. He wanted the move to be discreet, telling General Tim Williams, "No one is to talk about this...I want this to be kept quiet. If word gets out that the governor has called out the National Guard, every hatemongering lunatic in America will want to be there." McAuliffe ordered the Guard to be put on standby, but wrote that "the Guard wasn't doing much standing that day, they were on the move – and in big numbers." There were about 120 military police and 450 infantry soldiers put into place. When reporters asked about the Guard mobilization, the General attempted to deflect concerns by pointing out, truthfully, that a training exercise was going on at the time. [17]

Virginia Department Of Emergency Management

As early as August 1st, the Virginia Department of Emergency Management reported concerns to the CPD and VSP about what they perceived as inadequacies in their planning for various contingencies, potential communication challenges and concerns that the Command Center was too close to the rally site. Chief Thomas agreed to allow the VDEM to convene an Incident Management Team to assist with coordinating and planning.

---

17   McAuliffe, *Beyond Charlottesville*, pp. 73-74.

They consolidated plans among agencies and provided additional resources like GPS devices and radios. [18]

There were numerous meetings with personnel from various agencies over the next few weeks. Chief Thomas agreed to be incident commander. Despite vigorous efforts and thorough work on the Incident Action Plan (IAP) for the day, Chief Thomas reported to investigators that "no one in the Command Center looked at or operated from the IAP on August 12th."[19]

---

18   Heaphy Report, p, 107.

19   Heaphy Report, p. 109.

CHAPTER 3 QUICK LINKS:

 Heaphy Report. URL: qrs.ly/dpcvtcb

CHAPTER 4

THE OPPOSITION

"Information-gathering actions
were construed as harassment."

Counter-Protester Intelligence Gathering

LAW ENFORCEMENT ATTEMPTED to gather information from local groups that were likely to counter-protest Unite the Right. However, their efforts were not fruitful. Some groups, like Antifa, are nebulous and secretive by nature, making it challenging to contact representatives. Other relevant groups exist more openly, but even they were resolved not to cooperate with law enforcement.

According to the Heaphy Report:

> Efforts to contact local Charlottesville residents associated with counter-protester groups were met with extreme resistance. As described above, officers attempted to speak with members of Standing Up for Racial Justice and Black Lives Matter, resulting in demands by a local attorney that such contacts cease. As a result, detectives were instructed not to reach out to anyone affiliated with those groups. Officers told us that they were frustrated that their safety-focused information-gathering actions were

construed as harassment against vocal members of the community and by the resulting limitation in their ability to gather important intelligence. [1]

The attorney mentioned above who accused the Charlottesville Police Department of using "badgering inquiries [which] hearken back to the 1960s, when police harassed and intensely surveilled Black activists" was Pamela Starsia, an active member of SURJ and other left-wing organizations in Charlottesville. She was the same attorney that had represented Wes Bellamy when Kessler petitioned to have him removed from City Council.

The left-wing hotbed of Charlottesville was home to a wide range of activist organizations: Showing Up for Racial Justice, Charlottesville Black Lives Matter, Charlottesville Democratic Socialists of America, the Clergy Collective, Congregate Charlottesville, and Anarchist People of Color. Eventually they formed an umbrella organization called Solidarity Charlottesville through which they collaborated. (Associates of this group, including Don Gathers, Wes Bellamy, and Joe Starsia, were responsible for the May 14th "anti-racist" rally at which Kessler was assaulted and arrested.) Solidarity Charlottesville became the vehicle through which the Unite the Right counter-protests were organized.

Activists reached out through It's Going Down, Crimethinc, and the Antifa Torch Networks to network with some of the anarchist groups that had disrupted right-wing rallies in places like Berkeley, Portland, and Washington DC earlier that year. Left-wing militia Redneck Revolt was contacted by activists to assist with security for Unite the Right. Redneck Revolt posted a "Call to Arms" on their website which called for their members and allies in Antifa affinity groups to come to the Unite the Right rally and "dust off the guns of 1921," referring to an incident in which armed Communists murdered military and law enforcement personnel. They arranged for other communist militias to attend Unite the Right as well, including the Socialist Rifle Association and John Brown Gun Club. Redneck Revolt began preparing

---

1   Heaphy Report, p. 71.

for Unite the Right by setting up targets in a desert gun range depicting images of Alt-Right symbol Pepe the Frog and shooting them with semi-automatic rifles.

The comments of one left-wing organizer give insight into the discussions taking place behind the scenes around that time. "So there were a lot of heated internal conversations around how to confront the August 12 rally. APOC [Anarchist People of Color] organizers and other White accomplices were pointing out that these Nazis come with a lot of violent intentions... We wanted to make clear that under no circumstances were we going to allow that violent activity and we would need to defend ourselves by any means necessary. So with that a group of us wanted to establish an agreement towards diversity of tactics with respect to the different tactics such as open carry as a deterrent to violence, Antifascists blockading and basically any tactic that would go towards the goal of defending Charlottesville from fascists. People in SURJ [Showing Up for Racial Justice], people in the newly formed BLM chapter, clergy, liberal groups, progressive groups resisted that idea, and that strategy very strongly with the feeling that they would get bad press after the fact, that we would be putting people in harm unnecessarily, that people that were not consenting to being confrontational, so that led to a lot of tensions, that actually ended up in a lot, for example, APOC organizing separately from a lot of Antifascist networks, SURJ and BLM and other groups that were not signing on to diversity of tactics."[2]

George Lindbeck, MD, from the UVA Department of Emergency Medicine, UVA School of Medicine, was the head of emergency response for Unite the Right. He did a presentation for other physicians about lessons learned from Unite the Right. During this session, he remarked that the left-wing groups' distrust of government in some cases was extreme. "Some of these groups are very strongly anti-government. What we learned was if you wear a uniform - Fire, EMS - you're still part of the government and they are not interested in us. They're not necessarily interested in our services." Lindbeck said that some medics who were

---

2   Kessler, "Antifa Comms Director," BitChute.com.

affiliated with left-wing groups actively hid their patients from the authorities at Unite the Right. These medics view their role as being to protect protesters who suffer violence at the hands of the police, something they believe EMS responders do not adequately understand. Lindbeck also indicated that prior to the rally, there was chatter from left-wing activists to the effect that prior recent protests like the one at Berkeley had an **inadequate** amount of violence. Some thought an *increase* in violence was necessary to further their agenda.[3]

Antifa

By now most Americans are familiar with the term "Antifa," short for "Anti-Fascists," and the Black-clad street militants to whom the term is usually applied. However, the movement is relatively new in the United States, and is still not widely understood.

Independent journalist and author Andy Ngo has emerged as one of the most prolific writers and reporters on the subject of Antifa. Hailing from Portland, Oregon, a hotbed of Antifa activity, Ngo has since 2018 been reporting on the activities of the violent group. Sometimes he reports openly, walking amongst hostile crowds, Gopro in hand, through parts of town where it is not unusual to see "Kill Andy Ngo" scrawled in spray paint on the side of a building. At other times, he has dressed in black bloc and stealthily embedded himself amongst his subjects. Ngo has gained a great deal of respect for his real-time, on-the-ground reporting of Antifa riots. He has also become a target of the dangerous group, and is regularly the recipient of death threats. He has experienced night time visits to his home by mask-wearing, menacing figures, and on occasion suffered physical assaults. In 2019 he suffered a mob a beating so severe he was hospitalized with a brain bleed which left him requiring speech and cognitive therapy. Still, the courageous and tenacious Ngo, son of Vietnamese immigrants who fled communism, has remained undeterred in his goal of exposing the faces and deeds of Antifa.

---

3   Jason Kessler, "Head EMT at Charlottesville Rally Discusses Expectation of Left-Wing Violence," BitChute.com, video, posted Feb. 23, 2021.

Ngo explains the difficulty for law enforcement to gather intelligence about Antifa. "...Antifa is a phantom movement by design. It is leaderless and structured to be functional through small, independent organizations, known as affinity groups, and individuals. Only the ideology needs to be propagated for lone wolves or groups to be inspired... Antifa are trained to hide their political affiliations." [4]

He explains that Antifa uses extremely clever tactics to further their goals by draining the resources of the state and their other enemies while minimizing risk to themselves or severe public backlash. Notes Ngo, "They recognize that accelerationist tactics like mass killings of police or political opponents are too high risk. The goal is to inflict maximum damage without death... It costs little money to buy bear mace, brass knuckles, or batons. They can deploy a whole army to carry out smaller-scale assaults and vandalism at riots, making it difficult for police to make arrests and to maintain the illusion that 'Antifa has killed no one.' This is meant to mislead the public into thinking Antifa aren't dangerous."[5]

Though Ngo's reporting primarily focuses on Antifa in Portland and other parts of the northwestern U.S., some of the tactics he has observed were in play at Unite the Right in Charlottesville. For example, Ngo remarked that while he was covering protests in the Antifa-occupied territory known as CHAZ,

> What amazed me about the strategic choice of weapons – both purchased and homemade – was how innocuous they looked on camera and to bystanders. For example, one doesn't necessarily register a water bottle as a dangerous and potentially deadly weapon. However, black bloc rioters froze them to make them hard as rocks. Taking one to the head could lead to a serious brain injury or death... Other popular weapons

---

4   Andy Ngo, *Unmasked: Inside Antifa's Radical Plan to Destroy Democracy* (New York & Nashville: Center Street, 2021), p. 24.

5   Ngo, *Unmasked*, p. 160.

were slingshots. Rioters stood hundreds of feet back
and fired off marbles and metal ball bearings.[6]

In Charlottesville, innocuous-looking projectiles lobbed at Unite
the Right attendees included frozen water bottles, cement-filled soda
cans, and water balloons which contained acidic liquids. In Ngo's
book, he documents that Antifa specifically train for street violence.

Counter-protest groups had been making plans and rallying
reinforcements from allies all over the country. Prior to Unite the
Right, UVA professor Walt Heinecke (who has shared posts about
such topics as the fact that White people lack empathy) filed permits
to assemble in Justice and McGuffey parks on August 12, which
police later learned were to be used as staging areas for counter-
protesters. After initially indicating there were no police assets
available to provide security, upon Heinecke's request, Police Chief
Thomas agreed to provide some officers to monitor those areas.
Additionally, the park was guarded by communist militia Redneck
Revolt and private security which had been hired by Heinecke. The
morning of Unite the Right, several hundred people would gather
at those locations to sing songs and hear speeches.

One local activist that bears special mention is Emily (formerly
"Edward") Gorcenski. Gorcenski played a prominent role in the
events of Unite the Right and subsequent legal matters. Gorcenski
boasts an impressive resume - "she" has a degree in mathematics
and has also studied aeronautical and mechanical engineering.
"Her" personal website states "I work as a data science and data
engineering consultant for ThoughtWorks Germany, where I
help clients build high-quality data driven, intelligent software
applications efficiently." Gorcenski frequently speaks at conferences
on areas of expertise. One top hit for Gorkenski on YouTube is a
panel discussion called "Debunking Fake News and Fake Science"
for which "she" shared a stage with Sarah Jeong. Jeong is a NYT
technology reporter who was in the news for a time during 2018
when a series of old anti-White tweets were publicized. Examples of
Jeong's tweets include, "Dumbass fucking White people marking up

---

6   Ngo, *Unmasked*, pp. 65-66.

the internet with their opinions like dogs pissing on fire hydrants" and "oh man it's kind of sick how much joy I get out of being cruel to old White men" and "#CancelWhitePeople".

One way Gorcenski has used technology for activism is with the development of First Vigil, a database that tracks criminal cases of people on the far right. "She" has been given awards and featured in a number of written and televised national news stories and documentaries for "her" activism. Gorcenski has also contributed a number of articles and op-eds to outlets like *Slate, Teen Vogue*, and *Out*.

According to Ngo, "Gorcenski gained notoriety among Antifa and left-wing circles for identifying and releasing the personal details of people she says are Alt-Right. She has also expressed support for extremism on social media... She calls for the far left to embrace weapons"[7]

In the weeks leading up to Unite the Right, Gorcenski posted pictures of "herself" firing semi-automatic rifles with a message to rally demonstrators, "Antifa are watching you." Gorcenski called the rally "fascist," and declared, "...violence is justified to stop it." Gorcenski attended Unite the Right well-armed, and tweeted out a few weeks later, "I literally *pulled a fucking gun* on August 12th."

Clergy Groups

Some might assume clergy groups would be neutral parties in politically charged events, peaceful and loving towards all involved. But in Charlottesville, there are local clergy groups which work hand in hand with radical leftist activist groups.

One local clergy group, the Clergy Collective, formed after the June 2015 church shooting by Dylann Roof in Charleston S.C. After the July 8 Klan rally, the group split. The Heaphy Report states "Seth Wispelwey and Brittany Caine-Conley... formed a new group called Congregate Charlottesville. Wispelwey told us that the Clergy Collective was too close to the City "establishment" and lacked transparency. He explained that Congregate Charlottesville's

---

7   Ngo, *Unmasked*, p. 184.

goal was to 'equip faith leaders to show up on matters of justice.' They put out a call for 1,000 clergy to attend the August 12 event. In the weeks leading up to August 12, Congregate organized a series of trainings for nonviolent direct action... Members of Black Lives Matter and Showing Up for Racial Justice also attended the trainings." Some attendees of the training explained, "They wanted to be visible in the opposition to the right-wing groups and make it harder for them to have a platform to express racism."[8]

The attendance of BLM and SURJ members at the training is indicative of the clergy groups' willingness to work hand in hand with aggressive and sometimes violent left-wing activist groups.

---

8   Heaphy Report, p. 72.

CHAPTER 4 QUICK LINKS:

 Heaphy Report. URL: qrs.ly/dpcvtcb

 Jason Kessler, "Antifa Comms Director Luis Oyola on Charlottesville Conspiracy," video, June 19, 2020. URL: qrs.ly/4acvtbm

Jason Kessler, "Head EMT at Charlottesville Rally Discusses Expectation of Left-Wing Violence," video, Feb. 23, 2021. URL: qrs.ly/zxcvtfd

CHAPTER 5

NEUTRAL PARTIES

"Conversations could have reassured the community."

Local Business And Residents

ACCORDING TO THE HEAPHY REPORT, owners of businesses in the downtown Charlottesville area were concerned about Unite the Right and looking for guidance about how to prepare for the weekend's events: whether to close and board up their businesses, whether and under what circumstances they might deny service to customers, and what to do in case of emergency. They reached out to the city for information, but "there was no reciprocal outreach initiated by local government...Without effective communication, rumors easily spread."

Local neighborhood associations were likewise left in the dark about what to expect. "Conversations with neighborhood associations could have improved intelligence and reassured the community," the Heaphy Report concluded.[1]

---

1   Heaphy Report, pp. 75-77.

The Militias

Numerous militia groups were present the day of Unite the Right. Some of them reached out beforehand to let the CPD know of their intention to attend the event in a neutral, peace-keeping capacity. The CPD told them that they had a right to attend, but discouraged them from doing so out of concern that having more armed attendees would increase tensions.

Thankfully, the militia groups came to Unite the Right anyways. As it turned out, the militias provided the only semblance of peace-keeping and law enforcement in Charlottesville that day.

With regards to the militias, the Heaphy Report states, "In addition to the protesters and counter-protesters present for these events, we attempted to interview the militia personnel who appeared on August 12. In public statements and in conversations with us, the militia members claimed objectivity. They indicated that they appeared in Charlottesville to protect free speech and discourage violence on all sides. We had constructive discussions with several militia members, though we were unable to arrange formal interviews with any of them...the City's lawsuit against the militia groups halted our constructive efforts to obtain their cooperation. Once the lawsuit was filed, the militia groups told us they were no longer willing to provide information to our review." [2]

Some of the police had positive comments about the militia members. After observing some militiamen separating protesters and counter-protesters, one officer remarked, "I like those militia guys," to which his colleague replied, "Yeah, they're doing a good job."[3]

The militias firmly declared that they were neutral parties who intended to keep the peace between protesters and counter-protesters without favoritism to either side, and by most accounts they behaved in a very fair and responsible manner. However, on the day of Unite the Right, some assumed that the militia members, many of whom wore military garb or patriotic emblems normally associated with conservative beliefs, were in support of the rally.

2   Heaphy Report, p. 18.

3   Heaphy Report, p. 128.

Numerous media outlets described them as "far right," and some Unite the Right counter-protesters interacted with them in a hostile manner as if they were Alt-Right rally attendees.

CHAPTER 5 QUICK LINKS:

 Heaphy Report. URL: qrs.ly/dpcvtcb

CHAPTER 6

UNITE THE RIGHT ORGANIZERS

"Everyone turned against me before the event."

THE BILLED SPEAKERS for Unite the Right included:
- Richard Spencer
- Jason Kessler
- Mike "Enoch" Peinovich, host of The Right Stuff podcast
- Internet personality Tim "Baked Alaska" Gionet
- Christopher Cantwell, host of the Radical Agenda podcast
- Matt Heimbach of the Traditionalist Workers' Party
- Johnny Monoxide (aka John Ramondetta) of Identity Evropa
- Pax Dickinson, former CTO of Business Insider
- Augustus Sol Invictus (formerly known as Austin Gillespie)
- Dr. Michael Hill, President of the League of the South

Of those mentioned, Richard Spencer probably had the most name recognition. President of the think-tank National Policy Institute, and a telegenic, articulate, and well-dressed man, Spencer courted media attention and seemingly enjoyed being a lightning rod. Spencer is credited with coining the term "Alt-Right." Spencer had recently been featured in full-length articles in national media outlets and held a series of speaking engagements that drew massive, headline-grabbing protests, thereby becoming a household name during Trump's campaign and early presidency.

Conflicts developed behind the scenes during the planning stages of Unite the Right, which permit-holder Kessler had intended to control, as Alt-Right celebrity Spencer and others, such as Elliot Kline, aka Eli Mosley of Identity Evropa, sought to commandeer the event.

Augustus Sol Invictus had given a speech at a Boston event in May that included his first call to "unite the right," a plea for emergent groups on the New Right to put aside petty differences and unify around shared goals. He made a similar plea when he spoke at an event in Washington D.C. with Richard Spencer in June. Though viewed by some as extreme for eccentricities such as his pagan beliefs and practices, Invictus was not among the politically extreme, hard-right players in Charlottesville. Invictus is a Libertarian and was friendly with the "Alt-Lite" contingent of new right personalities.

"Alt-Lite" is a nebulous term used to describe people in the New Right who separate themselves from establishment conservatives and embrace American populism as civic nationalists. In other words, they believe in the founding ideals of the United States as defined by the Constitution, but believe that shared principles are the foundation of the nation and the race of citizens is unimportant. The Alt-Right, by contrast, is explicitly pro-White. On August 11, 2017, Richard Spencer posted a statement to his website (AltRight. com), that is sometimes referred to as the "Charlottesville Manifesto." It is entitled "What it Means to be Alt-Right." Based on an early draft by Invictus, the statement was recrafted by Spencer and some colleagues into a twenty-point "meta-political manifesto for the Alt-Right movement." The first of the twenty points declared: "Race is the foundation of identity," and defined "White" and "European." The statement further specified that Jews are distinct from Whites, that America was founded by Anglo-Saxon Protestants, and argued that "racially or ethnically defined states are legitimate and necessary."

At the time Invictus was associated with the Fraternal Order of Alt-Knights (FOAK), an offshoot of the Proud Boys. He had expected that the event in Charlottesville would bring the Alt-Right and Alt-Lite together on one stage. He states that originally some big name "Alt-Lite" personalities like Proud Boys founder Gavin McGinnis and FOAK leader Kyle "Based Stickman" Chapman were on board with the event, but that that they and others caved to pressure about sharing the stage with the Alt-Right. McGinnis banned the Proud Boys from attending Unite the Right. The Alt-Lite participants began to fall off, leaving only a few moderates like himself in the mix.

Invictus expected that everyone would make speeches and go home. "Having a riot was not on the agenda. I don't think anyone foresaw that." Invictus had expressed to the police that he had a keen interest in making sure Unite the Right was a successful event, because he was planning to use his speech to announce his candidacy to represent Florida in the U.S. Senate.

Trace Chiles, who hails from Richmond, Virginia was the East Coast Commander for FOAK. He arrived in Charlottesville with a group of about 80 men from all over the country, some from as far away as California. Chiles attended in part to provide security for Invictus, but also to show support for his heritage and for free speech which he believed were "going down the drain." He originally expected the rally to be peaceful, having heard that the counter-protesters would be assembling at a different park. But as the date of the event drew closer, he realized, "that wasn't going to happen."

Matt Parrot of the Traditionalist Workers Party was certain that the rally would be safe. "We were confident given the number of National Guard and State Police present, that this would be a monument protest with scheduled speakers." Prior to the rally, his group had a conversation about whether it would be safe enough for the women members of their group to attend. Parrot thought that because of the large police presence and the amount of planning that went into the event, "there would be no major violence... We had concluded it wouldn't be that dangerous an event." They decided it would be safe enough for the women members to attend.

Cooperation With Authorities

In contrast to the defensive and secretive counter-protester organizations, representatives of Unite the Right were in open communication with law enforcement in the weeks leading up the event.

According to the Heaphy Report independent investigation, "Jason Kessler was the most informative human source CPD had in advance of August 12." A number of other parties involved with organizing Unite the Right engaged in voluntary communication with the police, including designated security personnel for the event, Brian Brathovd and Jack Pierce. According to Heaphy, "Each told CPD that he expected a peaceful rally and hoped the police would protect Alt-Right groups from violent counter-protesters."[1]

Organizers began planning entry and exit of attendees to the venue, and to publicize the event as well as inform attendees how to prepare and what to expect in the way of counter-protesters. According the Heaphy Report, a planning document was circulated among various group leaders that provided guidance about what type of weapons were permitted by law. The document "advised against bringing knives, tasers, or masks. Shields, flags, and flagpoles could be brought, but attendees should avoid using anything that could be construed as a weapon, and shields could only be used 'defensively.' Helmets were recommended, and pepper spray was allowed – but they discouraged its deployment... With respect to conduct, the planning document advised all attendees to avoid violence "at all costs outside what is needed to defend our people."[2] There were color-coded contingency plans for various scenarios, depending on whether or not the rally permit for the park would be in place, and whether the police would secure the park or arrest attendees if they were to engage in civil disobedience by occupying the park. They also planned

---

1   Heaphy Report, pp. 71-72.

2   Heaphy Report, p. 79.

for vans to take attendees from a staging area to the park, and for attendees to march together using a shield wall for protection if they were required to be dropped off outside the traffic barricades.

Dysfunction Within

Relationships between the organizers of Unite the Right were rife with conflict right from the beginning, and continued to devolve as August 12th approached. By then, the parties involved were anything but united. Some were in open conflict, while others were scheming against each other secretly.

"Everyone turned against me before the event," maintains Kessler.

Disputes about who should be on the speaking roster caused some tensions. Because he wanted Unite the Right to attract mainstream conservatives, Kessler tried to moderate the influence some of the more notorious and extreme characters. For example, the League of the South member who was appointed to be the liaison for Unite the Right wanted David Duke to be featured. When Kessler refused to approve him as a speaker, believing that to do so "would stigmatize normal attendees," some parties revolted.

Questions about the participation of another incendiary figure, Robert "Azzmador" Ray, also created conflict. Ray, a contributor to openly anti-Jewish and fiercely provocative outlet The Daily Stormer, is known for his wild-eyed rants about Jews and the Zionist Occupied Government. Asked about Azzmador, Kessler explains, "I know I was trying to keep that guy away from UTR at the time of the event and then Eli Mosley - this was one of the reasons Eli Mosley turned against me - he really wanted Daily Stormer and Azzmador to have a prominent role at the rally, and I didn't."

"...so many of the people in the Alt-Right were like this guy Eli Mosley - that was Richard Spencer's right-hand man - starting all these rumors saying that I was Jewish, that I was mentally ill, whatever else, and he used those kinds of like rumors and things to seize control of the event from me."[3]

Invictus confirms Kessler's claim. Though Invictus was focused on recruiting speakers and attendees for the event and not directly involved with its logistics and security, he agrees that "there seemed to be a consensus that the Spencer camp was taking control of the event... they de facto took control."

Zarski believes the reason Kessler was edged out of leadership of Unite the Right was that "Jason was inconsistent. He was not prepared nor did he have the connections to make it happen."

Through discovery for some of the many lawsuits ensuing from Unite the Right, Kessler has learned a lot more about what was going on behind his back during the planning of the event. "[Mosley] ran his mouth a lot. He was not a good person. He was in text message with Richard Spencer saying that he had taken control of the event and all the leadership was referring to him. I also have other materials that I've obtained from Facebook messages - a group which was literally called 'The Coup' that I turned over to my attorney from a whistleblower that handed this over to me and it involved other people - Matt Heimbach and so forth - and they were basically just plotting how to take this event from me. And Eli Mosely made similar claims that he had stolen all of the leadership from me and that I was basically shadow banned at my own event."[4]

Some of the text messages made public show Spencer and Kline engaged in mockery of Kessler, and one text from Spencer to Mosley reads, "After c ville [sic], we need to drop him. He's just stupid and weird."[5]

---

3   "Were the Capitol Hill Riots Charlottesville II? A Jason Kessler Interview," LukeFord.net, Jan. 14, 2021.

4   *Ibid.*

5   Brett Barrouquerre, "'Let's just ghost him': Alt-Right leaders were leery of Jason Kessler before 'Unite the Right,'" SPLCCenter.org, Oct. 17, 2018.

Another large contingent, a loose confederation known as the Nationalist Front, broke away from the other planners entirely. The Nationalist Front included the Traditionalist Workers Party (TWP), the National Socialist Movement, (NSM) and the League of the South (LOS). Matt Parrot of the TWP says that neither Kessler nor Spencer's group were actually organizing. "Plans weren't very structured and mature." The groups of the Nationalist Front had a lot of experience with events of this nature, and decided to stay in control over their own organizations' roles in the rally.

CHAPTER 6 QUICK LINKS:

 Heaphy Report. URL: qrs.ly/dpcvtcb

 "Were the Capitol Hill Riots Charlottesville II? A Jason Kessler Interview," LukeFord.net, Jan. 14, 2021. URL: qrs.ly/e1cvtdi

CHAPTER 7

CHANGE OF VENUE

"I was on the phone for hours, trying to convince them."

SOME CHARLOTTESVILLE CITIZENS and members of local government hoped to cancel Kessler's permit for Unite the Right, but were advised by the City's attorneys that it would be next to impossible to do so legally as it would violate freedom of speech protections. Law enforcement reported that most of the threats of violence seemed to emanate not from Unite the Right-affiliated groups but from counter-protest groups, and to cancel the permit in response to counter-protesters would amount to a "heckler's veto," a violation of the First Amendment.

There was intense public pressure surrounding preparations for Unite the Right. The Heaphy Report notes, "City Councilors responded to this pressure by injecting themselves into the operational details of the City's response to this event – a function typically reserved for city staff." [1] After determining the rally could not be cancelled, the City began to consider moving it from Lee Park to McIntire Park, a larger, more open venue outside of downtown about a mile away. Lee Park, with shady trees,

---

1 Heaphy Report, p. 4.

crisscrossed sidewalks, and a statue of Robert E. Lee mounted in the middle, is on about an acre of raised land. It is surrounded on all sides by city streets - on the north by Jefferson Street, on the south by Market Street, on the west by First Street N.E., and on the east by Second Street N.E. By contrast, McIntire Park is an open area of about 130 acres.

Mayor Signer spearheaded the relocation effort, which he describes in great detail in his book about Unite the Right, *Cry Havoc*. He wrote, that a few days after the KKK rally, "my attention started turning to August 12. I started thinking we needed a big new idea... I felt there was no way hundreds or even thousands of protesters could safely coexist in the small park and densely compressed urban streets. It seemed like a recipe for havoc."[2]

He began calling associates for advice on moving the rally location. He spoke with numerous UVA Law School professors. He sought advice from South Bend mayor Pete Buttigieg and Houston Mayor Sylvester Turner and Virginia Governor McAuliffe. He spoke with a four-star general he knew, and the author of a book on counter-insurgency. He continued his mission for days, even while on vacation. "One any given day, I was on the phone for three to four hours. I repeatedly talked to my colleagues on the council, trying to convince them to move the event."[3] He tried to push a hybrid plan to allow the main event to take place in McIntire Park but permit small groups to shuttle to Lee Park.

A private legal firm, Boies Schiller Flexner, had been retained by the city at a cost of $30,000 to provide legal guidance for their case, which they were advised would be very difficult to win. Because of First Amendment protections, any successful legal attempt to move Unite the Right would require presenting content-neutral evidence that it was necessary – in other words, they must focus on public safety considerations and not allow it to appear as though they were motivated to move the rally based upon their objection to its message. Signer faults the city council and law enforcement leaders for being extremely resistant to his idea of changing the plans they

2 Signer, *Cry Havoc*, p. 162.

3 Signer, *Cry Havoc*, p. 174.

had been working to put in place. "If our government had presented credible evidence to a court that we would be unable to manage the rally safely at Emancipation [Lee] Park, our chances of winning would have been higher – according to our attorney. However, our staff did not seem to want to concede that the strategy already in place might not succeed. That would require specificity of evidence and humility in approach."[4]

A meeting was called by Mayor Signer for August 2nd to meet with lawyers about the issue. The lawyers advised the city that only evidence of a specific, credible threat that would legally justify moving the rally - generalized threats or statement of intention to use violence in self-defense did not meet that criteria. At the meeting, Chief Al Thomas expressed concerns about moving the rally at the late date after six weeks of work on developing plans centered around Lee Park. Despite the objections expressed, City Council voted by a 4-1 margin to move the scheduled event to McIntire Park. The final decision rested with City Manager Jones. On August 3rd, he announced his support for the change of venue.

On Monday August 7th, Kessler met with city officials, including City Manager Jones and Captain Wendy Lewis, at the Parks and Recreation office, where he was informed that his permit would be granted for McIntire Park, not Lee Park. Kessler was determined to hold the event at Lee Park. "The genesis of this entire event is this Robert E. Lee statue that the city is trying to move, which is symbolic of a lot of issues that deal with tearing down White people's history."[5] He indicated that he intended to fight the change in federal court. Furthermore, he expressed his intention that Unite the Right attendees would engage in civil disobedience and assemble at Lee Park even if McIntire Park was listed on the permit.

The City held a press conference later that day to announce that the permit rally had been granted for McIntire Park. Signer began speaking with a DC-based public relations firm that had been hired to assist in managing communications with the public. The next

---

4 Signer, *Cry Havoc*, p. 178.

5 McAuliffe, *Beyond Charlottesville*, p. 69.

day, Signer received an email from the Virginia ACLU and the Rutherford Institute demanding a retraction of the permit decision.

By that point, the city had used up their outside legal budget and were on their own for the next court battle. On August 10th, Kessler, represented by lawyers from the ACLU and Rutherford Institute, filed a First and Fourteenth Amendment lawsuit against the City of Charlottesville in Richmond federal court, arguing that moving the rally intended to protest the monument removal would "dilute and alter" its intended message.

On August 11th, Judge Glen Conrad granted Kessler's motion for a preliminary injunction against the move, allowing the permit for Lee Park to stay in place.

Governor McAuliffe recalls that he was "stunned" by the judge's decision which he found "unconscionable." He complains, "... the judge came right out and said he was blaming City Council members for posts on social media that showed they were against these right-wing extremists," which the judge took as proof that they were motivated to move the rally by objection to its content. McAuliffe imagined that the Alt-Right heard the ACLU declare the ruling a victory for the right to peacefully protest, and "laughed until they couldn't laugh anymore."[6]

The Heaphy Report states that the late decision to change the venue "had a negative impact on preparations for this challenging event" by increasing complications and frustrating communication with the public. [7] Furthermore, with his attempts to force a change of venue for Unite the Right, Signer was by his own admission stepping beyond what were understood to be the duties of his office. He wrote, "Through all of this, I was playing a far more active role than prescribed in my formal job description. I was directing legal calls, weighing in on political and legal strategy, and forming strategies myself... I was certainly coloring way outside the lines of my official job description."[8] He believed himself to be working

---

6 McAuliffe, *Beyond Charlottesville*, pp. 84-85.

7 Heaphy Report, p. 5.

8 Signer, *Cry Havoc*, p. 192.

to prevent disaster, but he knew that he was engaging in a long-shot legal fight, the results of which were likely to be disregarded by Unite the Right attendees even if he won. What did he actually accomplish, other than lining lawyers' pockets and taking time and attention away from meaningful planning?

Invictus believes that the attempted venue change contributed to the disastrous outcome of Unite the Right. "Everybody had security plans which were completely changed. The police had changed plans and didn't want to change again. They were sick of dealing with it. I don't know how Signer could say with a straight face that it would make things safer."

CHAPTER 7 QUICK LINKS:

 Heaphy Report. URL: qrs.ly/dpcvtcb

CHAPTER 8

THE ROAD TO CHARLOTTESVILLE

*"I thought we would picket
and get our side heard."*

Why Hold Unite The Right?

ON THE POLITICAL CESSPOOL podcast a few weeks before Unite the Right, host James Edwards asked Kessler about the purpose of the rally. He explained, "to destigmatize pro-White advocacy...To make sure our free speech rights are upheld... I want people to come out and support these monuments... this is an historic opportunity where you will not be alone. You will be greeted by hundreds, if not more, of your brothers and sisters and we are going to make news around the world."

Kessler continued... "This is an opportunity to reach out to the average conservative who knows that White people are under attack. Perhaps they're even as far as being a Confederate heritage supporter but they don't feel like they can stand up for their own interests. They feel like they need to hide behind the idea of a "rainbow Confederacy" or a very small minority of Black Civil War veterans... It's okay. You can stand up for your own history."[1]

---

1   "Radio Show Hour 1 – 2017/07/29," thepoliticalcesspool.org, podcast.

Think of the impact it would have on society if enough people embraced that simple statement: ***It's okay. You can stand up for your own history.***"

The day before Unite the Right, Kessler explained to Katie Couric, "The point of this rally is to protect this statue, because this statue is one of many statues that are in honor of the history of Western Civilization and European peoples that are being torn down... One of the ethnicities that is most in danger is the Southern White people."

Kessler is often described in the media as a "Nazi," "White Supremacist," or "White Nationalist," though he identifies as none of those things. He is sometimes thought of in connection to the Proud Boys, though his association with them was very brief and ended in mutual disavowals. Kessler identifies as a political moderate and civil rights activist that focuses on issues affecting White people. He believes that White people should be able to organize to advocate for themselves like all other racial groups. "I don't think that people should be treated unfairly because of their race or any other characteristics. I just feel this country's demographics should remain the same as they have been for the majority of history. But there seems to be this problem with the social justice people where they have a distinct hatred for White people... I would not say that they're pushing for equal rights. I think that they have long since passed the point where they have been going for anything approximating equality. They looking for special treatment for these groups. At this point, they want to have institutionalized discrimination against White people."[2]

The Rally Attendees

Why did a thousand or more people travel from all over the country to attend Unite the Right in Charlottesville on August 12, 2017?

Do you really know?

---

2 National Geographic, "See the Sparks That Set Off Violence in Charlottesville," YouTube video, posted Aug 19, 2017.

Have you heard anyone who was there that day explain it in their own words? If you learned everything you know about the rally from the mainstream news, the answer is almost certainly "no."

What do you make of the fact that few who were in attendance that day have ever been given a chance to tell their side of the story? Why was the media so disinterested in explaining all perspectives on what happened that day? Perhaps it was because they had already decided what they wanted the public to believe was the truth, and they didn't want create any sympathy for those they had cast as the "villain" in their story.

I interviewed several people who attended Unite the Right. I asked them about their personal and political backgrounds, their reasons for attending, their experiences of the event, and how their participation affected their lives afterwards. Some of them were willing to speak under their real names, but others requested that I use a pseudonym, since they were fearful of backlash from their friends, families, or employers. Still, they all believe that most of the public does not understand what really happened, and that it is important that the truth be told. Below, I introduce the attendees who bravely and generously shared their experiences with me so that I could share them with you.

Luke

Luke Gordon grew up in a paleo-conservative, multi-generational household with his grandparents and great-grandparents "in the sticks" outside of Richmond. A self-described family man, Luke is a graduate of the Virginia Military Institute. Formerly a pharmaceutical executive, he now owns his own business.

Though always conservative, he began to take in interest in the "dissident right" when he started to notice on the news a burgeoning hatred toward people that could be described as "Heritage Americans." Though he somewhat enjoyed the online trolling of the "transgressive Alt-Right," he mostly identified as a paleo-conservative with an interest in Southern Nationalism.

Luke's family had for many generations been in Virginia, and everyone he knew was against destroying historical statues of great men of history. He had visited Charlottesville as a child, and noticed that it changed since the late 1960s. It was now full of non-Virginians and radical liberals who "hate everything about the city, about the state, and about our history."

When Luke made his plans to go to Unite the Right, he "naively" assumed that everything would go well. He had only been to one protest before while in high school, a pro-life march, and the counter-protesters there had been peaceful. He knew that permits were in place for Unite the Right, and he had faith that the Virginia State Police would keep control. He expected to listen to speeches in a safe environment, and that the rally would go smoothly. He carpooled down with a large group of friends, about 15 or 20 people.

"I never in my wildest imagination thought it would turn out like it did."

He had an old photograph of his grandmother and great uncle in his WWII uniform in front of the Stonewall Jackson statue in Charlottesville. He kept the photo in his pocket throughout the rally to remind him why he was there. "I had to go for them." Later in the day when things got heated and he thought to leave, he would remember the photo in his pocket and resolve to stay.

Steve

Steve was raised in a typical Republican family that was not too political. For a long time, Steve has had an interest in politics and in dissident thought, but that has always taken the form of reading and writing, not activism. He was at one time a Libertarian with a passion for the ideas of Ron Paul and Ayn Rand. Eventually, he began to believe the "ancap" ideals he had embraced were too utopian and not workable.

When Donald Trump came to power, Steve began to realize that the "mainstream right" was not really right wing at all, but rather made up of "quisling opportunists." He came to believe that the "Alt-Right" were the only real representatives of right-wing beliefs. Furthermore, Trump's ascent to power had shocked leftists who had not expected their cultural and political dominance to be seriously challenged. "They went berserk."

Charlottesville had been Steve's hometown since he was a small child. He had lived out of state after college, but returned in his late twenties. Back in Charlottesville, he felt he was at home in the South again. Changes had taken place in the city while he was away. For a while, he was enjoying some of the changes, like the "cool cultural stuff." But the reaction of the city's leftists to the election of Donald Trump brought about other, less welcome changes. The town, which had been a liberal enclave for many years, became a lightning rod for left-wing opposition to Trump.

"I knew Charlottesville was going down a dark path. There were real rumbles of radical leftism." Mayor Mike Signer had dubbed Charlottesville "The Capital of the Resistance," and efforts were being made to remove historic statues like that of General Robert E. Lee.

"I grew up with that statue. I didn't want them to tear it down."

When he first heard about the proposed Unite the Right rally, he really liked the idea of it. "The philosophy behind 'Unite the Right' made sense to me - Let's get all hands on deck. No matter what particular ideological differences we may have, we all oppose the leftist assault on our identity as Southerners and other Heritage Americans. I think we all knew that it was an assault on White people in general... The initial drive to Unite the Right was 'Let's unite around this statue that represents all the other statues they want to tear down.' That was the whole reason the name "Unite the Right" worked with so many people, because all these different factions could get behind it. Statues are symbolic of something bigger, but let's start with the statues and protecting the integrity of the symbols."

The summer prior to Unite the Right, Steve didn't know much about the groups that were expected to be in attendance. He was slightly familiar with a few of them - some he liked, some he did not. However, "None of it seemed bad or crazy to me." He had recently attended a rally in Charlottesville held by MAGA candidate for Senate, Corey Stewart, in support of keeping historic statues, and remembered it as "a fun event."

Tom

Tom grew up in East Tennessee and was political from an early age. As an interested citizen participant in local government, he had found that traditional views were often laughed off. To defend his values, he became an active member of groups like the Council of Conservative Citizens. Tom had always felt that in politics, it was important not just to talk, but to take action.

When Tom heard about Unite the Right from a friend in the CCC, he thought it would be a good opportunity to stand up to what he saw as the ISIS-style destruction of Southern and American heritage. He liked the concept of "Unite the Right," with various groups coming together to fight the purge of history and to defend Western Civilization. Tom had been to dozens of street rallies in East Tennessee and across the Southeast. He expected "we would picket, and get our side heard," and that with about a thousand people saying "enough is enough," the message would be that much stronger. He hoped it would be the first step to building a "counter-revolutionary reaction" to the surge of leftist activism that had taken place during Donald Trump's presidency.

Tom thought that since the rally was permitted, it would be safe. One friend had offered him a shield to take on his trip, and another offered him a helmet. He declined both, believing "ain't nothing gonna happen."

Tom drove down with about five "nationalist, traditionalist" friends, and the group stayed at a cabin the night before the event.

Chris

Chris, a young man in his early twenties, grew up in Appalachia in a moderate conservative home. At time of rally, he considered himself to be a political moderate and a Trump Republican.

Chris had heard about Unite the Right on the Facebook page for the event before it was taken down. He believed it was primarily a pro-Trump "moderate conservative" rally in defense of the Robert E. Lee statue.

Chris drove down with 6 or 7 people the night before. He did not realize how big the event was going to be until he got into town and saw all the vehicles. He knew about Antifa, but didn't know much about the hard right except for what he had seen on TV, and he wasn't expecting to see much of it there.

Nathaniel

Nathaniel grew up in Delaware. A conservative since his teens, Nathaniel has followed a variety of political personalities over the years. He began listening to Rush Limbaugh, as well as other Republican commenters like Bill O'Reilly, Mark Levin, and Sean Hannity. His first vote was for Pat Buchannan in the 1996 Republican primary. As a young adult, he began to sour on the GOP for not following up on their promises.

Talking to real-life friends, and arguing, then later conversing, with online acquaintances made Nathaniel question many of the ideological assumptions he had held over the years. Nathaniel began to listen to Libertarians like Tom Woods and Ron Paul, and alternative media personalities like Stefan Molyneaux. He began to realize that even talk radio was "establishment," and to take an interest in more racially-conscious personalities like Chris Cantwell and Mike Enoch. Their talk about how the US was becoming like Brazil made a whole lot of sense. Around the time of Unite the Right, he had also been listening to "Alt-Lite" personalities like Lauren Southern, Gavin McGinnis, Paul Joseph Watson and Mike Cernovich.

One of the assumptions Nathaniel began to question was the "official" interpretation of the Civil War. He began to learn more about the Southern view of the conflict, and to develop respect and sympathy for the Southern cause.

He wanted to go to Unite the Right because he saw "Trump supporters getting their asses beat" and nothing being done about it, so he "wanted to push back against it." He thought the rally "seemed like it was going to be a lot of fun." He saw Unite the Right as an opportunity to meet online acquaintances in real life, and "take this to the streets."

It wasn't until two days before that he realized Charlottesville was a college town, and that they would be "going into the belly of the beast," a left-wing strong hold. However, because he knew the organizers had been working proactively with law enforcement, he was hopeful that both sides of the conflict would be kept apart. He had a can of pepper spray as his only weapon.

On the drive down to Charlottesville, Nathaniel was listening to "Clouds of Glory," a biography of Robert E. Lee.

He was part of a group of four online friends who were meeting in person for the first time. He had reserved the only hotel room he could find, one with modest accommodations that was usually reserved for hotel staff. When a friend offered him a spot in a nicer room, he gave his modest room to a stranger who had driven 10 hours to attend without having planned a place to stay.

Jim

Jim was born in New York to a family that was "fresh off the boat" from Ireland. He has lived all over the United States, but spent most of his life in Virginia and Florida. He was brought up to value his Irish heritage, but also with a strong belief in America as the Promised Land of opportunity for anyone who was willing to work hard. He was taught by his immigrant parents that to cherish the freedoms available in this country and to respect the Constitution as "sacrosanct."

For most of his life, Jim considered himself to be a typical American conservative. He joined the Marines at age 17, then went on to earn an MBA and become a husband and father. He was working in a professional, upper management position at the time of Unite the Right.

Jim's political beliefs began to change around the time of the Michael Brown riots. He believed that the media lied to fan the flames of racial tensions, and he was not happy to see that Obama gave support to the rioters and their Marxist narrative. Things became worse after the Dylann Roof murders. Jim remembers, "There was an almost instantaneous attack on all forms of Southern icons... I got infuriated." When Jim saw how rioters were celebrated as heroes while good Southerners were vilified, "It got my Irish up."

Having come from a family that fought for Irish independence, Jim recognized that the occupation tactics once used in Ireland were now taking place in the South. He wanted to see Southern heritage maintained. After the election of Trump, the left pulled out all the stops in their attacks on traditional America. Jim began to believe "the country that I was raised to adore was gone." He believed that a vestige of those values, however, still remained in the American South. At that point, he became active in the Southern Nationalist movement.

At the time of Unite the Right, Jim was a member of the League of the South. He had just moved to Florida and joined the chapter there. He explains, "Charlottesville was important for a lot of ideological reasons. The University of Virginia has been at the philosophical center of the South for 200 years." He believed the left was targeting Charlottesville because of its importance as the epicenter of Constitutional principles.

"I wasn't going to stand for it."

He meant to attend Unite the Right to defend the Constitution and the monument of the "great man" Robert E. Lee, then go home. He also planned to attend a few businesses meetings during his trip.

Bill

Retired from the oil industry, Bill has lived in Arkansas, Tennessee, Mississippi, and Louisiana. He is a Civil War history enthusiast and Southern heritage supporter, but he does not consider himself a Southern Nationalist.

Bill considered himself a yellow-dog Democrat for most of his life. He hadn't thought of himself as someone who would vote for Donald Trump - "I'm Southern and Trump is a brash Yankee" - but when faced with a choice between him and Hillary Clinton, he decided to vote for Trump.

For most of his life, Bill was not particularly political. Then in 2012, when people in New Orleans where he was living at the time began to push for changing the names of parks and the removal of monuments, he became involved with groups dedicated to preserving them. He became the moderator of a pro-monument Facebook group, and paid for a billboard calling to "Save Our Monuments." He personally attended the removal of statues of Beauregard and Lee.

Bill had met Jason Kessler and Augustus Sol Invictus on the phone, and they had supported his efforts to preserve the New Orleans monuments. He decided to go to the Unite the Right to reciprocate, because "those boys had helped me out." Bill knew of Kessler from some videos he had made about Antifa, and thought of him as someone who was not scared to stand up to Antifa and stand up for the monuments.

The night before the rally, Bill's group scoped out downtown Charlottesville and noticed the barricades and how "tight" the area was. Bill knew there would be a variety of groups of people at Unite the Right, and explains that "we didn't all get along with each other, but we were trying to make a statement," and to get as many people as possible together who weren't afraid to stand for the monuments.

"We didn't know how it was all going to play out."

Gene

Gene was born and raised in Nashville. He attended the University of Georgia on a track scholarship, then spent three years in the Marine Corps. He spent several years teaching at a high school and coaching high school football, then began working in sports medicine in the field of auto racing, including NASCAR and American LeMans.

Raised in a traditional Southern family, Gene was always a conservative. He had done a lot of reading about Southern history, so he knew the things the TV said about the South and the War Between the States were false. "That's not right. That's not historically accurate. I've read what the soldiers said." He wondered what else the mainstream media was lying about, so he started seeking out news and information from independent sources.

Gene planned to go to Unite the Right with a group of fellow League of the South members. He didn't know much about the rally or its organizers, but figured "if they're being slammed by the MSM, they must be the good guys."

The night before the rally, he and his group drove to downtown Charlottesville to check out the park and the parking garage. They talked about taking a tour of Monticello in the afternoon after the rally ended. At the camp where the League of the South was staying, Dr. Hill "laid down the ground rules" to make sure the group knew the state open carry laws and that wearing masks was forbidden. Hill emphasized to the members the importance of driving into town with a group for safety. Gene knew Antifa would be there, and he was expecting hostility and shouting, but not violence. He had never been physically attacked at a protest before, but took protective gear just in case.

Ayla

Perhaps better known by her online handle Wife with a Purpose, Ayla Stewart was among those who traveled to Charlottesville to attend Unite the Right. Known in Alt-Right parlance as a "trad wife," the mother of (at the time) six was famous for her social media posts and videos promoting traditional families, Christian homeschooling, and the celebration of European-American and Southern history.

Ayla first heard about Unite the Right on Twitter from online associates such as Paul Ramsey and Richard Spencer. She and her husband had frequently attended protests like anti-war rallies when they were younger and had fewer children, and she was excited that she might be able to attend the planned event in Charlottesville. "I loved the idea of getting together in real life, to see people face to face, hear their stories, and network." Because of her large brood, it had been impractical for her to attend the political rallies that had taken place in other parts of the country that year. However, she had family in Charlottesville and plans to be in the area around that time anyways, and thought it would be possible to go.

The fact that the rally centered around the Lee monument made her even more determined to attend. "The General Lee statue was super important to me because of my Southern heritage. I was reclaiming it." Her husband was from Utah, and she had tried to adapt herself to the culture while living there. After being doxed for her activism, she was rejected by Mormons, including those at the highest levels of the church, and gave up on trying to fit in. A native Tennessean, she decided, "Let's go back to where I am from." Respect for General Lee was a huge part of Southern heritage for Ayla. She had been given the middle name "Lee" in keeping with a family tradition meant to honor the great man. Bearing his name brought her derision in some parts of the country where she had lived, so she often found herself in the position of defending the honor of General Lee.

"I felt completely safe rallying behind this... I should be fighting for him," she explains. "This is erasing our history based on wrong information, and Charlottesville was particularly important to me."

CHAPTER 8 QUICK LINKS:

 The Political Cesspool Radio Show, Aug. 12, 2017. URL: qrs.ly/oscvtgt

National Geographic, "See the Sparks That Set Off Violence in Charlottesville," video, Aug 19, 2017. URL: qrs.ly/6ocvtgu

Part Two:

Unite The Right:
The Hour Arrives

CHAPTER 9

TORCHLIGHT RALLY

"It devolved pretty quickly."

AN UNFORGETTABLE EVENT took place in downtown Charlottesville on Friday August 11th, 2017, the evening before Unite the Right, when hundreds of Unite the Right participants marched after dark through the streets bearing tiki torches. The images of the torchlight processional - the aerial footage of a stream of lights winding its way through downtown Charlottesville, the close-ups of the torch-lit faces of young men in White polos, and the circle of lights surrounding the Thomas Jefferson statue on the University of Virginia campus - are some of the most indelible in the mind of the public when they think of the events of that August weekend.

The Plan And The March

Unlike the widely advertised Unite the Right Saturday rally, the Friday night event had been planned in relative secrecy on a private message board. Similar to the May torchlight protest that Richard Spencer organized, this gathering was meant to be a "flash-mob" style event for the purpose of preventing counter-protesters the opportunity to plan a response and gather in large numbers. The Thomas Jefferson statue was selected as the destination of the processional, Kessler explains, to make the point that not just Confederate symbols were under threat.

Local activist Emily Gorcenski spent a busy day occupied with monitoring the activities of Unite the Right organizers. In the early afternoon, Gorcenski, having learned from activist intelligence-gathering sources of a planned meet-up of Christopher Cantwell and some associates in a Walmart parking lot, took pictures of Cantwell at the meet-up and posted them to Twitter. Law enforcement followed up with Cantwell after receiving reports of a man with a firearm, but they declined to pursue charges after verifying that he and his associates had proper permits allowing them to carry the weapons. [1]

Shortly before the processional, the marchers learned Antifa had breached the private message board and become aware of the torchlight march plans. One leftist organizer explained, "The torchlit march was exposed through leaks and anonymous hearsay even weeks before August 12th we knew that they were planning a torchlit march somewhere in town. We knew this was something they were trying to keep secret and we knew this was an opportunity for the Charlottesville community to stand up to them and show them that we were not going to allow them to organize in secret again like they did on the night of May 13th."[2]

League of the South Public Affairs Chief Brad Griffin, who writes under the pen name Hunter Wallace, wrote that at around 5 pm on the day of the march, "I saw the news that the Antifa website "It's Going Down" had compromised the Discord group and found out about the torchlight parade to the Jefferson monument. I immediately called Jason Kessler to tell him the news. I recommended either canceling the torchlight parade or relocating it somewhere else like Monticello. It was still up in the air at this time."[3]

The Traditionalist Workers Party had told its members not to attend the march, concluding that it was too risky to attend the unpermitted event.

---

1 Heaphy Report, p. 112.

2 Kessler, "Antifa Comms Director," BitChute.com.

3 Hunter Wallace, "The Road to Charlottesville: Hunter Wallace Edition," Occidental Dissent.com, Aug. 31, 2017.

That same afternoon, an anonymous caller alerted the Charlottesville Police Department about the planned march. After a flurry of inter-agency communication, University Police Chief Michael Gibson doubled the number of officers on duty that evening, and instructed his staff to place officers near the Rotunda to monitor the march. He did not communicate information about the march to other first responder organizations such as fire and rescue, and he declined an offer of assistance from the Virginia State Police, large numbers of whom who had already arrived in Charlottesville to prepare for Saturday's rally. The Heaphy Report concluded that "[Chief Michael] Gibson's failure to fully engage and leverage the law enforcement resources at his disposal... resulted in a fragmented and disorganized response later that evening." [4]

Meanwhile, Kessler and several of the other Unite the Right organizers met at McIntire Park to discuss the agenda for the evening. There was debate amongst the parties about whether to proceed with the march at all since it was known that counter-protesters would be present. Cantwell proposed going ahead with the plan with the stipulation that law enforcement be notified of the plans in advance. Kessler agreed to place a call to the Charlottesville Police Department to inform them that the marchers planned to begin at Nameless Field and proceed to the Thomas Jefferson statue on the University of Virginia grounds. He then handed off the phone to Eli Mosley, who spoke with the police out of earshot of Kessler. (Kessler has since expressed regret at the trust he placed in other parties by allowing them to confer on their own with the police.)

Even after the police learned that counter-protesters would be present at the march, they issued no warnings to the students of the University of Virginia. However, some students learned of the planned event. UVA's Student Council Vice President for Administration, Alex Cintron, emailed Chief Gibson at 9:02 pm to express his concern. "Many students are alarmed and I was wondering if there is any safety information I can distribute to other student leaders and the student body at large?'"

---

4 Heaphy Report, pp. 112-113.

Gibson did not provide Cintron the requested safety information, but simply replied, "Thank you for writing me. UPD is aware of this information and is monitoring the situation very closely to make sure the Grounds stays [*sic*] safe."[5]

While Unite the Right organizers were getting ready for the events of the evening, hundreds of counter-protesters, including Cornell West and Mayor Mike Signer, were planning to attend an interfaith prayer service at St. Paul's Memorial Episcopal Church. Several hours in advance of the scheduled start time of 7:00 pm, a security team had arrived, including UVA professor Willis Jenkins and members of left-wing militia Redneck Revolt. Denied permission to bring firearms into the sanctuary, the security team guarded the building from the outside, monitoring the perimeter and posting guards at the doors. Jenkins admitted to Heaphy Report investigators that White males who attempted to attend the service were subjected to enhanced vetting and questioning before being allowed inside.[6] By the time the service began, the large sanctuary was full to overflowing. Though a few threats were called into the church, no violence occurred at the service.

Meanwhile, leftist activists were scrambling to respond to the impending march, as one organizer explains: "When the call came out on the day of for people to mobilize, there happened to be another call for nighttime prayer at that church across the street from the Rotunda which is where we found out the Nazis were trying to have their rally. The organizers in the city gave them a heads up, that the torchlit rally was going to happen at the same time and we also organized in whatever ways we could to disrupt the torchlit rally. When groups of Antifascists and other organizers showed up, we observed the torchlit rally had grown to over 300 participants, and at that same time we also were honestly very disorganized and scrambled with our comms, such that we weren't able to disrupt it, and they're en route to the Rotunda."[7]

---

5 Ken Klippenstein, "Emails Suggest UVA Police Downplayed White Supremacist Groups During Unite the Right Rally," ShadowProof.com, Sept. 1, 2017.

6 Heaphy Report, p. 114.

7 Kessler, "Antifa Comms Director," BitChute.com.

By about 9:20 pm, Unite the Right organizers and supporters had gathered at Nameless Field. A handful of University Police Department officers were stationed there, and Gorcenski was also observing as torches were passed out and instructions were given to marchers. The Charlottesville Police Officer who was in charge of their presence in the area asked the UPD if they required assistance, but he was told the situation was under control. Cantwell would later tell interviewers that he was shocked by the scant law enforcement presence at the event, remarking that "if you notify law enforcement that White nationalists were going to march on a public university with torches, you would think they would take an interest." [8]

The few police officers that were present at Nameless field followed the procession as it moved through town. A number of marchers, including Cantwell, were selected by the organizers to be "guards" who would walk on the outside of the line and fight physically with Antifa if necessary.

Invictus, who describes the procession as "one of the most epic things I've ever seen," remembers the march as going smoothly and proceeding in an orderly fashion as the stream of people made its way across the UVA campus. Most onlookers just stared as they passed by, but a few counter-protesters were following along and taunting them. Some marchers acted as "sheepdogs," maintaining order among the ranks and making sure nobody reacted to the counter-protesters' provocation. According to Invictus the march was "perfectly peaceful until we got to the statue and Antifa were there."

As the stream of torches came into view at the Rotunda around 10:07 pm, the CPD officer in charge once again asked the UPD if they required assistance, and once again was told "no." Gorcenski had run ahead and warned the small group of counter-protesters than a large contingent of torch-bearing marchers was on the way. Upon realizing the counter-protesters were greatly outnumbered and few police were present, Gorcenski went online, posted a video

---

8 Heaphy Report, p. 117.

of the stream of approaching torches, and lashed out at fellow activists for their absence.

"This is an entire fucking line of Nazis in 2017... hundreds of Nazis marching with torches. Folks this is the end. A handful of activists have linked hands around the statue. This is all we have. This is what we have to stand against them. Where the fuck are the rest of you? Where the fuck are the rest of you? Where the fuck are the rest of you to defend against this? This is twenty people. This is twenty people standing against what is coming. Where the fuck are you?"

Kessler recalls that as they approached the Rotunda, they didn't see the counter-protesters until too late. Conflict ensued, beginning with verbal taunts, then escalating into scuffles and clouds of pepper spray.

Hunter Wallace described the moment they arrived. "When we came down the stairs at the Jefferson monument, Emily Gorcenski was there with a group of about 20 Antifa. They had come to disrupt the torchlight parade. As we gathered around the Jefferson monument, a fight broke out when the encircled Antifa lunged with pepper spray. Several blows were exchanged and a cloud of pepper spray filled the air. I saw Christopher Cantwell with his hands in his eyes. The Charlottesville and UVA police had advance notice of the torchlight parade to the Jefferson monument and had failed to keep Antifa separated."[9]

Video of the event shows Cantwell spraying a man in a Black beanie in the face with pepper spray, then later sitting on the ground, rinsing his eyes, complaining of being maced by "commies." This skirmish with members of Antifa would result in his arrest a few days later after Gorcenski and one other person swore out a warrant against him for deploying a chemical agent.

Shortly thereafter, in front of the torch-encircled Rotunda, with chants of "you will not replace us," audible in the background, Gorenski informed live stream viewers, "There are no police. The police fucking abandoned us. The police abandoned us."

---

9   Hunter Wallace, "The Road to Charlottesville," Occidental Dissent.com.

When reporting about the conflict that occurred at the torchlight rally, many news outlets show the small, peaceful group of frightened University of Virginia students holding cardboard signs while singing "This is our state, Nazis are not welcome here." They have been portrayed heroically in the media for bravely standing up to throngs of "Nazis" who attacked them. Certainly, there were peaceful college students among the counter-protesters. However, what is omitted from most reporting is the small but vicious group of Antifa who antagonized marchers with pepper spray and other weapons. For example, one video captures an unidentified Antifa lighting and throwing a Molotov cocktail into a crowd of Unite the Right protesters.[10]

Studying video of the event, researchers have identified a number of known Antifa, some with serious criminal records, who were amongst the counter-protesters at the Rotunda that evening.[11] "The violence on August 11 was started by members of Philadelphia Antifa, Tom Keenan and Tom Massey, who were lunging into the crowd," according to Kessler. Massey was among those arrested in Washington D.C at Donald Trump's inauguration. Keenan and Massey later gained notoriety when they were arrested for assaulting two Marine Corps reservists in Philadelphia who they apparently mistook for members of the Proud Boys. The Marines, who are Hispanic, testified that Keenan and Massey were part of a mob of about a dozen people that beat them severely while hurling racial slurs. One of the victims testified that Keenan was "laughing, smiling, and having a good time" during the attack.[12]

Kessler and other researchers have also identified Brent Betterly, Paul Minton, Holly Zoller and Sean Liter as part of the Antifa crowd that opposed the torchlight march. Like Keenan and Massey, they were not UVA college students, and their histories provide reasons to doubt whether their intentions were peaceful.

---

10   Jason Kessler, "Antifa Throws a Molotov Cocktail During Charlottesville Torch March," BitChute.com, video posted June 29, 2020.

11   Jason Kessler, "Antifa Tom Massey Instigating Violence at Peaceful Torch March," BitChute.com, video posted June 19, 2020.

12   Victor Fiorillo, "Marines Testify About the 'Antifa Mob' They Say Attacked Them in Philly," PhillyMag.com, Dec. 13, 2018.

In 2012, Betterly was sentenced to six years in prison when he, along with two other men, was convicted for misdemeanor mob action and felony possession of an incendiary device with the intent to commit arson. When the three men's Chicago apartment was raided ahead of the 2012 NATO summit, police found pipe bomb instructions, an improvised mortar made from PVC piping, a crossbow, knives, throwing stars, a map of Chicago and four fire bombs. They were accused of planning attacks using homemade bombs made from beer bottles and gasoline. Planned targets included police stations, President Barack Obama's re-election headquarters, and Mayor Rahm Emanuel's house.[13]

Former skinhead Paul Minton, also of Philadelphia, pled guilty in 2000 to helping dispose of the corpse of a man his friend had killed by hitting him over the head with a hammer thirty times. Minton fled the state with the murderer, and was originally considered a co-defendant in the murder case, but ultimately testified against his former friend. The victim's mother called Minton's light sentence of parole and community service "a joke."[14]

Holly Zoller and partner Sean Liter, who appear in photos of the torchlight march with handguns, are members of the Louisville Anti-Racist Action group.[15] Zoller was arrested in 2020 when she was identified as the renter of a U-haul full of riot supplies (including "abolish the police" signs) at the scene of

---

13 Brendan O'Brien, "Men convicted of plot to attack during Chicago NATO get up to eight years in prison," Reuters, April 25, 2014.

14 Matt Archbold, "Man Sentenced for Role in Death of Skinhead," The Philadelphia Inquirer.

15 Danielle Grady, "Louisville Antifa: Inside Two Of The City's Most Militant Activist Groups," LEO Weekly, Feb. 19, 2020.

a protest related to the death of Breanna Taylor.[16] Zoller is also a "Bail Disruptor" for The Bail Project, a group championed by celebrities and funded by mega-rich financiers. Tucker Carlson reported that "[t]he Bail Project sends money to rioters and other violent criminals to help get them back on the streets as quickly as possible. The Bail Project as much as any other group is funding the violence we've been watching for the past few months... [it] is funding the riots that are destroying our cities.[17]

After fighting broke out around 10:16, the UPD finally called for support. The Heaphy Report explains, "Unfortunately, by the time UPD requested assistance, many of the disorders around the Jefferson statue were over and the participants were either dazed or fleeing."[18] Marchers continued to self-disperse while law enforcement tried to collect themselves and organize a response. They declared an unlawful assembly at 10:24 pm, and began to move in to disperse the remaining participants while EMS treated a few people for exposure to pepper spray. After the area was cleared, the service at St. Paul's church was released, about an hour later than planned.

The leftist protesters noted the police passivity at the torchlight event. Gorcenski confronted the officers that evening about their lack of intervention in the clashes at the Rotunda, and Cornell West reported afterwards, "We couldn't even get arrested. We were there to get arrested. We couldn't even get arrested, because the police had pulled back, just allowing fellow citizens to go at each other, you see."[19]

---

16 Cassandra Fairbanks, "EXCLUSIVE: Louisville Riot U-Haul Driver Arrested According to Leaked Internal Documents," TheGatewayPundit.com Sept 27, 2020.

17 Jeff Poor, "FNC's Carlson: 'The Bail Project Is Funding the Riots That Are Destroying Our Cities'," Breitbart.com, Sept 26, 2020.

18 Heaphy Report, p. 118.

19 Democracy Now, "Cornell West & Rev. Traci Blackmon: Clergy in Charlottesville Were Trapped by Torch-Wielding Nazis," YouTube video, posted Aug. 14, 2017.

One documentary records a Black counter-protester speaking with great agitation to a shoulder-to-shoulder row of motionless police officers standing near the scene. "You're trying to figure out what's going on now? It's too late bro! Y'all just be ready for tomorrow. Y'all couldn't help the couple people that was out here tonight. Just be ready for tomorrow at least!" he pleaded.[20]

The Unite the Right marchers were equally disgusted with the passivity of law enforcement. Hunter Wallace asked, "Is there some reason why Virginia State Police, Charlottesville Police and UVA Police couldn't have maintained the peace on August 11th with six hours advance notice?"[21]

Many mainstream reporting outlets described the marchers as aggressors against peaceful protesters. For example, the *Guardian* reported that protesters against the march were attacked with swung torches, pepper spray, and lighter fluid, but did not mention that some of the leftists present were themselves aggressive and violent.[22] It's interesting to see the leftists portrayed as victims of a "Nazi" attack considering that the Unite the Right organizers had planned the torchlight march in secret for the explicit purpose of avoiding conflict, then voluntarily informed the police of their plans after learning counter-protesters would be present. Are those the actions of people with malevolent intentions?

Social media quickly lit up with videos and reports of the event. As soon as these videos were posted online, they were thoroughly scrutinized. Some marchers were identified by internet users and their identities publicized. Kessler reports that some attendees of the torchlight event are still, to this day, being harassed by Antifa.

---

20 Vice News, "Charlottesville: Race and Terror," vice.com, YouTube video posted Aug. 14, 2017.

21 Hunter Wallace, "UVA Timeline Proves Police Had Advance Knowledge of Aug. 11 Torchlight March," OccidentalDissent.com, Sept 12, 2017.

22 Jason Wilson, "Charlottesville: far-right crowd with torches encircles counter-protest group," *The Guardian*, Aug. 12, 2017.

Kessler Speaks With The News

With torches surrounding the Rotunda behind him, Kessler spoke with reporters about the meaning of the event.

"Torches are to commemorate the fallen dead of our European brothers and sisters like Robert E. Lee, like Thomas Jefferson, like George Washington, who are under attack by these leftist cultural marxists who hate White people, who hate White people's history, who want to blame them for the things that happened in the past, things that every race on earth did, but only White people are being persecuted for. So this," he explained, gesturing towards the marchers in the background, "is to honor the fallen dead."

The interviewer asked, "Do you think Thomas Jefferson would have participated in something like this?"

Kessler replied, "Oh, absolutely. He was a revolutionary. We are too."[23]

How Did The Unite The Right Attendees Feel About The Torchlight March?

Nathaniel, who had driven down from Delaware for Unite the Right, had not been on the private message board where the torchlight march was planned, but he learned about it on Twitter shortly before it occurred and was able to attend. He remembers feeling pumped up about participating and "standing up for White people," and that crowd was energetic and larger than he expected. However, he thought the vibe was a little "cringey" and "LARP-y," and the "Jews will not replace us" chant was "dumb."

Nathaniel recalls seeing a few dozen Antifa and the clouds of pepper spray at the monument. "I am almost positive none of our people started it." One counter-protester had been beating people with a police baton, and Nathaniel's friend took it away from her and kept it as a souvenir. However, the event "devolved pretty quickly, so we didn't stick around." He noted that police who were

---

23 News2Share "Interview: Jason Kessler on UVA Torch Rally," YouTube video, Aug. 13, 2017.

there were not doing anything about the scuffles, though they did eventually disperse the crowd.

Nathaniel left the torchlight march left feeling pumped up and excited. He describes the mood as celebratory and fun, and he enjoyed the positive feedback in his Twitter stream as videos were posted later that evening.

At home in his Charlottesville apartment, Steve watched the whole, unedited live stream of the torchlight event. He was happy that the organizers were making a "firm, confident" stand for defending the monuments. He recalls the lived-streamed event become chaotic as scuffles ensued at the Jefferson monument. At one point he saw a cloud of gas appear in the air, and recalls being amused when he heard someone off camera yell: "Dude, Antifa just fucking gassed themselves... Way to gas yourselves you fucking idiots!"

At that point Steve was a little worried about the leftist protests, but not enough to be deterred from attending Unite the Right. He reasoned, "They got a permit, they're not doing anything wrong. It's a public speaking event." He was expecting some tensions between opposing sides, but not violence. Overall, he was still looking forward to hearing the speakers and lending support to the defense of the statue. There was "no dread of impending disaster. What happened the next day really rocked me."

Now he admits, "I was a little naïve... I thought law enforcement would do their due diligence to make sure everything went off peacefully."

Like Steve, Jim didn't know about the torchlight rally beforehand. He heard about it from a bartender while he was dining out with friends. He thought it seemed a bit silly and beside the point. Edgy theatrics were not the reason he was there.

Bill was not too happy about the torchlight march. "I was against that. They didn't let anybody else know... We kinda felt like we got used at that point... It was no longer about the monuments then to me. We got painted more as White supremacists."

When Luke found out about the torchlight march online, he was concerned that it would appear "Nazi-like," and that the fighting there had "primed the pump" for violence. Still, he was undeterred from attending the Saturday rally, reasoning that since the recent Charlottesville Klan rally had taken place without violence, that Unite the Right would also be safe. Also, thinking of his "long-past family," he concluded, "I don't have a choice. I have to go."

After that evening's events, some others did have safety concerns. Ayla had been planning to speak at the rally the following day. Because she was nursing an infant and could only attend for a short time, members of Richard Spencer's security team had made special arrangements to get her in and out of the event quickly, apart from the other scheduled speakers. That evening, they contacted her to let her know that based upon their observation of the huge Antifa presence in the city, they had determined that they could not guarantee her safety, and they advised that she not attend at all. She agreed.

"Jews Will Not Replace Us"

The aspect of the torchlight rally that brought the most horror to observers, and which caused many to interpret it as a Nazi march, was the fact that some of the participants were chanting "Jews will not replace us."

This had not been part of the plan.

Asked about the chants, Kessler replies," I remember being mortified when it happened and being embarrassed... A certain number of people, and it doesn't have to be a lot, and they're loud and aggressive and near video cameras and they change it from "You will not replace us" to "Jews will not replace us." Then they have essentially hijacked the message. And that's the way I feel about it."

He continues, "As the years go on, I'm more and more willing to say that. I think that was wrong and that's a bad focus. But what are you going to do? It does show how badly focusing on scapegoating a group of people is going to be perceived by the larger public. You always want to be seen as righteous defenders of your own people rather than aggressors looking to attack other people's cultures."[24]

After The March

Some things happened after the torchlight marchers dispersed were inauspicious, illuminating the intentions of the counter-protesters.

As Invictus and his friends were leaving the Rotunda, they noticed that activists dressed in clergy robes were following them back to their cars. The clergy took photos of license plates of marchers as they were leaving and posted them online.

Zarski has a favorable memory of her participation in the march. "It was an amazing night." But afterwards, she walked with some friends to a nearby church parking lot where their cars had been parked. They found that marbles had been thrown at the car windows. "Every window in every car was busted out, and every tire had been slashed. There was not a drivable car left in the parking lot." The victims filed a police report, but Zarski never heard the vandalism mentioned on the news.

---

24 Kessler Interview, LukeFord.net, Jan. 14, 2021.

CHAPTER 9 QUICK LINKS:

 Heaphy Report. URL: qrs.ly/dpcvtcb

 Jason Kessler, "Antifa Comms Director Luis Oyola on Charlottesville Conspiracy," video, June 19, 2020. URL: qrs.ly/4acvtbm

 Jason Kessler, "Antifa Throws a Molotov Cocktail During Charlottesville Torch March," video, June 29, 2020. URL: qrs.ly/imcvtiv

Jason Kessler, "Antifa Tom Massey Instigating Violence at Peaceful Torch March," video, June 19, 2020. URL: qrs.ly/7vcvtj5

Democracy Now, "Cornell West & Rev. Traci Blackmon: Clergy in Charlottesville Were Trapped by Torch-Wielding Nazis," video, Aug. 14, 2017. URL: qrs.ly/k7cvtje

Vice News, "Charlottesville: Race and Terror," video, Aug. 14, 2017. URL: qrs.ly/sacvtjp

News2Share "Interview: Jason Kessler on UVA Torch Rally," video, Aug. 13, 2017. URL: qrs.ly/xdcvtka

"Were the Capitol Hill Riots Charlottesville II? A Jason Kessler Interview," LukeFord.net, Jan. 14, 2021. URL: qrs.ly/e1cvtdi

CONVERGENCE ON LEE PARK

"We had to fight our way into the park."

THE UNITE THE RIGHT RALLY was set to begin at noon that muggy August day. Organizers, attendees and leftist counter-protesters began converging on the downtown area hours before. Early that morning, there were ominous signs already apparent.

The Charlottesville Police Department was ordered to be in place by 7:00 a.m. The Virginia State Police arrived later than expected, a little after 8:30. Because of the late arrival, the two groups did not have much time to coordinate, which contributed to the disorganized and feeble law enforcement presence.

Militias were assembling downtown as well. The Heaphy Report states, "CPD received several phone calls from concerned citizens that morning about the presence of armed militia at various locations. Police body camera footage shows the arrival of the Pennsylvania and New York Lightfoot Militias at 8:31 a.m. Around thirty members walked up 2nd Street NE and entered the public area of Emancipation [Lee] Park. After standing around for a few minutes, the militia left the park and formed a line along the southern edge of Emancipation [Lee] Park between 1st and 2nd Streets. A VSP trooper who arrived a few minutes later asked a colleague, "What are they, like military? They're more armed than we are."[1]

---

1 Heaphy Report, pp. 123-124.

Kessler recalls that "the whole day was a confusing cluster fuck." When he arrived at McIntire Park early that morning, he began to notice the first signs that things were not going as planned. He was surprised to find that there was no police presence. He noted that there were, however, busses parked there that looked like something that might be used by the police for prison transport. The shuttle system was not working. Most concerning, there was already a breakdown in communication between himself, the other organizers, and the police. Kessler reports that Richard Spencer's people had "insinuated themselves into conversations with the police" and a lot of people were reporting to Eli Mosley rather than to him.

CPD Captain Mitchell had planned for rally attendees to enter the park in a controlled manner through staircases on its southeast and southwest corners. An agreement had been worked out with Unite the Right organizers to allow security members for the event to act as "doormen" to prevent counter-protesters from entry to the areas designated for rally attendees. Shuttles were to drop off attendees about a quarter mile from the park. There were no plans for law enforcement officers to be placed along the route.

Transmission from McIntire Park to Lee Park was characterized by disarray.

There was confusion amongst the scheduled speakers and the police about whether and when the speakers would be escorted to the park, whether they would arrive in a group or separately, and from which direction they would enter the park. Discussions had taken place about the procedure for getting seventeen people who were scheduled to speak or otherwise designated as VIPs in and out. Unite the Right security personnel had planned to call the CPD the morning of August 12th with their exact location so they could be escorted to the venue. However, that morning they informed law enforcement that they had decided to decline the police escort.

General attendees were to be dropped off by shuttles in different areas around the park. Some would arrive to find that they were on the wrong side of the park and had to exit, march through streets full of counter-protesters and militias, and re-enter another way.

Throughout the city, attendees were getting ready for the day.

That morning was leisurely for Charlottesville resident Steve. He was not in a particular rush to get to the rally since it was "right in my back yard," a five-minute walk away from his apartment. He did notice that a crowd was gathering in the park earlier than he would have expected. As the people began gathering, Steve noticed a thump-thump-thump sound outside his window. He stepped outside to observe and found a very low-flying police helicopter circling over the park. He wondered, "What the hell is going on?" The helicopter was his first indication that something ominous was unfolding.

Command Centers

The many government agencies who had been planning for Unite the Right had set up stations to monitor the activities of the day. In a Wells Fargo building on Market Street across from Lee Park, a "Unified Command Center" reserved for key decision makers was set up for the CPD and VSP. Chief Thomas and his personal assistant Emily Lantz, who recorded scribe notes for the event, were among those present in the main room on August 12th. Others present were CPD Captains Mitchell and Lewis, Lieutenant Steve Upman, City Manager Maurice Jones, Superintendent of the Virginia State Police Colonel Flaherty, intelligence analysts from the FBI and Virginia Fusion Center, and ten VSP officers. The main room contained multiple screens displaying live feeds from pole cameras, helicopter units, and other live stream sources.

A second, adjacent room without live feed monitors was set up in the same building for CFD Deputy Chief Mike Rogers, EOC Coordinator Allison Farole, ACPD Captain Sean Reeves, UPD representative Don McGhee, City Director of Communications Miriam Dickler, VSP public information officer Corrine Geller, and various representatives from the National Guard and the Virginia Department of Emergency Management.

An Emergency Operations Center, meant to primarily focus on fire and medical operations, station was set up at Zehmer Hall on the grounds of UVA. People assembled there included Assistant City

Manager Leslie Beauregard, UVA President Teresa Sullivan, UVA Vice President and COO Pat Hogan, Albemarle County Executive Doug Walker, CFD Chief Andrew Baxter, UVA Director of Safety and Emergency Preparedness Marge Sidebottom, CPD Lieutenant Cheryl Sandridge, Albemarle County Fire Department Chief Dan Eggleston, and ECC Executive Director Tom Hanson. Dozens of UVA administrators were gathered in a nearby conference room.

The Incident Management Team assembled by the Virginia Department of Emergency Management was located at Charlottesville Fire Department Station 10 on Fontaine Avenue.[2]

The Organized Opposition

The groups that intended to oppose the rally were well-prepared. One left-wing communications organizer explained their plan. "We had come there with the strategy of organizing into affinity groups and having a very tight comm system so that even if affinity groups were spread about the area, we could very quickly tell each other what was going on. So we set up an outside location where we were able to have a dispatch that quickly communicated to others of police mobilization and fascist mobilization, so that we were able to in the most effective manner mobilize against the Nazi rally. In the morning, the earliest action was mobilized by a group called Congregate Charlottesville. They held a prayer in front of the only open side of the park that police were allowing people to stand on with the intention to then block the entrances into the park to prevent the fascists from coming in."[3]

Set Up At McIntire

A large pre-rally staging area for Unite the Right attendees was set up in the parking lot of McIntire Park about a mile and a half away from Lee Park. Around 8:45 am, a crowd began to gather there. The place was teeming with hundreds of people, some dressed and carrying flags for various organizations to which

2 Heaphy Report pp. 109-110.

3 Kessler, "Antifa Comms Director", BitChute.com.

they belonged, as well as lots of ordinary people. They were milling around, some catching up with old friends, and others meeting online acquaintances in person for the first time. They began lining up there to catch van shuttles to the rally.

Tom, the activist from Tennessee, began his day by grabbing a cup of coffee, and going to meet up with some friends in the parking lot. He recalls that there were a lot of people he knew from different conservative groups, and he roamed around mingling with them for a good while. He recalls it as "almost like a family reunion."

The VMI graduate from Richmond, Luke, arrived at McIntire Park with his friends around 9 or 10 a.m. He says, "There were a ton of people, various Alt-Right groups and some regular people, probably several hundred." They were lining up to get into vans. He drew upon his military training and tried to keep his group organized and in formation.

On the van ride to downtown, Luke began to realize there was miscommunication between the organizers and the police who were talking over radio. His driver was concerned that he was getting "radio silence" from the police. Luke surmised from the bit of conversation he overheard that the Charlottesville Police Department had dropped the ball. He heard one driver ask, "Why aren't they responding?"

Luke and his friends were expecting to be dropped off at the park, but the driver was told by the Charlottesville Police Department that they had to be dropped off several blocks away. Luke thought that the system did not seem "tight" which raised red flags in his mind. Luke wondered if they would have to go through a gauntlet to get to the park. He and his friends were dropped off with several other vanloads of people.

Walking through downtown, it seemed to Luke as though some citizens of Charlottesville were bunkered down as if for war, while others were enjoying the spectacle with more of a tailgate atmosphere. He recalls some downtown residents were screaming out of windows at them, things like "Kill yourself!"

When someone leading a group of rally attendees through the crowd asked a Charlottesville police officer where they should go to get in, Luke recalls the officer would not respond or even look him in the face - he was "like a toy soldier." Luke realized at that point that they were on their own.

Once they arrived at the park, Luke saw "liberal pastors in rainbow vestments" blocking the entrance, preventing about sixty rally attendees from getting in. He recalls that "the pastors were saying the vilest things: 'I hope you get fucked to death,' 'God hates you,' 'You're evil,' 'You're Satan.' Some clergy even spat on the attendees. Luke thought to himself, "These loving liberal pastors are big hypocrites."

With the clergy blocking the entrance, the Unite the Right attendees were in the streets, vulnerable to Antifa. There were "Antifa packs forming in the road, nipping at the edges of our group." Not wanting to linger in the dangerous setting, they pushed through the line of clergy.

Luke was in disbelief that pastors were blocking the entrance of the park, leaving attendees exposed to danger, and that the police were not ensuring that orderly entrance was protected.

"I was in a state of shock, trying to keep my composure."

Enrique Tarrio made his way to the park that morning with a small group. (At the time, Tarrio was a member of the Proud Boys. He became chairman of the national organization in 2018.) Proud Boys founder and leader Gavin McInnes had banned members of the organization from attending Unite the Right. Tarrio states that he wasn't planning to go, but was hired to film B-roll footage of the event. He remembers that on his way towards the park, "I started seeing kids shouting stupid shit like, 'Jews will not replace us.'" He saw a group of Antifa marching in to the sound of Islamic prayer music. When he noticed there was no real police line between the protesters and counter-protesters, he thought, "This is going to turn bad."

Peaceful Protesters?

The Clergy Collective had held "nonviolent direct action" training sessions in the weeks leading up to Unite the Right which some BLM [Black Lives Matter] and SURJ [Showing Up for Racial Justice] members attended. Heaphy Report investigators learned from attendees of that training that their goal was to "delay and obstruct the hate speech that they expected." and "to be visible in the opposition to right-wing groups."[4]

Heaphy Report investigators learned from Seth Wispelwey that of the clergy group members present that morning, "those trained in nonviolent resistance would stay behind to march to Emancipation [Lee] Park and engage in direct action... The direct-action group - whose goal was to encircle Emancipation [Lee] Park in a locked-arm barricade - numbered only about sixty."

Though the clergy group implied they were planning non-violent resistance, Antifa researcher Andy Ngo has noted that "[d]irect action" is a dog whistle for protest activity that includes violence."[5] One thing not mentioned by the clergy is that their obstruction of the right-wingers from the park would provide opportunity for the armed, militant Antifa throngs to attack them. Was this merely an accident that happened to play into the hands of the violent leftists in the crowd? Perhaps not.

When Antifa occupied a large area of downtown Portland, Andy Ngo observed Antifa employ similar methods in which seemingly peaceful protesters were used both to generate favorable publicity and for tactical advantage. (My emphasis below):

> When I was undercover on the ground, what I saw was a literal war zone with armed belligerents. On the side of Antifa were units of fighters with explosive fireworks, lasers, rocks, and loaded slingshots. They were joined by street medics, re-suppliers, tear gas leaf blowers, and human shields. Many were dressed in riot gear and gas masks. **Perhaps the most important faction was those labeled 'peaceful protesters.'** They stood arm in arm in the front to shield everyone behind them. The photographs of the 'Wall of Moms,' dads, and

---

4 Heaphy Report, p. 72.

5 Ngo, *Unmasked*, p. 89.

veterans against federal officers were propaganda. The 'peaceful protesters' were used as human shields to deter or delay law enforcement from taking action. It was incredibly effective. When officers inevitably responded... photographers were ready to capture 'moms' [many of whom were simply young Antifa women in yellow t-shirts] being tear gassed.[6]

There is reason to believe this tactic was in play at Unite the Right. In one tweet by Twitter user Anastasia Karklina (@mzfayya) posted on August 14, 2017 shows a photo of Reverend Osagyefo Sekou and Reverend Seth Wispelwey locking arms next to a group of red-flag carrying, Black-clad counter-protesters. The text of the tweet reads, "Press won't show Antifascists discussing tactics w/ @RevSekou before locking arms in front of clergy as Nazis approach. #Charlottesville #IWW. (The hashtag #IWW denotes Industrial Workers of the World). This tweet was "liked" by Reverend Wispelwey himself.

Some of the clergy were expecting to be arrested for blocking entry to the park, but no arrests were made. Some police officers later reported that they were under the false impression that the clergy meant to keep leftist counter-protesters out of the park to prevent confrontations between opposing groups.

Battling For Entry

The same morning, the Nationalist Front (including the Traditionalist Workers' Party, National Socialist Movement, and League of the South) gathered in the Market Street parking garage and prepared to march down Market Street towards Lee Park. They had made a decision not to participate in the shuttle bus plan, reasoning that dropping off attendees in small groups would leave them vulnerable to attack. They opted instead to line up together in a large formation to march towards the park. They were joined by a number other people who were not affiliated with any group. The ranks of angry, armed leftist counter-protesters had already

---

6 Ngo, *Unmasked*, p. 71.

filled the street between the parking garage and Lee Park, forcing attendees to make a treacherous march through a hostile mob before the rally was even supposed to have begun.

A few hours prior, Jim reports, he was present when the head of security for the League of the South and a few other of the organization's officers met with some uniformed Charlottesville police officers to discuss the group's entry to the park. League members were told to park on the top floor of the parking garage which was near the police station, and to follow a particular route to the park which they were told would be a cordoned-off zone.

Things did not go as they expected.

The League of the South members met at the parking garage as planned. There they assembled and got into formation. A few other people who were not affiliated with any organization asked to walk in with the group. Jim recalls one couple in particular, history buffs in their early eighties, who walked in with them. When Jim noticed that most of the young men were in the front of the procession, he and a few other men moved towards the back of the line to provide cover for the women, elderly, and civilians who were congregating there and who were relatively unprotected.

The group descended the parking garage ramp. Jim recalls, that once they reached the street, "pretty immediately I realized there was no police cover." He noticed a couple of uniforms in sight, but no real law enforcement presence like they had been led to expect.

"I realized there was going to be a fight."

As he marched in with the group of about 100, Jim recalls, "We were getting attacked from the sides." Counter-protesters were throwing punches. Some women got hit. The elderly history buffs were pepper-sprayed by a young man who seemed to be targeting them deliberately. The group continued forward.

"We were trying to get to the park. We assumed there would be safety there."

On the Political Cesspool podcast hosted by James Edwards later that evening, several attendees described this march to the park.

I mean we were the shock troops, everybody else was inside the pen, we had to fight our way in to even get adjacent to the pen where all the Alt-Right was kept away from Antifa and BLM. We had to fight our way through them to get even adjacent to that. --Michael Hill, President of the League of the South

Okay, let me tell you the story of what happened in Charlottesville. We all marched out of the parking garage towards Lee Park, right? The League of the South people and Traditionalist Worker's Party and a bunch of other people. We marched. So when we marched into Lee Park we had to march through a cloud of pepper spray, people pulling people into the crowd and attacking people, bear mace, they were throwing bricks. The police stood down and did not allow us to enter Lee Park. -- Brad Griffin, Public Affairs Chief for the League of the South

When I got there, there were at least 200 communists in a human wall facing us and I was on the front lines. So the first thing they did was begin to throw bottles of urine at us. And also, these, I don't know what these were - they were balloons full of pepper spray that had urine in them and all kinds of concoctions of deadly things, probably even diseases, and one of them hit me in the face, in my helmet, and the flag, my flag got soaked in it. I had to use my flag pole to keep the enemy away. It was kind of like a spear, per se, only I wasn't really doing anything. We finally made it through, and the enemy was continuously harassing us, they were encircling us, and basically raising all hell, as Dr. Hill said. --Chris, League of the South member

In the meantime, we had to literally fight our way up to the park. We were supposed to have the whole park according to the judge's order of the city to honor its permit to us. The police made no effort whatsoever to separate us from the Antifa, and stood around while they spat on us, threw stuff at us, and attacked us, and did nothing. At one point the cops disappeared, just flat-out went away. -- Rich

We had to fight our way into the park. We literally had to fight our way into the park. Our guys, two guys younger than my grandson, were pepper sprayed, were beaten with sticks, bloody, eyes all screwed up. We fought our way into the park. -- Eddie Miller, Political Cesspool correspondent

Of course we know any police force, particularly a riot police force, particularly a police force deployed specifically to an event of this nature would know very well that the first object would be to keep the two potential belligerents apart from one another and that didn't happen, and the police stood by and watched as we marched in good order, very decently and very respectably, I must say -- I must insist on that -- towards the grounds, and they just stood by and watched as these people ran in, and they hit our people, I say "our" though I was not in those ranks. I stood well aside, but I had some sympathy. -- Simon Roche, South African visitor who attended as an observer[7]

Gene remembers, "We got attacked about a block and a half before we got to Lee Park. They had all these big TV trucks parked on one side, so the road was one lane wide. We were easy targets for Antifa." The Antifa were throwing bags of feces and urine, and glass bottles full of nails and screws. They were spraying people in the eyes with pepper spray. "It was an all-out assault before we ever got to Lee Park. The police just stood there and watched while we were under attack."

Tom, the political activist from Tennessee, had caravanned to downtown from McIntire Park, and he walked from the parking garage

---

7 The Political Cesspool Radio Show, podcast aired Aug. 12, 2017, www. thepoliticalcesspool.org.

to Lee Park with the assembly. He and his small group of friends had wedged between members of a few more formal organizations.

One they got down from the parking garage to the street, Tom smelled tear gas, saw smoke, and heard counter-protesters chanting in unison. Crowds on the side of the street were screaming and cursing as they proceeded towards their destination. One of Tom's friends began to get nervous, but Tom was not yet worried. He pointed out some police officers and reassured his friend that things were under control.

Suddenly the procession stopped. Tom later learned that the entryway to the park had been blocked by counter-protesters, clergy members and others, who had locked arms to prevent their entry. He heard brawling in front of them, "smacking and crashing," but he couldn't see what was happening. After about 20-30 seconds, the line started moving again.

Chris, the young man from Appalachia, walked in with the same processional. "I'm not sure how we ended up with them," he recalls, but he had an "oh shit!" moment when he saw the huge throngs of counter-protesters lining the streets, including Black Lives Matter and Antifa, and decided it would be safer to march in with a large group. He noted that there were more news crews than police officers there.

Chris had not thought before that weapons would be needed, so the flimsy hardware-store flagpole which held his Confederate flag was the only thing he had to use for self-defense. He remembers that from the moment they exited the parking garage, his nose was burning and his skin was tingling from the tear gas and pepper spray in the air. When he noticed the helicopter circling above, it really hit home that "this was a big thing."

He recalls the procession coming to a halt because "Antifa and the League of the South were beating the hell out of each other." He notes that the guys in front of the procession were "ready to fight," having brought shields and helmets.

As far as the League of the South having been "ready to fight," President Michael Hill addressed that on the LOS website. "For several months we helped publicize the event on our website and social media. We also encouraged our members to attend what was shaping up to be a large gathering of right-wing groups in a show of solidarity in defense of our Southern inheritance. Knowing the violent history of Antifa (Anti-Fascist Action) and Black Lives Matter (BLM), both who promised to be there to oppose us, we encouraged our members and supporters to come with defensive gear such as riot shields (a dozen of which we provided), helmets, sturdy footwear, eye protection, etc. We also provided information regarding Virginia's gun and knife laws, and allowed our members to make up their own minds if they would arm themselves or not. In the end, we discouraged both long guns and knives, leaving open the option of concealed (with valid permit) or open carry of handguns. Most of our members chose not to bring any firearms or knives, having only legal pepper spray and flag poles (with flags attached) as potential "weapons." Our people carried with them NO objects that were intended to be thrown at the leftist protestors. Thus, we came ready to defend ourselves and our property but not to carry out any aggressive/offensive actions. We would respond but not initiate."[8]

One observer described the clash this way, "Wish y'all could've seen that clash out here a minute ago... it was pretty brutal. They ran into each other like Barbarians on a battlefield with their shields, riot shields and sticks and billy clubs, just beating on each other. Probably lasted about 30 seconds, 45 seconds then it broke up real quick. It was right here in the middle of this street. It went down this road right here about fifty feet, and stuff, then it broke up when the police started jumping the barricades and coming out."[9]

Matt Parrot of the Traditionalist Workers Party was part of the entourage as well. He wrote, "Southerners don't calculate odds the way we Yankees do, and the League of the South were directly in front of us in the line. With a full-throated rebel yell, the League broke through the wall of degenerates and TradWorker managed to enter the Lee Park venue itself while they were largely still reeling. Michael Tubbs, an especially imposing League organizer, towered

8 Michael Hill, "League of the South Statement on Charlottesville", LeaugeoftheSouth.com, August 23, 2017.

9 Jason Kubin, "Rob Kapp Shit's Gettin Real" YouTube video posted Aug. 12, 2017.

over and pushed through the Antifa like a Tyrannosaurus among raptors as League fighters with shields put their training to work."[10]

Parrot had been in the middle of the line, and could not see what was happening in the front. "The police had assured us they would secure the venue," he says, but when he started hearing combat noises, he realized they had not done so. Parrot notes that a formation that large cannot just reverse – the people in the front were being pushed ahead by those in the back who could not see what was happening. By the time he got near the park, the fight for entry was over and "Antifa were on the back foot."

Bill also walked in with the League of the South, who he described as "cornbread-fed boys you wouldn't want to mess with." He recalls that "they proceeded to start whipping the hell out of some people" after getting knocked down by counter-protesters while approaching the park. After the brawl subsided, Bill and his buddy kept moving towards the park. He noticed police halfway cordoned around the park. "They later proceeded to disappear."

Regarding the massive brawl, the Heaphy Report states, "Body camera footage shows that police officers in Zone 1 witnessed all of this. They called out the fight and observed that pepper spray had been deployed. Body camera footage shows people attacking each other in plain view of the officers. The officers stood behind the barricades and watched." Even after being exhorted by an observer to 'Take care of your people!' "[t]he officers continued to stand in silence. None responded. The cry for medics can be heard in the officers' body camera recordings."[11]

Chris asked a police officer which way to go to get into the park, and the officer pointed straight through a crowd of counter-protesters, which he describes as "some black bloc Antifa, some college-aged White liberals, and a few old hippies." They were shouting, "This is our town!" which made him feel that the Unite the Right protesters were not being treated as Americans who had the right to assemble. Chris was still determined to get into the

---

10 Matt Parrott, "Catcher in the Reich: My Account of my Experience in Charlottesville," Steemit.com, Aug. 15, 2017.

11 Heaphy Report, pp. 130-131.

rally at that point, but noted that even if he had wanted to turn back, breaking away from the large group in that situation would have been too dangerous. He recalls receiving a pot-shot from someone's fist on the way into the park - the first attack of many he received that day. At that point he brushed it off, not wanting to get into a fight.

The mismanaged entry into the park was a big contributing factor to the level of violence that occurred that day. One witness noticed a pattern to the conflicts. "As the Unite the Right groups approached Emancipation [Lee] Park, counter-protesters shouted 'Here they come!' and formed blockades. The demonstrators then used shields, flags, or fists to start skirmishes, all of which were eventually broken up by pepper spray. The crowd would then part and allow them entry into the park. That scenario played out at least half a dozen times... The witness was incredulous that police would allow the fights to go on."[12]

While giving a presentation about Unite the Right, George Lindbeck, MD, who was in charge of Emergency Medical Services for the event, displayed a photo of the column marching towards the park. "What you're seeing here is the permitted right-wing protesters surrounded basically on all sides by the counter protesters, and this is where most of the violence occurred, was in this area here... Later allegations and concerns were, why wasn't law enforcement prepared for this eventuality? Why were these groups not separated, physically as well as by law enforcement? Why did law enforcement not engage earlier when people got into fights along this route? I don't have answers for that."

He displayed another photo of Unite the Right protesters taken from a different angle. "You see the protesters walking in here surrounded on both sides by counter-protesters. And that's where things started to get kinda messy. So most of the injuries we saw that day occurred from these sorts of interactions along the ingress and egress routes. Blunt objects, sticks, that sort of stuff."

EMS had set up treatment tents about a block from the park. They quickly realized that treating protesters and counter-

---

12 Heaphy Report, p. 132.

protesters in the same space was a recipe for trouble, and pulled apart the tents apart into two separate sections.

Lindbeck remembers, "People would come in soaked with pepper spray from the tops of their heads to the bottom of their feet. The only way to deal with that was to have them disrobe, fully hose them down, and send them out in a Tyvek suit with their clothes in a plastic bag."[13]

---

13 Jason Kessler, "Head EMT at Charlottesville Rally" BitChute.com.

CHAPTER 10 QUICK LINKS:

Heaphy Report. URL: qrs.ly/dpcvtcb

Jason Kessler, "Antifa Comms Director Luis Oyola on Charlottesville Conspiracy," Video, posted June 19, 2020. URL: qrs.ly/4acvtbm

The Political Cesspool Radio Show, podcast aired Aug. 12, 2017. Hour 1 URL: qrs.ly/r8cvtl5 ; Hour2 URL: qrs.ly/r8cvtm1 ; Hour 3 URL: qrs.ly/9jcvtm3

Jason Kubin, "Rob Kapp Shit's Gettin Real" video; Aug. 12, 2017. URL: qrs.ly/yecvtm5

Jason Kessler, "Head EMT at Charlottesville Rally Discusses Expectation of Left-Wing Violence," video, Feb. 23, 2021. URL: qrs.ly/zxcvtfd

INSIDE LEE

"In a combat zone without a rifle."

NOT ONLY DID THE UNITE THE RIGHT attendees have to fight their way through a hostile crowd to attend the rally, but they were not even safe once inside the confines of the park. They found themselves surrounded by Antifa without and separated by barricades within. While throngs of police watched passively, attendees were attacked like caged animals. It was during this part of the day that Baked Alaska was sprayed in the eyes with a chemical agent which left him hospitalized and temporarily blinded.

When Kessler arrived at the park, having walked the last block on foot, he found that the sound crew who were setting up for the speakers were inaccessible to him due to the barricades that had been placed in the park. A line of Virginia State Police officers was also blocking entry. Kessler protested, but they refused to grant him access, saying that the Charlottesville Police Department, not they, were in charge. Kessler was unable to establish communications with the CPD to grant him access.

When Kessler saw that people were being smashed against the park barricades, he began to panic.

The chaos inside the park continued until about 11:30 am. The young man from Appalachia, Chris, put it this way: "Once we were inside the park, everything really went to hell. We had anyone with a shield, anyone able-bodied was in front holding back protesters so they couldn't take the park. They threw rocks, piss bottles, bricks, and paint bombs." Chris observed fist fighting and people being attacked with clubs.

Chris recalls that he was hit with "rancid piss" and paint bombs, despite the fact that he was trying to stay away from the front lines. After being pelted with objects for a while, he began to get angry, and decided to go up to the front to fight back. He admits that at that point, he got in "a couple of scuffles."

Chris spotted plenty of men in uniform, both police and National Guard, standing near the park. "They had the means to break it up ... They could've stopped it."

Eddie Miller reported a similar experience on the Political Cesspool podcast that evening. "What we found, you would not believe, once we fought our way into the park, we were barricaded on three sides, only one way out of the park... We were there for an hour and a half, taking all kinds of foreign missiles, bottles of water, sticks being thrown in, our people being spit, hit with pepper spray, they turned gas on us, they threw feces and urine on us. And you know what the police were doing? They were sitting there with their fingers up their rears, watching, some of them laughing. Watching us take all kinds of endless abuse."

On the same podcast, Brad Griffin of the League of the South reported, "When we got to the park, we found that Antifa was not penned by the police. The police allowed Antifa to attack our group. They attacked us with pepper spray, with bricks, with bear mace, with piss bombs, with literal human feces... The Antifa actually had like a canister of hair spray and a lighter, and actually turned it into a miniature flame thrower. I mean they had a literal flame thrower in Lee Park. They were throwing bombs and bricks. They were attacking our people... There were two dozen people on the ground, hit by mace, bricks, who were beaten trying to get into the park."[1]

Gene recalls being fenced in to a "little bitty" area with "all this stuff flying through the air." There were nurses in his group who

1 The Political Cesspool Radio Show, podcast aired Aug. 12, 2017, www.thepoliticalcesspool.org.

were pouring milk in the eyes of people who had been pepper-sprayed. He did not see anyone in Nazi or Klan garb or any swastikas amongst the crowd.

Bill and his friend took cover under some oak trees on the south side of the park which deflected most of the projectiles. Bill had worn protective gear, but he took it off to get relief from the intense August heat.

While milling around the park, he and his friend talked to a few people. He spotted Kessler and a lot of different groups there. He recalls being amidst a thick crowd, "pretty much hemmed in." At one point, part of the barricades were pushed down to assist some people who were being attacked that were trying to get into the park to safety. He noticed that the police were not separating the protesters and counter-protesters. He also noticed National Guard members atop a bank across the street. "There was a big police presence, but they didn't do a thing."

When Tom and his friends got into the park, they could see state troopers and cops. "There were barriers in the park between us and Kessler and his crowd." Tom got hit with a balloon full of blue paint, and his friend got hit with a hard projectile which they later identified as a condom filled with cement.

Tom remembers noticing, "Cops were just sitting there just chilling, and I guess they're not gonna do anything. And we're being assaulted here." He began to wish that he had not turned down his friends' offers of the shield and helmet. "I felt kind of exposed." The Iraq War veteran said, "I felt like I was in a combat zone without a rifle. Then it became survival mode."

"[Antifa] were coming in waves trying to push into the park. I kept seeing them come and come and come. They are horrible, ineffectual fighters... a bunch of wimps."

The leftists then began to come at the park from a different angle. Tom and his friends went to stand in the unguarded area. They stood on a hill which provided a good vantage point, but most of the fighting didn't come their way. He recounts that they were yelling at late arrivals that were being swarmed by counter-protesters while trying to get to the park. "It was pretty hectic."

Tom also said "The League of the South are the ones I remember because they really kept Antifa out of the park."

Other observers noted that the League of the South shield wall was critical in protecting rally attendees from the surrounding mob. Simon Roche, the visitor from South Africa, heartily praised the League of the South members who guarded the park entrance:

> And once we occupied the park after much ado, the police stood by and watched as the Antifa attacked the people, our people, over and over and over again. Eventually, marvelously, I saw how a group of about twelve young, young, young men, very young men, took it upon themselves to form a barricade between the Antifa and the rest of us. They were all that stood between us and the Antifa, and nigh on one thousand of the people who had come there to defend their culture, their history, their values, and their norms, because that's what it comes down to. And I tell you, if there's an impression that I'll leave with from the USA, it is that of these young men who took it upon themselves, who volunteered to stand at the foot of these steps under the direction of Michael R. Tubbs and defend all those people by themselves, and over and over and over again they were hit and they were smashed, and one Black man ran up with a great pipe and he smashed one man on the side of the head in front of everybody before running away into the crowd. They were spat on. And feces was thrown on them - some feces landed on me. And there was urine and there was some evidence of condoms filled with seminal fluid. And it was just tremendous for me to see with my own eyes how a thin line of young men, 19, 20, 21, 22, stood there and withstood everything that was thrown at them. [2]

---

2 The Political Cesspool Radio Show, podcast aired Aug. 12, 2017, www.thepoliticalcesspool.org.

Another attendee echoed Roche's praise, saying, "it was precisely the group most stigmatized by the MSM, the armored Alt-Righters with shields, who created what order existed."[3]

One member of the Traditionalist Workers' Party who had paramilitary experience helped manage the shield wall securing the park. Parrott was switching out people from wall duty as they needed to be relieved. "There was a mess outside the shield wall," he remembers, and he stayed busy for half an hour or so, venturing into the crowd to find injured people and pull them back into the park. When he was uncertain which side someone was on, he would ask them, "Are you a commie or a Nazi? That usually worked." He laughs remembering how one man was offended and refused to pick either category. He eventually deduced the man was a Libertarian and pulled him to safety in the park.

Once their large entourage arrived in the park, Jim recalls, some of the female League of the South members were acting as medics for those who had been injured on the way. Some Sons of Confederate Veterans and older folks were already there. He noticed "weird gates separating the middle of the park," and about 200 or so cops standing around in riot gear doing nothing.

"The park was surrounded by crazed Marxists," Jim recalls. They were throwing balloons with some kind purple irritant that caused a light acid burn, as well as used tampons, urine, feces, and water bottles. The League of the South Members who were manning the shield wall would occasionally pull in stragglers who were arriving late and being attacked. "It was a scrum."

When Luke arrived at the park, he found himself on the side with the League of the South and some "Nazi weirdos," and thought "I do not want to be near those people." He saw rally attendees scuffling with a handful of Antifa that had gotten into the park, and one large Black man screaming at people. At one point, the Black man put his hand on his pistol grip. "I almost hit the deck."

Luke told his friends, "This is nuts. We've got to get out of here."

---

3 Charlottesville Survivor, "The System Repudiated: City's own report confirms Charlottesville Police, Politicians conspired to suppress Unite the Right Rally," Vdare.com, Dec. 3, 2017.

One the other side of the park, they spotted a more clean-cut crowd with Confederate and American flags and some young, polo-clad Alt-Righters. Because of the barricade down the middle of the park, they had to exit back into the crowd of protesters to get to the other side. Luke and his party exited the way they had come in, then proceeded to walk around the park with their group in a square formation, with women and the elderly in the middle. They walked stone-faced forward, not wanting to start a fight by catching the eye of anyone of the surrounding sea of Antifa, who Luke describes as being "like a pack of hyenas. You can smell them ten feet away... They are gross people."

As the group proceeded around the park, an Antifa jumped out and attacked one of their men out of the blue, choking him. "Holy shit!" thought Luke. A militia member intervened, and forced the Antifa to stand back.

"I'm very thankful for the militia guys. They did more than any law enforcement officer that day."

They finally reached the other side of the park, where another shield wall was being manned by a polo-and-khaki-wearing Alt-Right crowd. Luke remembers that it was extremely hot while he and his party were waiting inside the park for the rally to start. The cops were ambling about, not really doing anything, while the Antifa that encircled the park were "acting as if possessed" and throwing things - gas bombs, smoke grenades, bottles of urine - and there were rumors among the crowd that others were being hit with even more dangerous chemicals. Luke himself had already been pepper sprayed by this point.

Luke spotted a counter-protester hanging from a tree screaming at people. Concerned that she might fall, he approached a state trooper and suggested he do something about it. When the trooper failed to act, Luke reminded him "I pay your salary." The trooper smirked and walked away.

The chaos continued. Asked about his concern level, Luke described it this way: "If 1 is chilling, and 10 is Kandhahar province, I would say 7.5. It was as though a fort was being created in the middle of the park. Outside are crazy people who want to tear you apart, and the cops aren't doing anything."

A left-wing organizer described the fighting during this part of the day, and indicated the Alt-Righters took the brunt of the abuse. "As we got closer to noon, the Antifascist block was successful in drawing away the most heavily shielded contingent of Nazis. They were successful in drawing them away from the park and make them more vulnerable. As that happened, many people were in the line of fire of projectiles, of pepper spray, of tear gas. A lot of people were hurt and beaten on both sides. I can't speak for being on the ground but from what I observed from my street, it was mostly Nazis that were getting beaten at that point."[4]

One attendee described his experience as the victim of the aforementioned tactic. "An Antifa toady stole the hat of one of our comrades, which served as both physical and dox protection. Naturally he sought to retrieve his property, in the process getting mobbed by the crowd and receiving a nasty laceration... (This is a common Antifa tactic – to provoke and isolate an individual, then swarm him.) I entered the fray to recover the hat and prevent my friend from being swallowed by the crowd, and in the process receiving a series of clubs to the head and torso in a surreal sort of baptism into politically-motivated leftist American street violence."[5]

---

4 Kessler, "Antifa Comms Director," BitChute.com.

5 Max North, "Anarcho-tyranny's Unequal Justice: Why Charlottesville Patriots Can't Prosecute Antifa Thugs," Vdare.com, Sept. 8, 2017.

CHAPTER 11 QUICK LINKS:

The Political Cesspool Radio Show, podcast aired Aug. 12, 2017. Hour 1 URL: qrs.ly/r8cvtl5 ; Hour2 URL: qrs.ly/r8cvtm1 ; Hour 3 URL: qrs.ly/9jcvtm3

Jason Kessler, "Antifa Comms Director Luis Oyola on Charlottesville Conspiracy," Video, posted June 19, 2020. URL: qrs.ly/4acvtbm

CHAPTER 12

DISPERSAL

"Where the freak do we go?"

AROUND 11:00 A.M., as fighting intensified, Captain Shifflett reported to the Command Center that 2nd and Market Street were "getting ready to erupt any second now," then a moment later, he reported another fight of "about forty people going at it, they're using sticks." At 11:08 a.m., Maurice Jones and the Regional Policy Group declared a local and regional state of emergency. At 11:10, CPD officers in Zones 4 and 5 were ordered to withdraw from Lee Park to put on riot gear.

Governor McAuliffe writes that he was watching the turmoil on the streets of Charlottesville on TV while communicating with Colonel W. Steven Flaherty, the Superintendent of the Virginia State Police, and Secretary of Public Safety Brian Moran, who were both on the scene. Though eager to declare a state of emergency, he refrained from doing so since normal protocol was for local authorities to make the call. McAuliffe writes that at 11:15 Moran called him and said, "Governor, you've got to declare a state of emergency. This is out of control... We can't wait for Charlottesville.

Screw protocol." At 11:28 a.m. McAuliffe authorized a state of emergency via text message.[1] At 11:31 a.m. Chief Thomas called for the declaration of unlawful assembly.[2]

At that moment, Unite the Right attendees were waiting for the speeches to begin, when unexpectedly, the police made an intercom announcement. "This has been declared an unlawful assembly. If you do not disperse immediately, you will be arrested." (The delay between the 11:08 a.m. decision to declare a state of emergency, and the 11:31 announcement is attributed to the time it took the VSP to bring in their mobile field forces, and their insistence on extracting their undercover officers from the crowd prior to the announcement.)[3]

There was mass confusion in the park. Organizers of the rally huddled together, conferring with businesslike concern. Kessler could be heard yelling "We're marching to McIntire!" A large number of Unite the Right attendees joined a train of people formed by the rally organizers and marched in a line back to McIntire Park. Others were forcibly dispersed into the unruly crowd in a disorganized manner and forced to fend for themselves.

At 11:42 am, Kessler explained to a documentary crew at the park, "The Charlottesville Police Department comes in an hour and a half after our permit started at 10 am, and declares an unlawful assembly. It was a heckler's veto. We, our people, were not being violent. They were being violent to us. And from my understanding, our people were tear gassed. After they declared an unlawful assembly, our people left immediately, and they still tear gassed us."[4]

A member of Kessler's security team then approached him. "All right. We're moving." He was escorted away. Invictus was with Jason in the first group to leave the park, which missed all the fighting.

---

1 McAuliffe, *Beyond Charlottesville*, p. 95.

2 Heaphy Report, p. 133.

3 Heaphy Report, p. 134.

4 National Geographic, "Violence in Charlottesville," YouTube.

At 11:44a.m., a line of Virginia State Police in riot gear arrived at the park. At 11:49a.m., they begin to move forward into the park to push out those who had not already voluntarily dispersed.

Enrique Tarrio of the Proud Boys remembers the park had one exit point – a small set of stairs only wide enough for three or four people at a time. When the unlawful assembly was called, "The shit hit the fan... there were gigantic fucking clashes on the way out." He witnessed an older man getting pushed down by Antifa, who tried to stab him with a broken flag pole. Fortunately, the man was wearing body armor and was not seriously harmed. During the attack, Tarrio saw a police officer standing about fifteen feet away, watching disinterestedly with his arms crossed. Tarrio was glad he had worn body armor and was carrying book bag, which protected him later when he was hit with a pole.

Other attendees describe their reaction to the unexpected order to disperse.

"We were just trying to peaceably assemble as we came to do when the police declared our assembly unlawful. And right then and there I was infuriated. I was really, really surprised by this," said Chris on the Political Cesspool podcast that evening.[5]

Nathaniel was angry as well. As the riot cops moved forward and forced his group into the crowd, he was hit in the face with a shirt soaked in urine and pepper spray. He told his friend, "I think I see a gun."

His friend said, "Move!" and then they heard a gunshot. He later learned about the warning shot towards a man wielding a flamethrower that had been fired by Richard Preston and was surprised to discover how close he had been to the flamethrower.

Gene was even closer to it. "That Black guy came running at us with the homemade flame thrower... Police were literally pushing us out of the park. They pushed us off the top of the wall. We had to jump four feet to get to the sidewalk. Now we had to fight our way three or four blocks to the parking garage."

---

5 The Political Cesspool Radio Show, podcast aired Aug. 12, 2017, www. thepoliticalcesspool.org.

Bill recalls, "The police came in on the north side and told everybody to leave. They pushed everybody out the narrow entry way out into those people." He also recalls that the retreat was "fairly well organized."

Jim remembers that when the unlawful assembly order was called. "Riot police began marching down on us, pushing UTR attendees out of the park and into the mob." Some people had taken down the middle gates to help them get to the safer side. "It was bedlam." The guys from their group who had been manning the shield wall went towards the parking garage. The rest of the League of the South, and others who were in their group, were trying to get through "one little pathway that was available." There, they confronted Antifa armed with aerosol torches and slingshots that were being used to launch water bottles full of urine.

They faced a choice. "We either go through the gauntlet or we walk around the city." They chose the latter. Some of the elderly members of the party were not up to the lengthy hike in the hot summer sun. Jim called a van for them and escorted them to a police officer to protect them until their van arrived. The officer told them, "You can't stay here." Jim got the officer's badge number and threatened a lawsuit if any harm came to the older people, who he later learned were able to get home safely.

By the time Tom heard the unlawful assembly order, the barrier in the middle of the park between groups of attendees was down. He was glad to see it since he felt it would allow for more safety in numbers. Tom recalls "That was the first time I saw law enforcement move" as they were pushing into the park to push the attendees out.

"Where the freak do we go?" he wondered. There was no good answer. Still, he saw no choice but to leave. "We followed orders. I didn't want to get arrested. If we have to battle our way out, that's what we have to do." At that point it began to occur to him that this was almost like a set-up.

After the dispersal order, Luke and his friends decided it was time to leave. They repositioned into square formation with the women and elderly on the inside to begin their "battle retreat" out of the park. After the barricade opened and they started leaving, Antifa was "picking people out on the edges." He was thinking, "We have to get out of here in one piece... Police allowed pandemonium to ensue."

On the Political Cesspool, host Eddie Miller reported, "Well our Vietnam vet ex-marine told one of the cops we'd be happy to leave the park and go back to the parking garage the way we came in. He was told, 'Get the hell out of here. We're not gonna clear a path for you.' The way we had to go was straight forward into Antifa. I think we were outnumbered four or five to one. We had to fight our way out of there... Well as you can imagine, all hell broke loose... It was just total chaos, fighting, fighting, fighting, fighting. We broke up. All our guys got separated all over Charlottesville. We were scattered all over."

Another guest of the Political Cesspool, Mike, told a harrowing story about being dispersed from the park. "I was part of a group of five people who got cut off from the rest of our entourage by the police shield wall. They kept pushing us forward toward the Antifa. I tell them 'What are you doing? There are five of us, and there was at least 200 of [the Antifa] standing over here.' Two of the guys tried to dive down to get past the police, and one of them got rewarded for it with a hit in the back with a baton loud enough that I was able to hear it from six feet away. They were both coated in mace. I got coated in mace. I turned around. I had a shield, I told them to follow me, we were going to try to force our way through the Antifa, and one of the police officers nailed me in the back with his shield, tried to knock me down the steps and two of the other guys tumbled right beside me... They intended us to fall. So finally they got up and we made our way around. We were pressed up against a wall by I don't know how many of them, one of the guys took a blow to the head, he had blood pouring down the side of his face from it. We finally made it to the medic line."[6]

After they issued the dispersal order, explains Chris, the young attendee from Appalachia, "Riot police came up behind us near the statue." At that point he concluded "It's time to go. I'm getting out."

---

6 The Political Cesspool Radio Show, podcast aired Aug. 12, 2017, www.thepoliticalcesspool.org.

He recalls that Richard Spencer approached, and asked for anyone who was willing to be arrested to follow him. Spencer's contingent moved down towards the riot police. Chris went the other way, following the crowd to McIntire.

As police pushed them into counter-protesters, the violence escalated. Chris explained that at that point, "I'm just trying to get out of there before something insane happens." Out in the street, he was attacked by "a real tall Black guy" who started pushing him. Some skinheads who happened to be nearby jumped in to help fight off the attacker. He continued marching, ready to go home.

Darren, a caller to the Political Cesspool podcast, did not escape so easily. "The police were clearly on the side of the enemy. They attacked us. They were not on the side of law and order. It was planned, obviously, orchestrated by the city government. The police, they moved in without provocation. They attacked us with pepper spray. I personally was pepper sprayed from head to toe – my eyes, my arms, everything was on fire. And you know it was rough, but that's the reality we live in."[7]

Consistent with the many eyewitness accounts presented here, the independent Heaphy Report confirms, "Much like the plan for entry to Emancipation [Lee] Park, the dispersal of crowds following the unlawful-assembly declaration did not ensure separation between conflicting groups. Rather, the mobile field force units pushed the Unite the Right protesters right back onto Market Street, where a larger group of counter-protesters were waiting for them." One Lieutenant described the dispersal as 'the most messed up thing I ever saw... causing confrontations and pushing [the Alt-Right] right into their enemies'"[8]

Drone footage publicized in 2021 provides further evidence of the provocative dispersal in vivid visual form, proving that "the pro-Lee protesters looking to protect a statue of Robert E. Lee from being taken down were literally pushed by Democrat police agents and funneled through a hostile crowd of left-wing agitators" and

---

7 Ibid.

8 Heaphy Report, p. 135.

that "militant Antifa, 'alternative left' Communists, outnumbered pro-Lee protesters by 10:1...you can see as Virginia State Police and Charlottesville Police push the protesters out of the park directly into the waiting crowd of Antifa and left-wing protesters. There was zero police crowd control of the left-wing elements."[9]

"Police were eerie in their organized, planned lack of engagement," says Parrot, describing them as having had "stony, blank looks."

Remarked one rally attendee, "Speaking just for myself, this was the moment when I was convinced I was going to have to fight for my life."[10]

One alley way on Market Street, protected from aggressors by militiamen, became a safe zone for injured attendees.

Meanwhile, the left-wing groups had been monitoring the happenings in the park and become aware of the dispersal. "Speaking from the point of view of dispatch, we decided to hop on to Kessler's Periscope live feed where he was rambling about the fact that the police were not allowing people to come into the park, and he was very, very upset about that... Shortly after that, he in his Periscope denoted that a police officer from CPD was coming up towards the rally and the police officer informed them that, one, a state of emergency had been declared in Charlottesville, and, two, their gathering had been declared an unlawful assembly... Because we were able to catch that in dispatch that, we were able to communicate that immediately to teams on the ground, and they were able to mobilize immediately. And we were also able to communicate immediately that Kessler was planning to move to McIntire Park as a backup."[11]

---

9 Ben Wetmore, "EXCLUSIVE: Never-Before-Seen Drone Footage from Charlottesville 2017 Protests Reveals Enormous Extent of Media Lies and Propaganda," TheGatewayPundit.com, May 5, 2021.

10 Charlottesville Survivor, "The System Repudiated," Vdare.com.

11 Kessler, "Antifa Comms Director," BitChute.com.

At 12:06 p.m., Governor McAuliffe declared a state of emergency. By 12:13 p.m., the park had been cleared.

Return To McIntire Park

A large group of Unite the Right attendees arrived at McIntire Park around 12:20pm. Hundreds of people were milling around, most in confusion, searching their phones and exchanging information with one another, trying to figure out what was going on. Rumors spread through the crowd – some people believed the rally had been relocated, while others thought the National Guard was on the way to make arrests. Richard Spencer, David Duke and Mike Enoch made some brief impromptu remarks. Eli Mosley then advised everyone present to get in their cars and leave before counter-protesters or the police arrived. Most attendees were willing to leave, but many who had become separated from other members of their parties, or who were far away from their cars, were uncertain what to do next.

On the Political Cesspool podcast, Brad Griffin of the League of the South, reported, "They declared our gathering an illegal assembly, and made us march two miles to McIntire Park. And once we arrived in McIntire Park, we were isolated from our vehicles. The Governor of Virginia declared a state of emergency, which meant that we couldn't have a public assembly anywhere in the state of Virginia... The various people who were with our group, after the police ordered them to disperse or face arrest by the police, were attacked by Antifa... The police basically stood by and allowed Antifa to attack us, and then completely shut down our constitutional rights. It's outrageous. I'm furious. I've never been through anything like this."[12]

There was lots of confusion, Nathaniel recalls, as he marched with the large group in a line back to McIntire. He remembers warning others who were walking on the outside of the line to be

---

12 The Political Cesspool Radio Show, podcast aired Aug. 12, 2017, www. thepoliticalcesspool.org.

careful. The walk took a while. When walking through the Black neighborhood, he got lots of dirty looks, but at least one "supportive" honk from a passing car.

Nathaniel recalls while at McIntire, word was spreading through the crowd that everyone had to either disperse or face arrest for a felony. At the park, he was excited to meet a few people he followed online - James Allsup, Nick Fuentes, and Eli Mosley. Nathaniel and his friends hung out a short while, wondering, "How do we get back to our car?" Eventually, one of them got an Uber and brought the car back to pick up the others.

After walking to the other park, Tom heard a rumor the National Guard was coming to arrest anyone who had not dispersed. He was parked at a garage that was two miles in the other direction. He began to wish that he had brought water. He had to walk through jeering protesters but experienced no violence. After walking for a while, some fellow rally attendees saw them and offered them a ride back to the parking garage.

He began to realize "It was definitely a set-up. It could not have succeeded." By then, word of the rally had made the news, and friends from home were calling to check on him.

Eddie Miller reported on the Political Cesspool, "We got back to McIntire Park. There were about 200 people there. Met up with some of our guys. We had been given the green light earlier by the state to meet there. After going about three miles to McIntire Park in the hot sun, the governor says, we have to get out of McIntire, if we don't evacuate McIntire Park, then we're going to be arrested."[13]

Luke took a water break on the outskirts of McIntire. A liberal woman who was visiting the park with her kids was screaming things like "I hope you die!" and "You're evil!" at the attendees. She wouldn't let up. He thought to warn her to leave it alone for her own and her kids' safety, but before he could, "some Nazi-looking dude" pepper sprayed her. A medic tried to help her, but she refused.

---

13 *Ibid.*

By the time Chris arrived at McIntire, he had been separated from all but one friend from his group. At that point he heard about the State of Emergency, the car accident, and the helicopter crash. He knew then that it was over and he needed to go, but didn't know Charlottesville very well and he had no clue where the rest of his friends were.

At 12:38p.m., Richard Spencer tweeted, "My recommendation: Disperse. Get out of Charlottesville city limits. State of emergency has been called."

Shortly before noon, Charlottesville resident Steve was outside in his driveway waiting for his friend to arrive. They were planning to walk up to the park and arrive around noon when the rally was scheduled to begin.

To his surprise, Steve saw a stream of people, mostly men, walking down the sidewalk away from the park. The stream of people appeared to be rally supporters. There was no violence or unruliness - Steve said that if he had to use one word to describe the crowd, it would be "subdued." Some were walking casually, others were slumped over and looking down. Many of the endless stream of people seemed overwhelmed from having just gone through the gauntlet. Some seemed defeated, others angry.

He thought, "This isn't right. What's going on?"

Steve walked down his driveway to meet his friend that had just arrived. The two began questioning the evacuees to determine what had happened. After a while, about four or five people from the exodus accumulated in his driveway, talking about the events of the morning. Eventually, the group decided to head back downtown to survey the scene. The chopper was still circling overhead, so Steve knew things were not yet over.

Civil Disobedience

Pax Dickinson had been scheduled to speak at the rally. In the Daily Caller, he wrote about what he experienced after the Unlawful Assembly order was issued.

We were instructed to leave the park, and told that anyone refusing to do so would be arrested. Attendees began attempting to leave via exits 1 & 2 and were set upon by Antifa as they attempted to do so. After a quick consultation, a small group of rally headliners and attendees decided to engage in civil disobedience and get ourselves arrested, myself included.

We told our security teams to leave the park to avoid arrest, while Virginia State Police began forming a shield wall at the north end of the park. The pens were nearly empty at this point, except for those planning to be arrested and a few people still attempting to run the Antifa gauntlet at the stairs to escape from the park.

The VSP shield wall began advancing south, and we linked arms and held our ground. We told police we refused to leave and planned to engage in civil disobedience. We were respectful and informed them we would not resist arrest but we refused to leave the park willingly.

The shield wall advanced on us and began to shove our line. We stood firm and held our ground for a few minutes. Police on the line did not say a word and refused to arrest us while shoving with their shields and swinging them at us.

After a few minutes of shoving, our line was pepper-sprayed from a cop behind the police shield wall, and our resistance crumbled. Being near the end of the line, I was not sprayed directly. The spray drifted in the wind onto my arms and face, but my eyes remained clear.

We retreated through the western barricade but police on 1st St. would not let us onto the street forced us to retreat south. We're pushed through the barricade at the south end of 1st St. and onto Market St., which was lined on both sides with mobs of screaming Antifa with no police presence whatsoever.

We ran west on Market St, running a gauntlet of Antifa throwing bottles, sticks, and rocks. Two people I believe were nearly blinded by pepper spray. I followed them closely but then dropped back as the crowd hurled everything they had at another protest headliner, luckily missing with most of it.

After running a few blocks west, we reached the intersection of Market and Preston, where a shield wall had been set up by rally attendees on a grass strip alongside Market St. Casualties were being tended there, including multiple heavily bleeding scalp wounds and pepper spray injuries. Luckily all the injuries seemed superficial except one man with a very bad head injury who seems to be going in and out of consciousness.[14]

On the Political Cesspool podcast, James Edwards asked Evan McLaren of the National Policy Institute about this encounter. "Can you speak about the treatment that Richard Spencer experienced? I think many of us probably saw his live video stream in which he very bravely stood his ground and said that he would not resist the police but that he was not going to move. He was not ultimately arrested, but it looked as though he may have been roughed up a little bit. Is that accurate?"

McLaren replied, "Yeah, I think that is accurate. I was with him. I was arrested early on. Richard took the lead, but the decision was a group one to simply say that we were not going to leave, we had the right to be there. So the riot lines formed, the riot police, and some of us were pushed out, that was what happened to Richard. I was knocked down and arrested right away. That turned out to be the safer course for me, because Richard and the others were

---

14 Pax Dickinson, "Here's How Virginia State Police Facilitated Violence At Charlottesville," DailyCaller.com, Aug. 14, 2017.

pushed out into the crowd, they had to flee through Antifa and had things thrown at them, were attacked, so it was a very dangerous situation. The police did much less than fail to do their job. They did the opposite of their job and they put us in danger. And to the question that you asked earlier, I ask you, if this is what can happen, then really what is the state of the constitution in this country? It's very much in question right now."

Edwards remarked that based on his viewing of the live stream, "It did look as though police were actively kicking our participants, kicked you and Richard."

"Yeah." McLaren replied.[15]

Matt Parrot described his experience of the dispersal:

I was walking a fighter back to the medics when I heard the police announce over the megaphone that it was now an "unlawful assembly" and that everybody was to disperse... Bear in mind while reading this that we were entirely trapped in the park. Fighting was not optional. This was classic self-defense in the most simple and direct manner. The police had deliberately removed our ability to protect ourselves while not offering us protection. As the police began forming into a straight line preparing to vacate the park, I yelled at an officer, "How are we supposed to exit?! How the fuck do we peacefully exit the park?!

He smiled smugly and pointed in the opposite direction of our entrance, through their barricades, and through a human sea of degenerates open-carrying with open sores... Most of the Antifa had become so discouraged at this point that they had retreated back. Only a handful of their heartiest fighters, positively exhausted, fumbled aimlessly,

---

15 The Political Cesspool Radio Show, podcast aired Aug. 12, 2017, www. thepoliticalcesspool.org.

half-blinded by their own chemical weapons, lashing out at the nationalists who were being forced into them by the encircling riot cops...

For everyone but me, the lethally dangerous job of working through the maze of Antifa mobs, police blockades, and contradictory police directions back to their vehicles was just beginning... I wrote a status update on my Facebook wall, "We will not be replaced." and then put my phone away. Shortly afterwards, I was zip-tied and led into a wagon which took me to the police department directly beside our parking garage and released. They attempted to have me sign a form promising not to return to the park, which I refused to do... The police immediately let me out. I was only a political prisoner for about 20 minutes, not nearly long enough to write my manifesto. Fortunately, the jail was right beside my parking garage and my civil disobedience had earned me a free pass out of the most dangerous part of the whole event... I called up [Matthew] Heimbach to find out where everybody was... [h]e explained that "Everybody is lost. Everybody. The police are chasing small groups of both sides in random directions and into blockaded blind alleys."

I had thought all my adrenaline had been expended already, but the thought of my men being herded into dozens of traps in the narrow streets and alleyways of Charlottesville frightened me all over again.[16]

Walking away from the park, Cantwell, red-faced and shirtless, spoke to a reporter who had been following him all day as part of a documentary about Unite the Right. "We're here obeying the law. We're doing everything that we're supposed to do, trying to express opinions. And the criminals are over there getting their way... I'm

---

16 Matt Parrott, "Catcher in the Reich," Steemit.com.

not even saying that we're nonviolent. I'm saying that we did not aggress. We didn't initiate force against anybody. We're not nonviolent. We'll fucking kill these people if we have to."[17]

Meanwhile, other event organizers were strategizing how to evacuate their people from the park. One documentary records Eli Mosley on the phone, saying "I need to speak to the police captain immediately. Right now we have guys, right now we have people on the ground at the statue with equipment. And they're being told they're not allowed to have a vehicle come through and pick them up, or anybody come and pick them up. I'm about to send about 200 people with guns to get them out if you guys do not get our people out... [pause] Thank you. Tell them to call me. They have my number."[18]

Trace Chiles was hit in the face with wasp spray on his way out of the park. He fought to keep his large group together while Antifa tried to break them into smaller groups. They had to fight their way through the unfamiliar streets, with "the police nowhere to be found." Chiles remembers chaos and confusion the whole way back to their vehicles, and notes that while it had taken them about fifteen minutes to walk from their vans to Lee Park that morning, it took about two hours to get back.

---

17 Vice News, "Charlottesville: Race and Terror," YouTube.

18 *Ibid*.

CHAPTER 12 QUICK LINKS:

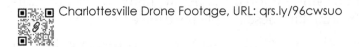 Charlottesville Drone Footage, URL: qrs.ly/96cwsuo

 Heaphy Report. URL: qrs.ly/dpcvtcb

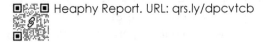 National Geographic, "See the Sparks That Set Off Violence in Charlottesville," Video, posted Aug 19, 2017. URL: qrs.ly/6ocvtgu

The Political Cesspool Radio Show, podcast aired Aug. 12, 2017. Hour 1 URL: qrs.ly/r8cvtl5 ; Hour 2 URL: qrs.ly/r8cvtm1 ; Hour 3 URL: qrs.ly/9jcvtm3

Jason Kessler, "Antifa Comms Director Luis Oyola on Charlottesville Conspiracy," video, June 19, 2020. URL: qrs.ly/4acvtbm

Vice News, "Charlottesville: Race and Terror," video, Aug. 14, 2017. URL: qrs.ly/sacvtjp

CHAPTER 13

ANARCHY

"The police had completely lost control of the city."

UNITE THE RIGHT ATTENDEES were forced from the park and into a hostile crowd with a warning that they would face arrest if they did not disperse. At the same time, groups of counter-protesters were roaming around the area with impunity. Some were engaging in fights with Unite the Right attendees who were trying to leave, while others were organizing into groups to march. The combination of these warring groups wandering through downtown Charlottesville along with police passivity led to chaos, confusion, and wanton violence. The results were catastrophic both to the individuals involved, and to the psyche of the nation.

Pax Dickinson wrote about what happened after the dispersal. "From there the bulk of the rally attendees were able to march north and eventually reached the relative safety of McIntire Park, about two miles away, but many had been scattered throughout the city by the chaos of the dispersal. At that point the police had completely lost control of the city. The State of Emergency order meant that any public gathering was de facto illegal, but Antifa were still allowed to roam freely bearing weapons and attacking people. This chaos ultimately led directly to the vehicular incident that killed a woman and badly injured more than a dozen others."[1]

---

1 Pax Dickinson, "Virginia State Police Facilitated Violence," DailyCaller.com.

Enrique Tarrio describes the hostilities he saw in the streets of Charlottesville after the dispersal. "I saw a bunch of nasty shit. People fighting each other like they weren't human. They were going for faces and putting each other in choke holds. I'm surprised there weren't more deaths and serious injuries. Super surprised." Tarrio interprets what he witnessed. "I saw polarized America - people fucking hated each other that never met each other."

Tom recalls that after the dispersal order was given, "we made a train and we walked out of town." He noticed that law enforcement wasn't pushing the left out of the street. They were being allowed to impede traffic. "A thousand leftists blocked up the whole road." He had been to dozens of other rallies and never seen anything like it. "Leftists were dancing in the streets. The police were sitting there not even clearing the streets."

One caller to the Political Cesspool podcast reported, "After we were driven out of the park, the people who had the permit, guess what? One of our people came back thirty minutes after we were driven out of the park and the Antifa were still there. They were lounging around like having a holiday."[2]

Additional evidence from drone footage "makes clear the 'alternative left' could protest anywhere, assault anyone, and police would not stop them...you can see the harassment and assault upon departing protesters by left-wing extremists in the bottom left of the screen, as the police march in to shut down the protest in the upper right. There was total legal impunity for the left to assault people trying to leave the location...The double standard obvious on video is appalling"[3]

Chris recalls that he and his friend walked back to the parking garage, intending to return to their cars. When they turned onto the street where they were parked, they found it full of counter-protesters sitting on their knees, listening to a man with a bullhorn describing the car accident that had just happened as "a terrorist

2 The Political Cesspool Radio Show, podcast aired Aug. 12, 2017, www.thepoliticalcesspool.org.

3 Ben Wetmore, "Never-Before-Seen Drone Footage from Charlottesville," TheGatewayPundit.com.

attack" and saying that we needed to have an uncomfortable conversation about racism.

"There was no way we could get through." They had to take a roundabout path through the unfamiliar city. By chance, they ran into another band of about 5-10 Alt-Righters who they had never before met who were facing the same problem of being unable to return to their cars. The group walked around for about 45 minutes before making their way back to their cars. Part of their trek took them through the ghetto, which Chris described as "very uncomfortable."

Meanwhile, some counter-protesters heard that Alt-Righters were seen in Black neighborhoods. They headed to those neighborhoods as well with the intention of protecting the minority residents, under the false impression that the Alt-Right had gone there deliberately to cause trouble. In fact, the Alt-Right were wandering through Charlottesville, a town unfamiliar to most of them, as a result of the disorganized dispersal.

As they trekked back towards the parking garage, Black Lives Matter protesters were attacking members of Gene's group from behind, so he moved to the back of his group and walked backwards to guard the rear. Gene had a Confederate flag on a wooden flagpole which he used "like a hockey stick" to fend off attackers, though he recalls that "the young guys did most of the fighting." Once they got back to the parking garage, they realized that two members of their party were missing. As they waited for their missing friends, Antifa attacked one member of their group until the sheriff's department intervened. Once the missing members rejoined the group, they got into a van and drove away. Shaken by the events of the day, they discarded their plans for an afternoon visit to Monticello.

While driving away, Gene observed about ten or fifteen busses lined up a few blocks from Market Street. He supposed they had been used to transport counter-protesters to the rally. Questions arise about who was organizing and funding the hordes of counter-protesters. Charlottesville native Hannah Zarski remarks, "The organization for Unite the Right was so far beyond anything that could have been arranged here. It was very well coordinated." She points out that the swarm of Antifa were carrying professionally-printed signs mounted on thick wooden dowels. "Those things are not cheap."

Parrot spent the aftermath of the dispersal trying to account for the whereabouts of his compatriots. "I drove back and forth repeatedly from the parking garage through the city sweeping up comrades and driving them to safety. Like a catcher in the rye, I spent most of my time at both the melee itself and the period afterward frantically racing around trying to account for everybody's safety."[4]

"It was kind of fun," remembers Parrot. "It was kind of a movement unity thing," with people from different right-wing groups that were not always friendly all working together and helping each other get to safety. Parrot notes that James Fields had been doing the same thing at this time – helping displaced rally attendees get to safety.

An organizer for left-wing groups that day who described the event from his point of view did not portray the Alt-Right as the aggressors. "It was during this dispersal that some of the more violent hand-to-hand clashes happened and as groups of Nazis were leaving the area, and Charlottesville residents alongside Antifasists from all over the US demonstrated to them that they were not welcome. They were chased up to the parking lots, they were chased down towards McIntire, and through leaks in their internal chats, the Nazis admitted they were defeated, and they should take refuge as soon as possible."[5]

Steve, the local who was still at home when the stream of people leaving the park marched past his house, had been walking towards Lee Park to explore what was happening. He arrived in the downtown area not long after the car crash. He recalls, "seeing my hometown reduced to a war zone was devastating... At that point it was complete chaos." There were hundreds of leftists wandering "wherever they saw an easy target," carrying protest signs and screaming obscenities. Impromptu marches were beginning to

---

4 Matt Parrott, "Catcher in the Reich," Steemit.com.

5 Kessler, "Antifa Comms Director," BitChute.com

form into what Steve later surmised, after studying video of the event, was a literal victory lap. They were chanting, "Same enemy, same fight. Workers of the world unite." Some carried Hammer and Sickle flags.

Steve continued past the park, and headed towards downtown where he heard a "dull roar" of activity. Upon arriving on Market Street, he learned about the car crash from a bystander. He was unsurprised that something like that had happened since there was so much chaos and so many people in the streets. There were some police present, he recalls, "but as God is my witness, they were not doing a damn thing." He fumes, recalling how they had forced evacuation from the park "in the most dangerous direction possible," then did nothing to reign in the chaos. "I cannot recall them doing a damn thing to take charge... The police presence may as well have been non-existent."

By chance, he encountered an old friend of his from high school with whom he had reconnected after moving back to Charlottesville. "She was and is a big leftist." Steve knew she had come to counter-protest the event, but the two were having a friendly conversation. He asked her jokingly, "You know we're on different sides, right?" He noted she was holding a small cardboard sign that read, "Jesus was brown." He knew his friend had anti-Christian views, and had in fact dabbled in paganism and witchcraft. He thought to debate the assumptions that caused her to think that particular sign would trigger right-wingers, but decided instead to try to keep things agreeable.

While they were talking, a fight broke out in the street just a few yards away between some White right-wingers and Black leftists. He saw the White guys start to run away. The Black guys started throwing large blocks of ice, which seemed to have materialized from nowhere. Steve described the blocks as being about 10 to 20 pounds each, big enough that if someone received a solid hit, they could have been killed. Someone hurled a big block of ice towards a fleeing man which narrowly missed Steve's head.

As he watched it shatter, his friend cheered, "Yeah, get em, boys!" He was taken aback by her reaction considering how close he had come to being struck by the potentially deadly projectile. While he was still standing there "shell shocked," one of the guys from the group that he had walked up with came up and admitted that they had been taunting the Black men, who responded violently.

Steve and his female friend ducked into a nearby bar for shelter where he found himself in a group with her friends. He was dressed neutrally and they didn't recognize him as a Unite the Right attendee. They seemed to be hyped up on adrenaline. His impression was that they were excited and happy about the chaos and riots, even though the car crash had taken place shortly before. "They were getting what they wanted."

Eventually Steve left, and went out wandering the streets, looking for the friend that had come to his apartment to join him earlier in the day and from whom he had gotten separated. Oddly, he noticed that his cell phone did not work for about an hour even though he was in the heart of downtown, and he wondered if someone was signal-jamming, though he had no idea who would do that, or why.

He had brought a loaded .38 to be safe, but never pulled it out.

Jim and his party arrived back at the parking garage, after a mile or so walk. They were met by 100 police officers blocking them from entering. Jim approached, explained that they were trying to leave and comply with orders. The commander agreed to let them enter to get into their cars. Some of his group were angry that the police had blocked their entry, but Jim encouraged them not to engage the cops and just keep walking. Once at the top of the parking garage, they found out about the Deandre Harris incident, in which Unite the Right attendees who were attempting to leave were assaulted by a Black counter-protester. Their response to Harris' attack produced one of the most viral photos of the day and resulted in the arrests of several men.

Jim recalls that people were cleaning themselves up then getting into their cars to leave. His own shirt was covered in urine and he had been burned by an irritant. After cleaning up, Jim tried to leave, but realized that he had lost his car keys at some point during the chaos of the day. While trying to break into his own car, he was rushed by police officers. Though he was able to prove that the car was his own, there was another problem – the pistol in his cargo pants pocket. While he had a carry permit, it was for Virginia, while his drivers' license was for Florida where he had recently moved. Jim was arrested for carrying a gun without a permit.

Jim was taken to the state troopers' station at the courthouse. While there, he overheard the troopers complaining about how Governor McAuliffe had wanted to have a police helicopter there "all for show." They felt he was responsible for the deaths of the two men killed in the crash. The officers were also complaining that the City of Charlottesville hadn't been doing its job of communicating with the Virginia State Police. One officer remarked, "This wasn't how it was supposed to go."

Jim was placed in a cell next to a clean-cut looking young man who he later learned was responsible for that day's fatal car crash – James Fields. Jim recalls, "He looked to me like a preppy kid who got a DUI or something." He watched as police officers took a statement from Fields, and had him sign some things. They were telling him, "Admit what you did."

Jim's observation was that Fields seemed "shocked." His face was red. Was it from shame? From terror? He looked as though he had been crying. Though the arrestees had been instructed not to speak to each other, Jim offered, "Good luck, Brother" as they escorted Fields away. Fields did not reply.

Because he still had a Virginia residence, Jim was able to be released without bond, with instructions to return to court the next Monday.

Late in the afternoon, a Virginia State Police helicopter that had been used for aerial surveillance crashed, killing two officers. The tragic deaths of Lieutenant H. Jay Cullen and Trooper-Pilot Berke M. M. Bates, though later attributed to mechanical problems with the helicopter that were unrelated to Unite the Right, increased the trauma associated with the rally and furthered the nation's impression of it as a "deadly" event.

CHAPTER 13 QUICK LINKS:

 Charlottesville Drone Footage, URL: qrs.ly/96cwsuo

The Political Cesspool Radio Show, podcast aired Aug. 12, 2017. Hour 1 URL: qrs.ly/r8cvtl5 ; Hour2 URL: qrs.ly/r8cvtm1 ; Hour 3 URL: qrs.ly/9jcvtm3

 Jason Kessler, "Antifa Comms Director Luis Oyola on Charlottesville Conspiracy," video, June 19, 2020. URL: qrs.ly/4acvtbm

CHAPTER 14

CAR CRASH

"I need an ambulance right now!"

AS MENTIONED BEFORE, the deficient plans in place for traffic management in downtown Charlottesville did not leave the streets well-fortified to handle the massive crowds present on the day of Unite the Right. Most are now well familiar with the tragic consequences of this failure: a car plowed into a crowded street, resulting in the death of 32-year-old counter-protester Heather Heyer.

Earlier that day, the Heaphy Report explains:

> ...Officer Tammy Shiflett, a school resource officer, was available to work after having spent most of June and July recovering from elbow surgery. So on August 11, Lewis replaced Sandridge with Tammy Shiflett, which freed up Sandridge to take over Durrette's role as a roving traffic supervisor. Officer Shiflett was told about her assignment at Market Street and 4th Street NE, but she did not receive any instruction other than that she would be "doing traffic." She understood that her role was to prevent "anything coming down East Market Street" to Emancipation

[Lee] Park... Video footage shot around 10:30 a.m. on August 12 shows Officer Shiflett standing at her post next to her squad car in Market Street as scores of Unite the Right attendees streamed past her towards Emancipation [Lee] Park. The video also shows that the southbound route on 4th Street SE was obstructed by a single wooden sawhorse that spanned only the middle third of the road.[1]

After the unlawful assembly order was called before noon, Shifflett found herself standing alone, with no protective gear, as Unite the Right attendees streamed past her away from the park. The Heaphy Report explains further,

She felt she was in danger. As people started to pass, they made profane and aggressive statements toward her. She smelled pepper spray in the air. Just as Sergeant Handy and his unit arrived at the Market Street garage, Shiflett radioed Captain Lewis and said, "They are pushing the crowd my way, and I have nobody here to help me." Lewis radioed to Sergeant Handy and instructed him to help Shiflett. Sergeant Handy and Officer Logan Woodzell started to move towards Shiflett's location, and Handy radioed Shiflett to walk towards them. Woodzell's body camera footage shows Shiflett leaving 4th Street and jogging to the two officers. But she forgot to lock her car, so Handy instructed her to go back and move her car. Shiflett hustled back to the car, got in, and moved it out of the intersection to Market Street near the parking garage. Officer Shiflett ultimately ended up with Lieutenant [Dwayne] Jones as he handled the Deandre Harris incident. Lieutenant Jones told us that he was asked by either Handy or Woodzell to let Officer Shiflett stay with him because she did not have any protective gear. Neither Shiflett nor Jones

---

1 Heaphy Report, p. 91.

notified the traffic commander or the Command Center that she was no longer at her assigned post at 4th Street NE and Market Street. As a result, all that remained there was a wooden sawhorse barricade.[2]

The street that was abandoned by law enforcement was soon to become the setting for the infamous car crash that killed one person and injured dozens of others.

Faith Goldy Livestream

The following is a transcription of raw footage from the Periscope live stream of Faith Goldy, who was reporting on the Charlottesville rally for Rebel Media. Her video captured the James Fields car crash and its immediate aftermath.

Faith Goldy is walking through the crowd in downtown Charlottesville in the aftermath of the rally dispersal. She is wearing a black baseball cap and a black shirt and has a large backpack on her back. As she is walking through the thick crowd, woman in a Black Lives Matter shirt follows her, screaming "Are you with the Alt-Right? If you're with the Alt-Right, get away from here! Get away from here! Get away from here!"

As Goldy walks away, the woman fades into the background. Goldy speaks to the camera. "Very inclusive. I'm looking to learn about inclusion, guys. I'm just looking to learn about inclusion and diversity. I'm here to learn about multiculturalism, and I'm here to learn about how diverse groups lead to very high-trust societies." A steady, loud murmur can be heard from the surrounding crowd of various ages, races, and clothing styles that is milling around her. Some are carrying bright red flags.

"All right, here you go." Goldy taps the camera to turn the camera view from herself to crowd.

Briefly, the focus is on a group of people who are marching with red flags chanting "Our streets! Our streets!"

Goldy remarks, "It's a full-on demonstration."

---

2 Heaphy Report, pp. 139-140.

Suddenly, screaming and a thunderous crash is heard. Abruptly, a car jolts into frame and hits another car which plows into the crowd. More screaming erupts.

Goldy reacts in shock. "Holy shit, holy shit, holy shit, holy shit. Oh my God, oh my God, oh my God, oh my God." The video shows a crowd in chaos, with lots of yelling, screaming, and running.

The time stamps below indicate the minutes and seconds that have passed in the video since the car crash.

0:03   Fields' Dodge jolts backwards out of the frame.

        The camera jerks around wildly. People are running around, and much screaming can be heard.

0:23   "I need to find a safe space, guys. I need to find a safe space." says Goldy.

0:31   Goldy turns the camera back to herself. She is visibly shaken. "Someone, some cars just ran over a whole bunch of protesters. A lot of people got hit. A lot of people got hit. That doesn't look good, that does not look good, that does not look good, that does not look good."

0:46   Goldy turns the camera back to the crowd. There are lots of people moving around. Some seem to be wandering aimlessly. Others are just standing.

0:59   The camera is on a woman in blue shirt who is sitting on the ground. One woman is kneeling beside her holding her hands, and another is standing behind her, helping hold her upright, while a few more concerned people hover around. Goldy remarks, "She is badly hurt. She is badly hurt."

1:08   The camera pans to a motionless silver car. A few people are leaning through the open window towards the driver, who does not appear to be moving. "There is a Black woman driving here."

1:16   "We need medics, we need an ambulance. I'm gonna go see if I can find someone that can find us an ambulance. Hold on a sec. There's like a high level of bystander apathy affect here right now."

1:23   The camera pans to another person on the ground with people kneeling next to her. One kneeling man is yelling, "We need an ambulance right now!" as screaming and chaos continue.

1:33   Goldy says, "I'm getting right off the street right now."

1:42   "There's chaos. There's chaos. Where the hell are the police? Literally there are no police for the first time today. There we go. Oh my God. We need medics here right away."

2:04   The camera pans back to an injured woman in a car. "There's a Black woman driving here. I do not know what happened there. Her car obviously was seriously rammed."

2:13   The camera pans back to another group crowded around an injured person on the ground. "There is someone that looks like they are in very bad shape over there. They're trying to stop the bleeding."

2:17   In frame is yet another injured person on the ground, with a man who appears to be a civilian medic kneeling beside her. "There's another woman over here. Holy smokes." A woman is leaning over the injured person, shouting her name.

2:26   "You're gonna be okay, ma'am, you're gonna be okay," reassures Goldy amidst the melee. The camera zooms around almost 360 degrees. People are everywhere.

2:34   Goldy calls out, "Are you a medic? This way, this way, this way! This woman right there - it looks like they're trying to stop the bleeding. Right there!"

2:40   An unseen person shouts, "If you're not a medic, please back up!"

2:43   Goldy seems to be directing the medic to the injured person. "Ma'am, right over there! Right over there!"

2:50   Goldy tells viewers, "All right, some of the medics are coming through right now." The camera shows a milling crowd and still cars.

2:54   "Holy smokes, if you guys were watching that on my Periscope right now, that was terrifying. What just happened?"

3:05   The camera turns back to another woman on the ground with a group kneeling beside her.

3:08   An unknown voice says, "We're gonna have to clear the streets guys."

3:13   Others join in screaming. "Clear the road! Clear the road!" Members of the crowd start to move out of the road and onto the sidewalk.

3:18   The camera turns to a street which is now mostly clear of pedestrians. A single state police car may be seen slowly approaching from a few blocks away. "Okay, cops are coming now. Here they come. Here they come."

3:30   Goldy tells the viewing audience, "I saw one girl that looked like she got herself right in between two of the cars there. Oh my God."

3:39   The police car stops and its door slowly opens. The camera turns back towards the intersection, showing stopped cars and lots of people still standing around, though mostly on the sidewalk. "This is an absolute failure of police. An absolute failure. They were here the whole time in riot gear, and as soon as Antifa starts marching, they decide it's time to stop patrolling."

3:56   The camera pans to people sitting on curb. Goldy notes, "There are these little pockets like this everywhere." Sirens can be heard in the background, and plenty of people are still milling around. Unseen people may be heard shouting, "Get out of the road!"

4:09   Goldy observes a large dent in a maroon-colored car that is stopped in the middle of the street. "I wonder what happened there. I wonder if that was a human that created that dent right there."

4:16   "I'm getting on the sidewalk guys. I don't know who the hell else has any fancy ideas over here."

4:28   "All right guys. So we're here right in the thick of it." Sirens wail in the background. "Cops are now coming in. Some ambulances I'm hoping. There are some just impromptu medics folks who walk around with red crosses on them. Not I think part of the actual Red Cross, but just medics."

5:04   Sirens grow louder.

5:14   A fire truck with sirens wailing pulls into the intersection and stops.

5:38   The camera is on milling the crowd. "People are understandably very shooken up. That was crazy."

5:55   "Oh, yeah, now the cops are here," Goldy remarks, as two police officers walk slowly into the intersection on foot. One is wearing a yellow vest, the other is pulling his yellow vest on as he walks.

6:07   One of the cops gestures for the crowd to move back.

6:18   More sirens sound, and an emergency vehicle pulls into intersection. Emergency workers in several different kinds of uniforms are milling around, looking at the accident scene. Civilians are also milling around and gawking.

6:38   "For you guys that are just tuning in right now, there was a two or three car pile-up into a very crowded street. Someone, I don't know if it was deliberate, or they just slammed on the accelerator because it was a high-stress situation, I do not know, but I did see one woman who was inside a car that was really badly rear-ended, I saw at least one girl who seemed to get stuck in between the two cars."

7:05   "Now after having absolutely no emergency crews on the ground at the initial moments of this, there is an absolute swarm of them. We've got state police, we've got fire, we've got a giant military vehicle over there." The camera frame shows a sea of people as far as the eye can see, both emergency workers and civilians.

7:23   Unseen voices demand, "Make a hole for the medics!"

Goldy says, "I'm sorry, I'm gonna get out of the way here."

7:27   People are holding hands in front of a person on the ground. "You see people creating human, like, fences to protect - I think that's the girl that I saw get caught between the cars to be honest. My God, I don't think she's responsive."

7:38   Unseen voices yell, "Get back, get back."

7:43   Goldy can be seen on camera again, walking down the street away from the center of activity. "We're being told to move back. I'm going to be respectful here. They've got the flatbeds right now. I saw this one girl that was bleeding in the back of her thigh. It looked like they were trying to stop... One girl who looked to have a deformed leg of sorts, I don't know if it was just a lump or if there were actually bones that were [grimaces]."

8:16   She turns around the camera to show another person on the ground with people kneeling beside. "Some people as far as out here seem to be injured, about 50 meters out."

8:35   "There have got to be, shy of a dozen I'd say, people who seem to be injured here."

8:48   Goldy stops to talk to a passerby. "Faith - nice to meet you. Did you see what happened over there?"

An unidentified man in gray t-shirt replies, "Yeah, there was a car that came down right through that alley way, probably about 40 miles an hour. It just came down, mowed a whole bunch of people, hit a couple of cars. I was right there. I was about ten feet away. It backed up, then it just reversed, hit some more people on the way out, then it was gone."

9:05 "What the hell? Did you see who was driving it? What kind of car it was?"

Man, shaking head, "Uh, it looked like a Dodge Charger. It was gray and black or something like that."

9:18 "Maybe we should tell some officers. What do you think?" Goldy asks. A uniformed officer can be seen walking by. "Excuse me? Officer, officer? I wanted to just let him know, because if the car's still in the area it's probably a good idea that they find that car." She fails to get the attention of the officer.

9:33 An off-camera voice yells, "Free water, free water!"

9:47 People are standing along the street. There is a fire truck parked in the intersection. "People are just bewildered, standing around."

9:56 "Well we've learned at least one important lesson today. When cops don't show up to these things, it's not good news for anyone."

10:18 Goldy begins to speak to the viewers of her live stream. "The car is on your reply fam. Can you guys rewind in the video? Does Periscope even allow you? Does anyone even remember what we saw? Maybe we'll get out of this video and I'll go find it and report it to the police, because I imagine, wow." The camera shows a thick crowd, with cops visible among them. "These are some horrific images here." There is much shouting heard among the crowd which is full of police, emergency vehicles, and workers.

11:05 Goldy begins again to respond to her live stream commenters. "Grey Charger, right? Ok, thanks guys. Thanks guys."

11:15 Goldy approaches a policeman. "Officer just so you know, a lot of people got it on camera, and it would seem that it was a grey Charger that did the damage."

The officer replies, "We know."

Goldy remarks, "Ok they know. Cool."

11:30 She responds to the questions of her live stream viewers: "Where is the National Guard? Good question guys. Yeah guys, feel free to rip this video and share it. I don't mind whatsoever. You have the license plate? If you guys want to DM me the license plate, whoever got it, my DMs are open."

12:08 "Ok guys I'm gonna end the stream."[3]

[LIVE STREAM ENDS]

Emergency Response

George Lindbeck, MD, who was in charge of Emergency Medical Services for the Unite the Right, describes the experience for the first responders there immediately after the crash. "The crowd situation was growing exponentially. The impact was loud, screaming, yelling. People were attracted to that. So this situation was growing both in terms of volume, chaos, and numbers exponentially."

The EMS person in charge during the immediate aftermath concluded that there were adequate resources to deal with the injuries, thus decided to make it his first priority to remove Heather Heyer from the scene. Her condition was grave, and he feared the reaction of the crowd if they saw that EMS had ceased compressions and thus made it apparent that she was dead.

Lindbeck reports, "They were able to clear that scene in about 20-22 minutes. Everybody was gone. They turned it over to law enforcement as a crime scene at that point." There were 26 event related transports to UVA hospital that day, 20 as a result of the

---

3 Faith Goldy - Raw Footage from Charlottesville (Aug 12 2017), "... of record," YouTube Account, posted Dec. 4, 2017.

car crash. Martha Jefferson hospital saw 15 event-related patients total, with 11 being victims from the car crash.[4]

The Heaphy Report praised the Charlottesville Fire Department and UVA health system for the "remarkable feat" of their speedy management of the emergency caused by the car crash, remarking "[t]his prompt, effective response represents a bright success on a day largely filled with failure."[5]

---

4 Jason Kessler, "Head EMT at Charlottesville Rally" BitChute.com.

5 Heaphy Report, p. 7.

CHAPTER 14 QUICK LINKS:

 Heaphy Report. URL: qrs.ly/dpcvtcb

 Faith Goldy - Raw Footage from Charlottesville (Aug 12 2017), "... of record," Posted Dec. 4, 2017. URL: qrs.ly/zxcvtny

 Jason Kessler, "Head EMT at Charlottesville Rally Discusses Expectation of Left-Wing Violence," video, Feb. 23, 2021. URL: qrs.ly/zxcvtfd

Part Three:

The Aftermath

CHAPTER 15

JUGGERNAUT: THE FALSE NARRATIVE

"It was the opposite of the truth."

The Governor Speaks

THE EVENING AFTER UNITE THE RIGHT, Governor Terry McAuliffe held a press conference to grandstand while the eyes of the nation were on Virginia. "I have a message to all the White supremacists and the Nazis who came into Charlottesville today. Our message is plain and simple. Go home. You are not wanted in this great commonwealth... You came here today to hurt people, and you did hurt people... But my message is clear. We are stronger than you. You have made our commonwealth stronger. You will not succeed... There is no place for you here. There is no place for you in America."

McAuliffe's statement is appalling for many reasons.

His characterization of all Unite the Right attendees as "White supremacists and Nazis" meant to inflame ire against even the most benign participants.

His assertion that the citizens who he personally disfavors should not be allowed to exercise their constitutional rights to assemble and speak, as they were attempting to do peacefully.

His imperious order that protesters in Virginia "go home" when in fact many attendees did count Virginia as their home, and at any rate he has no right to forbid citizens of other states from travelling to Virginia.

His utterly unjustified accusation that attendees "wanted to hurt people."

Worst of all, think of the implications of this statement: "There is no place for you in America." With his words, McAuliffe is implicitly embracing the cultural cleansing of his political enemies, many of whom are regular Heritage Americans who want to protect their culture and history. If these people have no right to exist in America, what does one imagine is to be done with them? The answer is chilling.

The Media Speaks

The following are samples of the headlines that were all pervading TV and the internet the weekend of the Unite the Right rally. Note the characterization of the event as "White Supremacist," "White Power," "White Nationalist," usually with the implication that the rally attendees were to blame for the violence.

Charlottesville Reels After a White Supremacist Rally Turns Deadly - Politico

Events Surrounding White Nationalist Rally In Virginia Turn Fatal - NPR

Charlottesville officials: 1 dead, 19 injured after crash near 'Unite the Right' rally - CNN

Bipartisan condemnation for 'Unite the Right' rally – CNN

Car Strikes Protesters During White Supremacist Rally in Charlottesville - Washingtonian

Shocking Photos From The Violent White Supremacist Rally In Charlottesville – BuzzFeed News

Two Virginia state troopers killed in helicopter crash tied to White supremacist rally – Fox News

3 Dead and Dozens Injured After Violent White-Nationalist Rally in Virginia – Intelligencer

Man Charged After White Nationalist Rally in Charlottesville Ends in Deadly Violence – New York Times

Top Naval Officer Condemns 'Shameful Events' in Charlottesville – Daily Caller

White nationalist rally in Charlottesville, Virginia sparks violent clashes, turns deadly – ABC News

3 arrested in connection to violence at Charlottesville White nationalist rally, police say – CBS News

Ted Cruz Condemns Charlottesville Terror: 'The Nazis, the KKK and White Supremacists are Repulsive and Evil' - PJ Media

Man charged with murder after driving into anti-far-right protesters in Charlottesville – The Guardian

How A White Power Rally in Charlottesville Turned Deadly – The Daily Beast

White Nationalist Rally in Charlottesville Shut Down Due to Violence – Reason

House Speaker Paul Ryan Condemns Alt-Right Chaos in Charlottesville, VA – RedState

Car Slams Into Protesters At White Nationalist Rally – The Daily Caller

Violent Clashes Turn Deadly in Charlottesville During White Nationalist Rally – Time

Violent clashes erupt at 'Unite the Right' rally in Charlottesville, Va. - Yahoo News

Terror in Charlottesville: Woman killed as car rams into anti-racist protesters at White nationalist rally – Salon

Blackburn: Charlottesville Riot, Violence Has 'No Place in Civil Society' - NewsMax

Charlottesville 'Unite the Right' rally turns deadly – Al Jazeera

Apple CEO Tim Cook condemns Charlottesville mayhem, says 'Violence and racism have no place in America' - MacDailyNews

Car crashes into crowd, protesters draw blood, toss urine at violent 'Unite the Right' rally in Charlottesville – USA Today

Kessler Versus The Blitzkrieg

Kessler had spent the evening after Unite the Right at the home of family members, assuming that it would be safer than going back to his own residence. He recalls watching the events of the day reported on Fox news. "It was so fake."

By the next day, the whole country was ablaze with talk about the events that took place at Unite the Right in Charlottesville. The shock of what was portrayed in the news as a White Supremacist uprising, combined with the anger and grief over the death of a protester and two police officers, left emotions raw and inflamed all over the nation.

Kessler would spend the subsequent days trying mightily to speak out against the bogus account of Unite the Right that was inundating the news cycle. He called a reporter he knew who was with the Fox affiliate in Charlottesville, Doug McKelway, to ask for an opportunity to address the public. McKelway informed him that the station had deemed him "too toxic" to be allowed on air. Kessler appealed to McKelway further, suggesting that they put him in a contentious setting, such as on an opinion show like Tucker Carlson, so it would not appear the station was sympathetic to him. "I don't care if they want to yell at me. I can take it. I just want a chance to speak." McKelway said he would pass along the suggestion. Kessler never heard back.

He managed to secure interviews on a few alternative news outlets, speaking with hosts like Alex Jones and Gavin McInnes. Even on the few alternative outlets that would interview him, the reception was frosty if not outright hostile. They seemed more interested in distancing themselves from Kessler and Unite the Right than presenting the other side of the story to the public. Kessler recalls, "They wanted to slit my throat."

Almost four years later, Kessler has yet to present his side of the story to a national audience. "I've never really been able to have a platform to explain myself. You would think with a major news event like that, Fox News or somebody would come and ask me, 'What is your perspective on what happened here?' But it was so easy to blame the people who were the political dissidents, who had speech that people didn't agree with, rather than to look at this real government conspiracy to shut down people's civil rights."[1]

The Press Conference

The day after Unite the Right, public fury was nowhere more explosive than at ground zero in downtown Charlottesville.

Kessler sought to address the public and to stand up for the organizers and attendees against the false impression created by the media of what had happened that day. At 2:00pm on Sunday, August 13th, he scheduled a press conference in front of City Hall in Charlottesville. A podium with dozens of microphones attached was placed in front of the building, and dozens of police officers, some equipped with riot gear, held back a frothing mob of angry protesters. A sniper kept watch from the roof of the nearby bus station.

Wearing a Black blazer, Kessler emerged from around the side of the building, and stood near the podium. He shifted from foot

---

1 "Charlottesville — Unite the Right — the Aftermath podcast with Jared Taylor," Podcast on AmRen.com, May 13, 2021.

to foot while waiting to speak. The mob began to chant, "Shame, shame, shame."

Many stood with middle fingers extended. Kessler remembers, "There was a bloodlust in the air from those people."[2]

"Filth! Filth!" screamed one middle-aged man with a red head band. "Come on a little closer, Jason!"

Shouting and drumbeats emanated from the crowd in an attempt to prevent his words being heard. Kessler approached the podium and attempted to speak over the clamor. "The noise you hear around you is the anti-White hate that fueled what happened yesterday.'

A man in a black shirt and red scarf approached the podium and stood inches from the microphone bank. "Fuck you, Jason!" he yelled.

Another man approached, "Indict for murder now! He invited these people!"

A third chimed in. "Get the fuck outta here!"

He continued, "It really is a sad day in our constitutional democracy when we are not able to have civil liberties like the First Amendment. That's what leads to rational discussion and ideas breaking down, and people resorting to violence."

Kessler found himself in the middle of an angry throng. He attempted to keep speaking, but his words were drowned out by the shouts of the encroaching of the mob. The police ignored his pleas for help as the crowd, swarmed closer and closer. Kessler was spat upon by one man. He was punched in the head by another. Nearly surrounded, Kessler was forced to flee through the grass around city hall, tackled by a small woman as he plunged through shrubbery to escape the scene.

About a dozen police officers in yellow vests stood between him and the crowd, yelling, "Get back, get back!"

A member of the crowd began to chant "Nazis go home! Nazis go home!" and many others joined in.

---

2 *Ibid.*

As Kessler retreated at a jog, flanked by two police officers, some protesters pursued on foot. Close on his heels, one man shouted after him. "Her name was Heather, Jason! Her blood is on your hands!"

Zarski had been perched atop a wall above the fray, live-streaming the press conference. She was shocked by the number of protesters. When a group of female Black Lives Matter supporters strolled by armed with baseball bats, she was in disbelief of what was taking place in her hometown, and asked herself, "Where am I?" Zarski watched in horror as the crowd pushed through the media line to mob Kessler. She describes the press conference as "one of the scariest moments of my entire life."

After Kessler left the scene, the counter-protesters milled about. A woman with the Revolutionary Communist Party seized the opportunity to hold court and expound on the benefits of communism.

Writing about the press conference, attorney Sam Dickson, who attended Unite the Right, remarked, "If the Governor of Virginia believed that the situation in Charlottesville was so horrific as to require the declaration of a state of emergency, it makes no sense that over a full day later a mob of violent people was still being allowed to perpetrate assaults and shut down a press conference. The fact that this incident took place in the presence of many uniformed police officers shows that the authorities were still refusing to provide protection to those whose views they dislike."[3]

Later in the day on August 13th, Kessler released a video statement condemning the leftist protesters and Charlottesville police and other officials for the violence of the day. "All of the carnage that happened was because the Charlottesville city government would not recognize our right to assemble."

The next day, Richard Spencer expressed a similar sentiment at his own press conference at which he was joined by Nathan Damigo of Identity Evropa. Spencer was forced to host the gathering in his own apartment after two other venues at which he had scheduled it cancelled on him. He denied guilt for the carnage at the rally,

---

3 Sam Dickson, "Sam Dickson's Statement to Charlottesville Inquiry," VDare. com, Nov. 30, 2017.

denouncing Antifa and the Virginia police. He also attempted to distance himself from Kessler, implying that he was not involved in with organizing the rally. "I accepted an invitation."[4]

Text messages from August 13th that were released pursuant to a civil suit give insight into the dynamic between Spencer and Kessler at that point in time, and suggest that Spencer's involvement went beyond merely accepting an invitation. In a message discussing a post-rally press conference, Kessler suggested to Spencer, "Let's take it right to the enemy. Let's do a press conference today in front of the Charlottesville Police Department."

Spencer replied, "I'm sorry, but I won't attend the press conference today. You're not listening to leadership."

Kessler replied, "What do you mean? We agreed on it and I placed it on the national press."

Spencer replied, "I won't be there."

Kessler asked, "Do you want me to announce the details of tomorrow's press conference today?"

Spencer replied, "No. You won't be speaking at tomorrow's presser."

Kessler shot back, "Now is not the time for us to be divided man."

"You should have let us lead," Spencer responded.[5]

No-Platform

After Kessler was assaulted and driven from his own press conference, leftists celebrated one of their enemies having being denied his right to speak.

The faith-based organization Congregate Charlottesville posted an image of Kessler during the attack with the message, "No platform for fascism!"

Attorney Pam Starsia shared the video with the message, "Super proud of Charlottesville no platforming Nazis again today."

---

4 Rosie Gray, "The Alt-Right's Rebranding Effort Has Failed," *The Atlantic*, Aug. 13, 2017.

5 Brett Barrouquere, "'Let's just ghost him'," SPLCCenter.org.

JUGGERNAUT: THE FALSE NARRATIVE

Activist Emily Gorcenski tweeted, "Truly there is never a bad opportunity to watch Jason Kessler get chased through the bushes and blindside tackled..."

South Side Anti-Racist Action shared a video of the attack with the message, "No platform."

The Antifa principle of "no platforming," is denying the right to speech to anyone they choose to label as a Nazi, fascist, or White supremacist.

When asked about the fundamental tools of Antifa, Mark Bray, the author of *ANTIFA: The Anti-fascist Handbook*, replied (my emphasis),"

> One of the most fundamental principles is: "No platform for fascism." In short, this slogan means that fascist, neo-Nazi, and White supremacist politics and organizing **should be shut down at every opportunity** before they can expand into murderous movements or regimes, as they have in the past. It rejects the liberal notion that fascism is a school of thought worthy of open debate and consideration.

> After the "Unite the Right" White power rally in Charlottesville, many of the racists in khakis with tiki torches have been doxed—that is, had their identities publicly revealed—and are now shocked that marching in a Nazi procession might earn them some enemies. Antifa also organize educational campaigns, build community coalitions, monitor fascists, pressure venues to cancel their events, organize self-defense trainings, and **physically confront the far right when necessary**. Though this last facet of anti-fascism gets the most attention, it is actually only a small fraction of the thankless drudgery that is committing oneself to tracking the scum of the earth.

> The framework of "free speech" assumes this liberal construct; it is based on an expectation that fascism

157

and anti-fascism will always co-exist and therefore should arrive at mechanisms to accommodate each other. In contrast, **Antifa view fascism and White supremacy as enemies that must be destroyed.** Therefore the notion of allowing fascism certain liberties misses the point of the underlying political project.

Understanding that point helps to frame the relationship between "no platform" and "free speech." I have an entire chapter in Antifa about anti-fascism and free speech that unpacks the arguments with much greater subtlety than we have room for here.

I do want to note that **Antifa don't call on the police or the state to do anything other than cease and desist in their operations immediately.** "Censorship" is a governmental action — ironically, one that's been most frequently applied to the left historically. So Antifa never call for censorship.

Finally, we should be wary of those who are more distressed about alleged violations of the speech of fascists than the actual violence they perpetrate.[6]

In other words, not only do Antifa not agree that their opponents have a right to free speech, they believe they are *obligated to take action* to prevent them from speaking. Charlottesville exemplified that tactic in action, and the result was carnage.

Slight Justice

Though he was attacked in broad daylight in a public place in front of dozens of police officers, Kessler struggled to bring the perpetrators to justice. "It's really been a difficult thing. You would think that the police would have prosecuted those people that attacked me right away but in fact I had to pursue it myself. I had

---

6 Melville House, "No platform for fascism: A Q&A with Antifa author Mark Bray," MHPBooks.com, Aug. 22, 2017.

to pull them kicking and screaming to investigate these people... And I was eventually able to get them to do their jobs. The police, anyways. The Charlottesville prosecutor wanted nothing to do with the case. We actually had to get a special prosecutor from a conservative district, Goochland, a guy named Mike Caudill came out and he was just all business."

Kessler was unsurprised by his difficulty getting justice in Charlottesville. "That's par for the course. I've been attacked multiple times in Charlottesville. I've had my recording equipment destroyed. I've been stalked through the streets. I've been attacked by police even who've destroyed my equipment as I was filming. And the prosecutors never want to go through with the case. And when the evidence is so profound that the case has to go forward, they will recuse themselves and appoint somebody from another district."[7]

In February of 2018, three people were convicted of assaulting Kessler at the press conference. High school teacher Phoebe Stevens, who claimed when she tackled Kessler to the ground that she was trying to hug him and shield him from the mob, was convicted initially, but appealed. At the appeal, Kessler recalls, "My attorney said, 'This is the worst jury pool I've ever seen. These people are laughing like it's a joke. And they are going to let this woman go.' So we had to settle for this woman apologizing essentially even though she had assaulted me on camera in front of the entire world..."[8] Stevens was sentenced to fifty hours of community service, contingent upon her issuing the apology which she delivered in an equivocating manner. ("I apologize for making you feel like you were tackled.") Afterwards, she told reporters that she believed Kessler to be "a deeply disturbed individual," but said she had forgiven him for accusing her of assaulting him.[9]

Activist Jeffrey Winder and Public Housing employee Brandon Collins were each given suspended sentences for assaulting Kessler.

---

7 "Aftermath podcast with Jared Taylor," AmRen.com.

8 *Ibid.*

9 Samantha Baars, "Too much love: Apology for unwanted hug settles Kessler case," C-ville.com, Feb 19, 2019.

Prior to the trial, UVA professor Walt Heinecke had encouraged people to "Pack the court room for Jeff and Brandon!"

Afterwards, Kessler told reporters that "[t]he judge made the right decisions," but complained that "[t]he Charlottesville Commonwealth Attorney and police department consistently tried to sabotage the cases by improperly investigating and failing to submit the proper orders," citing the delay in the trial for a fourth defendant, Kenneth Litzenberger, for allegedly spitting on him.[10]

Winder appealed his conviction, and in September of 2018 was again found guilty of punching Kessler. The jury fined Winder one dollar, and he received no jail time.[11]

More Than Bias

One thing many Unite the Right attendees complained about was the fact that the media implied that all of the violence was perpetrated or at least initiated by the right-wing, when they were almost always acting in self-defense against armed protesters. The fact that the coverage was lopsided should be no surprise. Speaking of media coverage of Antifa violence, Andy Ngo reports,

> ...no one does propaganda for Antifa than sympathetic journalists and useful idiots. In my first year covering the Antifa beat, one of the things that shocked me as much as street violence was the alternate reality local and national press presented on Antifa... The American public has been inundated with nonstop propaganda that obfuscates and lies about Antifa, simultaneously presenting them as anti-fascists fighting racism and a figment of the right's imagination. But something different that I observed in my years of reporting on Antifa is the existence of whole networks of writers and so-called

---

10   Andrew Blake, "Three convicted for assaulting Jason Kessler, Charlottesville 'Unite the Right' organizer," *The Washington Times*, Feb. 3, 2018.

11   Joel Shannon, "Man gets $1 fine for punching Unite the Right organizer in the head, reports say," *USA Today*, Sept. 5, 2018.

journalists who intentionally spread pro-Antifa messaging.[12]

Living In Infamy

With fury about Unite the Right engulfing the country, Kessler was already the object of nationwide animus. Making matters worse, a week after Unite the Right, Kessler posted a tweet insulting the woman who was killed in the car crash. On Friday, August 18, 2017 at 9:25 pm, he tweeted "Heather Heyer was a fat, disgusting Communist. Communists have killed 94 million. Looks like it was payback time."

The tweet was met with widespread condemnation, not just from the public in general but from fellow Unite the Right personalities like Baked Alaska and Richard Spencer. Spencer took the opportunity to further distance himself from Kessler, quoting the offending tweet with the remark "I will no longer associate w/Jason Kessler; no one should. Heyer's death was deeply saddening. "Payback" is a morally reprehensible idea."

At 4:52 am, Kessler deleted the tweet and posted, "I was hacked last night. I apologize for the tweet sent from my account last night."

Later that morning at 10:45 am, he replaced that tweet with another:" I repudiate the heinous tweet that was sent from my account last night. I've been under a crushing amount of stress and death threats. I'm taking ambien, xanax and had been drinking last night. Sometimes I wake up having done strange things I don't remember."

Despite the apology, this misstep increased the stigma he faced.

Kessler describes the effect on his life of having been branded as a villain.

> People who I knew who I was friendly with from college, or whatever, would suddenly start writing long Facebook posts denouncing me... and

---

12 Ngo, *Unmasked*, pp. 216-217.

remembering things from our relationships in the past in a negative light. Like, it's weird. It's kind of like the propaganda that you see from Soviet Russia where they're disappearing the guy next to Stalin. So that's a thing that can happen. But also, they can completely change who you are. The second you become a political enemy, a real political dissident, attacked by the media, you're not who you are anymore. You're a villainous caricature.

People would give out my phone number, so I'd just be bombarded with like threatening and lewd text messages and calls constantly. I had to move out of the apartment I where was staying at the time because folks were coming by in vehicles, slow rolling, leering at me. Journalists were trying to break into my apartment when they didn't know I was there. They'd come up and jiggle the handles and try and get in. Angry, angry people would come looking for fights outside my apartment. So, it was a huge mess, and just, uh, the stress of waking up every day and not knowing what's gonna happen from a legal situation, getting fake, phony criminal charges - I beat all of them - coming at me one after another, lawsuits coming one after another. And just being lied about.

The thing that still haunts me to the most to this day is what I get from the conservatives or the right wing, who I mostly agree with on most issues, but they spread all these conspiracy theories about me. You know, saying that I worked for Obama, that I was paid by Soros, that I'm an Occupy Wall Street activist, that we set it up to make Trump look bad, that the Antifa and the Alt-Right were getting off of the same bus, a lot of this coming from very prominent people like Alex Jones. And there's just no way to fight that. And suddenly you are defined in the public consciousness by conspiracy theories, which are, like, extremely hurtful, and you get your identity stolen from you, essentially.[13]

Unite The Right Attendees React To The Coverage

The evening of Unite the Right, Rich, a caller to the Political Cesspool podcast remarked on the narrative that was already forming in the media. "People need to wake up. This is what's going on. If you read the news media and you see the narrative that is being developed, there is none of the representation of our side, and it's all trying to blame us for the violence that occurred that was clearly started by the Antifa."

Sam, another caller to the show who had been monitoring the day's media coverage said, "David Duke was the only person they would name as an organizer, supposedly, of this Unite the Right." [In fact, Duke was neither an organizer nor slated to speak, though he did attend the event.] "Everyone else just fades into nothingness in the eyes of the main stream media. They're basically stuck in the sixties. They also said the Alt-Right is just a synonym for the KKK."[14]

Rally attendee Steve fumes, "Everything people saw in the mainstream media was not only false, it was the opposite of the truth." He also notes that the talking heads were complaining about "hate speech" and attributing horrible motives to Unite the Right attendees, despite the fact that nobody who was associated with Unite the Right was ever allowed to speak.

Invictus describes it this way: "It was like the media created a parallel universe where they made up this crisis that did not happen. It was divorced from reality... They were saying the right wing was rioting. Obviously, the left wing was a mob and out of control." He notes that the people who were present in Charlottesville have a

---

13 "Dissident Mama, episode 27 – Jason Kessler," Podcast on DissidentMama.n et, Jan. 22, 2021.

14 The Political Cesspool Radio Show, podcast aired Aug. 12, 2017, www. thepoliticalcesspool.org.

completely different perception of the event from the people who only heard about it.

Chris spent the rest of the day looking at the news and social media. He felt that some of the media coverage was accurate, and some was biased. Chris complains that it was portrayed as if "everyone was hard right or a neo-Nazi," with no mention of the Robert E. Lee supporters, and that out of thousands of people present, "all the focus was on the swastika guy."

"One sided and terrible," Bill says of the media coverage of Unite the Right. "All lies... Everybody is a White supremacist. It's bull crap. 'Unite the Right' means a bunch of different groups. They're not all the same."

When asked about the media coverage, Tom sighs. "I knew they would find a way to twist it." He laments that "nobody listened to our side about whether we were really White Supremacists."

Trace Chiles describes the media coverage as "obviously one sided all the way around," explaining that though some attendees "were yelling stupid stuff, the majority of them were there for the right reasons."

Of the media coverage of Unite the Right, Gene says "what I've seen is just total fiction that they made up. How can you say the Alt-Right was stirring up sedition? The Alt-Right positions were made up by the media. We never got a chance to speak."

Jim thinks there was no chance the coverage would have been fair. "I think they had their narrative before the day even started... It's nonsense that we were there to attack... That whole media picture was painted well before we got there. It was straight-up wrong, straight-up B.S."

Watching the news back at his hotel, Nathaniel remembers that for a while he was "riding high," thinking that the images of chaos would be good for the right, since he knew the counter-protesters and the authorities were at fault. But after seeing news reports of the car crash that was attributed to a Unite the Right participant, and then the Governor's press conference, "That's when we knew we were effed." He recalls that the media lies were so convincing, he almost bought them himself.

After the dispersal, Parrot went back to a mountain cabin with his compatriots, some of whom were bandaging their wounds. At first the atmosphere was somewhat festive, with the group celebrating, "We made it out alive!" The news was playing on a big-screen TV in the background. When they heard rally-related deaths announced, and the rally being described as a terrorist episode, a chill fell on the gathering. The group had been no strangers to public events with fighting, but at that point it began to dawn on them that this was going to be an historic event on a scale they had not anticipated.

Parrott explained the media narrative this way: "The liberal political class and the government are shrieking so loudly at me and mine right now precisely because they know they're guilty, know they're caught red-handed, and know that the only way through this is to steamroll over us with a nationwide hysteria."[15]

Tarrio explained the media portrayal of Unite the Right simply. "What sells is fisticuffs."

After deciding not to attend Unite the Right, Ayla and her children had met up with a friend for lunch at an Amish bakery, and then spent time at a public park. Throughout the day, the friend was getting some text messages about the events of Unite the Right, but other than that, Ayla was not giving it much thought.

It wasn't until the next morning, while eating breakfast in her hotel lobby, that she heard the media's spin on the day's events. Watching the news, Ayla was aghast, in such shock that she dropped some of the food in her hands. She yelled at the TV as she stood in the dining area. "They're lying! They're lying!"

"They were saying the most outrageous things. I wasn't there, but I knew these people!" She knew that they were there to support the statue, but the media was describing them as Nazis. She recalls that her husband practically had to drag her out of the room.

---

15 Matt Parrott, "Catcher in the Reich," Steemit.com.

Nazi Flag

Though only one or two people among thousands were carrying Nazi flags, the photos of attendees with swastikas accompanied scores of news articles.

Asked about the Nazi flags, Kessler replies:

> I think it was only two people, and only one who was actually within the protest area. The other guy I think was carrying it in McIntire Park... I've seen the guy in McIntire Park around, and he had actually brought that flag to me at one point like after the protest. I saw this guy at like a party or something. And he said, 'Sign this flag for me.' And I said no, I'm not gonna do that. And that was pretty much the end of it.

> But the guy who was in the famous pictures. Everybody said he was like a federal agent, they said, 'Look at the creases on his flag!' But first of all. If people thought it was that bad, why didn't anybody step in and say, 'Take that thing down?' They should have. And now people have an understanding of how bad that looked. But that was just an unfortunate thing that so many people involved in the Alt-Right movement thought that was okay. They should've told him to take it down.

> I do think he was a genuine person because I went to a conference in Tennessee at one point... and this couple came up to me and was talking to me... and for some reason it came up. And they said, "Oh, that's our son. He lives with us."

> And I was like, 'What? Really? Seriously?' And since that time, I've reviewed so many pictures and video footage of the event, and I saw an image of that guy with the swastika flag that I'd never seen before, and there in the back I saw the two people who said they were his parents. I think this was a weird autistic

kid that spent too much time on the internet... and just didn't have any connection to the real world and thought it would be okay to bring something like that to a public rally.[16]

An attendee commented on the presence of the Nazi flag, "Both Alt-Right detractors and supporters have criticized the event organizers for not better regulating its optics – including the presence of at least one Nazi flag... If the police had done their jobs, there would have been ample time to regulate the event symbolism, including among the representatives of national socialist movements in attendance. (There were a few, but...[t]he largest group was probably sincere Southern heritage supporters).[17]

---

16 Kessler Interview, LukeFord.net, Jan. 14, 2021.

17 Max North, "Anarcho-tyranny's Unequal Justice," Vdare.com.

CHAPTER 15 QUICK LINKS:

 "Charlottesville — Unite the Right — the Aftermath podcast with Jared Taylor," Podcast, May 13, 2021. URL: qrs.ly/qucvto3

 "Dissident Mama, episode 27 – Jason Kessler," Jan. 22, 2021. URL: qrs. ly/cycvto9

The Political Cesspool Radio Show, podcast aired Aug. 12, 2017. Hour 1 URL: qrs.ly/r8cvtl5 ; Hour2 URL: qrs.ly/r8cvtm1 ; Hour 3 URL: qrs.ly/9jcvtm3

 "Were the Capitol Hill Riots Charlottesville II? A Jason Kessler Interview," LukeFord.net, Jan. 14, 2021. URL: qrs.ly/e1cvtdi

CHAPTER 16

TRUMP, NAZIS, AND VERY FINE PEOPLE

"There were very fine people on both sides."

Trump Statement And Reactions

MANY OF TRUMP'S DETRACTORS complained that he did not address the public quickly enough once news of the "deadly White supremacist rally" hit the news.

Governor McAuliffe remembers, "I kept waiting, and still there was no Trump press conference. An hour later, still no Trump. He had just talked to me, the governor of Virginia, and I had given him updated information... The nation was waiting. Who else did he need to consult? I can't say. I can't account for the missing hours." [1]

Trump would later explain the delay. "Before I make a statement, I like to know the facts."

The words spoken by President Trump with regards to the events in Charlottesville on August 12, 2017, were some of the most memorable and controversial of his Presidency. The day of Unite the Right, Trump said "We're closely following the terrible

---

1   McAuliffe, *Beyond Charlottesville*, p. 3.

events unfolding in Charlottesville, Virginia. We condemn in the strongest possible terms this egregious display of hatred, bigotry and violence, on many sides."

"On many sides."

Though he condemned hatred in general, that phrase, while completely accurate, would be evoke horror in many Americans who are used to having the blame for racial conflict exclusively cast upon their favorite boogeyman, "White Supremacists."

"Trump fails to condemn White supremacists in statement on Charlottesville violence" an article on *Politico* complained.

Mother Jones noted that "Trump's stunningly milquetoast response to the Charlottesville protests" neglected to denounce Unite the Right protesters, who had legally secured a permit for their demonstration, as forcefully as he had denounced the disruptors who had plagued his own rallies. [2]

Perhaps unsurprisingly, many gutless members of his own party condemned Trump for failing to single out "White Supremacists" for blame.

In a series of tweets, Senator Marco Rubio remarked, "Very important for the nation to hear @potus describe events in #Charlottesville for what they are, a terror attack by #Whitesupremacists... The organizers of events which inspired & led to #charlottesvilleterroristattack are100% to blame for a number of reasons. They are adherents of an evil ideology which argues certain people are inferior because of race, ethnicity or nation of origin. When entire movement built on anger & hatred towards people different than you, it justifies & ultimately leads to violence against them." Rubio's statement is flawed in numerous ways, but especially in his unjustified assertions that Unite the Right attendees were motivated by an "evil ideology," and were the perpetrators of the violence.

Senator Cory Gardner tweeted, "Mr. President - we must call evil by its name. These were White supremacists and this was domestic terrorism."

---

2 Inae Oh, "Trump's Stunningly Milquetoast Response To The Charlottesville Protests," *Mother Jones*, Aug. 12, 2017.

Senator Orrin Hatch denounced the protesters forcefully as well. "We should call evil by its name. My brother didn't give his life fighting Hitler for Nazi ideas to go unchallenged here at home."

How did these politicians justify condemning, with absolute certainty - on the very day of the rally as the facts were still coming in - the attendees of Unite the Right as "Nazis" and "White Supremacists" who were entirely to blame for the events of the day? It's almost as though their primary concern was not conveying the truth to the public, or assuring the accurate and just assignment of blame, but posturing and virtue signaling for their own benefit.

At a contentious press conference on August 14th, two days after Unite the Right, Trump doubled down on his assertion that parties on both sides were to blame for the violence. Furthermore, he pointed out that many of the Unite the Right protesters were in attendance to show support for the statue of Robert E. Lee, the purge of which he correctly predicted would escalate to a purge of markers of the United States' Founding Fathers. His assertion that some of the statue supporters were "very fine people" would become a defining moment of his presidency.

Following is a partial transcript of the press conference where the remarks were made (emphasis mine).

"Reporter: "Let me ask you, Mr. President, why did you wait so long to blast neo-Nazis?"

Trump: "I didn't wait long. I didn't wait long."

Reporter: "Forty-eight hours."

Trump: "I wanted to make sure, unlike most politicians, that what I said was correct — not make a quick statement. The statement I made on Saturday, the first statement, was a fine statement. But you don't make statements that direct unless you know the facts. It takes a little while to get the facts. You still don't know the facts. And it's a very, very important process to me, and it's a very important statement. So I don't want to go quickly and just make a statement for the sake of making a political statement. I want to know the facts. If you go back to —"

Reporter: "Was it terrorism, in your opinion, what happened?"

Trump: "As I said on — remember, Saturday — we condemn in the strongest possible terms this egregious display of hatred, bigotry, and violence. It has no place in America. And then it went on from there. Now, here's the thing — Excuse me. Excuse me. Take it nice and easy. Here's the thing: When I make a statement, I like to be correct. I want the facts. This event just happened. In fact, a lot of the event didn't even happen yet, as we were speaking. This event just happened."

"Before I make a statement, I need the facts. So I don't want to rush into a statement. So making the statement when I made it was excellent. In fact, the young woman, who I hear was a fantastic young woman, and it was on NBC — her mother wrote me and said through, I guess, Twitter, social media, the nicest things. And I very much appreciated that. I hear she was a fine — really, actually, an incredible young woman. But her mother, on Twitter, thanked me for what I said."

"And honestly, if the press were not fake, and if it was honest, the press would have said what I said was very nice. But unlike you, and unlike — excuse me, unlike you and unlike the media, before I make a statement, I like to know the facts."

Reporter: "Nazis were there. David Duke was there."

Trump: "I didn't know David Duke was there. I wanted to see the facts. And the facts, as they started coming out, were very well stated. In fact, everybody said, 'His statement was beautiful. If he would have made it sooner, that would have been good.' I couldn't have made it sooner because I didn't know all of the facts. Frankly, people still don't know all of the facts."

"It was very important — excuse me, excuse me — it was very important to me to get the facts out and correctly. Because if I would have made a fast statement — and the first statement was made without knowing much, other than what we were seeing. The second statement was made after, with knowledge, with great knowledge. There are still things — excuse me — there are still things that people don't know. I want to make a statement with knowledge. I wanted to know the facts."

Reporter: "Was this terrorism?"

Trump: "Well, I think the driver of the car is a disgrace to himself, his family, and this country. And that is — you can call it terrorism. You can call it murder. You can call it whatever you want. I would just call it as the fastest one to come up with a good verdict. That's what I'd call it. Because there is a question: Is it murder? Is it terrorism? And then you get into legal semantics. The driver of the car is a murderer. And what he did was a horrible, horrible, inexcusable thing.

Reporter: "Sen. (John) McCain said that the Alt-Right is behind these attacks, and he linked that same group to those who perpetrated the attack in Charlottesville."

Trump: "Well, I don't know. I can't tell you. I'm sure Senator McCain must know what he's talking about. But when you say the Alt-Right, define Alt-Right to me. You define it. Go ahead."

Reporter: "Well, I'm saying, as Senator — "

Trump: "No, define it for me. Come on, let's go. Define it for me."

Reporter: "Senator McCain defined them as the same group — "

Trump: "Okay, what about the alt-left that came charging at — excuse me, *what about the alt-left that came charging at the, as you say, the Alt-Right? Do they have any semblance of guilt?*"

"Let me ask you this: What about the fact that they came charging with clubs in their hands, swinging clubs? Do they have any problem? I think they do. As far as I'm concerned, that was a horrible, horrible day. Wait a minute. I'm not finished. I'm not finished, fake news. That was a horrible day —"

"I will tell you something. I watched those very closely — much more closely than you people watched it. And you have — you had a group on one side that was bad, and you had a group on the other side that was also very violent. And nobody wants to say that, but I'll say it right now. You had a group — you had a group on the other side that came charging in, without a permit, and they were very, very violent."

Reporter: "Do you think that what you call the alt-left is the same as neo-Nazis?"

Trump: "Those people — all of those people — excuse me, I've condemned neo-Nazis. I've condemned many different groups. *But not all of those people were neo-Nazis, believe me. Not all of those people were White supremacists by any stretch. Those people were also there because they wanted to protest the taking down of a statue of Robert E. Lee.*"

Reporter: "Should that statue be taken down?"

Trump: "Excuse me. If you take a look at some of the groups, and you see — and you'd know it if you were honest reporters, which in many cases you're not —

but many of those people were there to protest the taking down of the statue of Robert E. Lee."

"So this week it's Robert E. Lee. I noticed that Stonewall Jackson is coming down. I wonder, is it George Washington next week? And is it Thomas Jefferson the week after? You know, you really do have to ask yourself, where does it stop?"

"But they were there to protest — excuse me, if you take a look, the night before they were there to protest the taking down of the statue of Robert E. Lee."

Reporter: "Should the statues of Robert E. Lee stay up?"

Trump: "I would say that's up to a local town, community, or the federal government, depending on where it is located."

Reporter: "Mr. President, are you putting what you're calling the alt-left and White supremacists on the same moral plane?"

Trump: "I'm not putting anybody on a moral plane. What I'm saying is this: You had a group on one side and you had a group on the other, and they came at each other with clubs — and it was vicious and it was horrible. And it was a horrible thing to watch."

"But there is another side. There was a group on this side. You can call them the left — you just called them the left — that came violently attacking the other group. So you can say what you want, but that's the way it is."

Reporter: (Inaudible) "... both sides, sir. You said there was hatred, there was violence on both sides. Are the — "

Trump: *"Yes, I think there's blame on both sides.* If you look at both sides — I think there's blame on both sides. And I have no doubt about it, and you don't have any doubt about it either. And if you reported it accurately, you would say."

Reporter: "The neo-Nazis started this. They showed up in Charlottesville to protest — "

Trump: "Excuse me, excuse me. They didn't put themselves — and you had some very bad people in that group, but *you also had people that were very fine people, on both sides.* You had people in that group. Excuse me, excuse me. I saw the same pictures as you did. You had people in that group that were there to protest the taking down of, to them, a very, very important statue and the renaming of a park from Robert E. Lee to another name."

Reporter: "George Washington and Robert E. Lee are not the same."

Trump: *"George Washington was a slave owner. Was George Washington a slave owner? So will George Washington now lose his status? Are we going to take down — excuse me, are we going to take down statues to George Washington? How about Thomas Jefferson? What do you think of Thomas Jefferson? You like him?"*

Reporter: "I do love Thomas Jefferson."

Trump: "Okay, good. Are we going to take down the statue? Because he was a major slave owner. Now, are we going to take down his statue?"

"So you know what, it's fine. You're changing history. You're changing culture. And you had people — and I'm not talking about the neo-Nazis and the White nationalists — because they should be condemned totally. *But you had many people in that group other than neo-Nazis and White nationalists. Okay? And the press has treated them absolutely unfairly."*

"Now, in the other group also, you had some fine people. But you also had troublemakers, and you see them come with the black outfits and with the helmets, and with the baseball bats. You had a lot of bad people in the other group."

Reporter: "Sir, I just didn't understand what you were saying. You were saying the press has treated White nationalists unfairly? I just don't understand what you were saying."

Trump: "No, no. There were people in that rally — and I looked the night before — if you look, there were people protesting very quietly the taking down of the statue of Robert E. Lee. I'm sure in that group there were some bad ones. The following day it looked like they had some rough, bad people — neo-Nazis, White nationalists, whatever you want to call them."

"But you had a lot of people in that group that were there to innocently protest, and very legally protest — because, I don't know if you know, they had a permit. The other group didn't have a permit. So I only tell you this: There are two sides to a story. I thought what took place was a horrible moment for our country — a horrible moment. But there are two sides to the country."

Reporter: "Mr. President, have you spoken to the family of the victim of the car attack?"

Trump: "No, I'll be reaching out. I'll be reaching out."

Reporter: "When will you be reaching out?"

Trump: "I thought that the statement put out — the mother's statement I thought was a beautiful statement. I will tell you, it was something that I really appreciated. I thought it was terrific. And, really, under the kind of stress that she's under and the heartache that she's under, I thought putting out that statement, to me, was really something. I won't forget it."

There were numerous important truths noted by Trump which shocked members of the public who were used to hearing only leftist narratives spoken aloud by public figures. These truths include:

- The fact that there were benign supporters of the Robert E. Lee statue represented among the Unite the Right attendees.

- The fact that the Unite the Right attendees had a permit to assemble, unlike the counter-protesters.

- The fact that there were people on both sides responsible for violence, including an aggressive left-wing contingent.

- The fact that the removal of Confederate statues would likely progress to the removal of tributes to the United States Founding Fathers.

Unite The Right Reaction

Despite the media's insistence that Trump was emboldening and giving cover to "Nazis" and "White Supremacists," actual Unite the Right attendees and other right-wingers did not all perceive it that way. Their reactions were quite varied.

Kessler was initially "ecstatic" when he heard Trump's remarks, which he described as "speaking simple truths that the American public had not been given." It provided him a ray of hope at the time, and for a moment he was optimistic that the tide would turn on public opinion.

Hunter Wallace had a drastically different reaction. "I felt like vomiting after watching this video," he wrote. "The Alt-Right attempted to hold a peaceful rally in Charlottesville, VA... We were attacked by violent Antifa while the police stood down and watched. Gov. Terry McAuliffe declared a 'state of emergency' and riot police pushed us into hordes of violent leftists who attacked dozens of people... In response to this outrage, Donald Trump has condemned us, praised the Virginia State Police and said nothing about the actions of violent Antifa groups who will only be further emboldened to attack his supporters all over the country... Sadly, President Trump's chilling message will only stoke the flames of the violent Left and will strike fear into all those who dare to speak out against it who know they will inevitably be attacked now and portrayed as wicked racists by a vicious and hostile media cartel. Donald Trump has given a green light to Antifa. He has sided with a group of people who attack us on sight and attempt to kill us and for that the Alt-Right can no longer support him. What Donald Trump has done today is an unforgivable betrayal of his supporters."[3]

On the Political Cesspool podcast, co-host Eddie Miller remarked, "Well the President's response was disappointing. I think he is attempting to placate people who will never be placated."

Unite the Right attendee Bill, the pro-monuments activist, said that Trump's "very fine people" statement was "exactly correct." Bill estimates that 80-85% of the Unite the Right attendees were there for the monuments.

Attendee Chris agrees, "Trump was right - there were violent radicals on both sides, as well as a decent amount to counter racism or protect the statue from a normal standpoint."

Gene had a different view. "Trump's statement wasn't accurate. We didn't go to pick a fight. We went for a peaceful meeting to urge the state of Virginia to save the statue of a native Virginian."

Attendee Tom appreciated Trump's "fine people" statement, adding, "Our side held ourselves very well. I didn't see one person attack unless it was in self-defense."

Enrique Tarrio agreed with Trump's assessment. "There was a small group that were there that just wanted to fucking start trouble, and they did." He also saw some people from different sides of the spectrum just talking to one another.

---

3   Hunter Wallace, "Donald Trump's Horrifying Charlottesville Statement," Occidental Dissent.com, Aug. 14, 2017.

The Very Fine People Hoax:
The Best Persuasion Play Of The Year

Scott Adams first came to fame as the creator of the wildly popular Dilbert comic. He is also an author, trained hypnotist, and expert in the subject of persuasion. It was his expertise in the latter that brought him recognition as a political commentator. Early in the 2016 election season, when most pundits were still treating Trump's campaign as a joke, Adams recognized that The Donald was a master persuader, and correctly predicted his now legendary drubbing of the dozen-plus seemingly more qualified GOP politicos in the race for that year's party nomination.

After Trump's use of the phrase "very fine people" to describe some Unite the Right attendees, Adams addressed the media's interpretation of it as a statement of support for Nazis. In February 2018, he blogged about the phenomenon:

> Now that some time has passed, and emotions have subsided a bit, I can tell you about the best persuasion play of the past year. The credit goes to the anti-Trump media. They convinced much of the world that the President of the United States referred to a bunch of racists with tiki torches in Charlottesville as "fine people."... What President Trump did say is that some "fine people" were at the event. I see only two ways to interpret that statement. One interpretation is completely ordinary and the other is batshit crazy...

> Amazingly, the anti-Trump media successfully persuaded half the public in this country that President Trump intentionally and publicly took sides with racists who have intense hatred for his family and close advisors. President Trump clarified soon after his first statement on Charlottesville that he disavowed the racists. But the haters didn't believe it. They were locked in their hallucination bubble...

I don't blame the public for falling for this well-orchestrated persuasion scheme by the anti-Trump media. Their collective persuasion on this point has been solid. Lately, the people opposing Trump simply list Charlottesville as one of the many "proofs" of his racism, as if no further explanation is needed. I can't tell if the pundits believe their own interpretations or if they simply think the public will. It would look the same.[4]

On July 9, 2019, Adams engaged in a heated Twitter debate with Charlottesville counter-protester Reverend Seth Wispelwey. When Wispelwey posted a link that disputed Adams' conclusions about Trump, Adams responded, "All fake news. The press that leans right reported it correctly in most cases. You can see (with no doubt whatsoever) by looking at the full transcript and full video. This situation has no ambiguity whatsoever."

Wispelwey replied, "I've never said 'fuck you' #onhere or [in real life] (and meant it) because pastor stuff and posture and so on, but I did today and it turned out it was to the creator of Dilbert. Who it turns out is a #Charlottesville Conspiracy Theorist. So yeah, fuck you Scott. In Jesus name."

Adams responded with words many were probably thinking. "You might be the worst pastor of all time."

Shortly thereafter, in response to the explosion of replies to his posts, Wispelwey added this comment to the Twitter thread: "Since my account is getting trolled to the max today, might as well give y'all some more fodder: Jesus is Antifa."[5]

The false interpretation of the events in Charlottesville so impacted American political discourse that it played a spotlight role in next Presidential election. Joe Biden, when announcing his candidacy for President in April, 2019, immediately cited Trump's remarks about Charlottesville as having been his motivation to run.

---

4 Scott Adams, "The Charlottesville Fake News Was the Best Persuasion Play of the Year," ScottAdamsSays.com, Feb. 14, 2018.

5 Chris Gregory, "Scott Adams Debunks Charlottesville Hoax, Cursed Out by Pro-Antifa Pastor," Cultture.com, July 9, 2019.

CNN reported, "The first words Joe Biden spoke as he announced his presidential campaign on Thursday were "Charlottesville, Virginia." The former vice president entered the race with a video that framed the 2020 campaign as a battle to redeem the soul of the nation from a Donald Trump presidency he cast as 'an aberrant moment in time.' And he chose to highlight the President's reaction to White supremacists' August 2017 march in Charlottesville and the killing of a counter-protester." [6]

Breitbart Senior Editor-at-Large Joel Pollack termed the repeated misrepresentation of Trump's Charlottesville comments the "Very Fine People Hoax." In August, 2019, he confronted then-Presidential candidate Biden about his use of the false narrative as a talking point during his campaign, prompting the following exchange:

"Mr. Vice President, are you aware that you're misquoting Donald Trump in Charlottesville? He never called Neo-Nazis very fine people."

Biden replied, "No, he called all those folks who walked out of that — they were Neo-Nazis shouting hate, their veins bulging."

"But he said specifically that he was condemning them," Pollak insisted.

"No, he did not. He said — let's get this straight — he said there were very fine people in both groups. They were chanting antisemitic slogans, carrying flags," Biden said, before storming away."[7]

On January 20, 2021, Joe Biden was inaugurated as President of the United States. If not for the media drumbeat of the false narrative about Unite the Right, how might the outcome of the election, and the fate of the nation, have been different?

---

6 Eric Bradner and Maeve Reston, "Joe Biden takes Trump head-on over Charlottesville in announcement video," CNN.com, April 25, 2019.

7 Jerome Hudson, "Media Spin for Biden, Deceptively Omit Trump's Condemnation of Neo-Nazis in Charlottesville Remarks," Breitbart.com, Aug. 8, 2019.

No Love Lost: Trump And The Alt-Right

The media and the left-leaning public often repeated claims during the Presidency of Donald Trump that he emboldened White supremacists and that he was admired by Nazis. Though he publicly renounced White supremacy many dozens of times, had Jewish advisors, Jewish grandchildren, and was arguably the most Israel-friendly President in history, the belief was seemingly intractable.

After Charlottesville, the media's portrayal of Unite the Right as an uprising of violent White extremists proved to be confirmation of what his detractors had feared - that Trump had awakened the demons of racism that lurked within the American psyche with his dog-whistles of encouragement to "Nazis" and "White supremacists."

It is true that Trump both benefited from, and gave momentum to, the wave of populist sentiment that was already rising against the aggressive leftward cultural shift that happened during the Obama era. It is true that nationalists, including those who embraced White identity, saw that the policies promoted by Trump – particularly that of curtailing immigration – as convergent with their interests. However, it is also true that the most hard-core nationalists were the first to become disgusted with Trump when the actions taken early in his Presidency diverged from his campaign rhetoric.

Take, for example, one of the most well-known nationalist pundits, Ann Coulter. Early on, when most others considered his campaign to be a joke, she identified Donald Trump as her pick for the most likely to become the Republican nominee. She correctly recognized that his anti-immigration, anti-war message would resonate with the "forgotten" middle American voter. Her faith in his message, despite her distaste for his personality, was great enough that she penned a book in support of his candidacy: *In Trump We Trust*.

Despite Coulter's early and enthusiastic support of Trump, she lost patience with him fairly quickly. In December 2016, before he had even taken office, she sent an email to Steve Bannon warning that Trump's reported appointment selections would be disastrous and lead to a failure to deliver on central campaign promises. "Trump will be dead," she told Bannon.[8] On June 16, 2017, she tweeted, "Yesterday, the Trump administration kept in place Obama's unconstitutional executive amnesty. This daily Trump melodrama is worth it ONLY if he's really going to build the wall, cut off Muslim refugees and deport illegals." She added another tweet: "Today's BORDER WALL CONSTRUCTION UPDATE: Miles completed yesterday–Zero; Miles completed since Inauguration–Zero. NEXT UPDATE TOMORROW." Disgusted with his failure to deliver the promised wall, she would repeat the "construction update" tweet many times over the course of the Trump Presidency.

Similarly, the less mainstream, even farther-right nationalists and identitarians of the Alt-Right were clear-eyed about the fact that Trump's actions did not match his rhetoric. Some turned away in disgust immediately after he failed to initiate his expected agenda on day one. Others developed serious reservations, but held out hope that some good may still come from his tenure as President.

Most of the public is unaware that some members of the Alt-Right attended a rally in Washington DC organized by Richard Spencer on April 8, 2017 to protest Trump's decision to bomb a Syrian air base, a betrayal of his promise to resist military intervention in foreign countries.

The New Republic reported in April 2017, "It is a disorienting time to be in the Alt-Right. Mere months after seeing its champion ascend to the height of power, the movement is going through a painful and public break-up. The members of the Alt-Right feel they played a large part in making Donald Trump president, and now he is giving them the cold shoulder. 'It certainly feels like a parting of ways,'" [Richard] Spencer told me. "A lot of us feel disillusioned and even burned by Trump.'"[9]

Any remaining loyalty towards Trump, and any residual hope amongst the Alt-Right that he would help populists, was dealt a

---

8   Jose Nino, "Flashback: Ann Coulter Warns Steve Bannon About Trump's Hires During 2016," BigLeaguePolitics.com, Jan. 17, 2021.

9   Vegas Tenold, "The Alt-Right and Donald Trump Get a Divorce," *The New Republic*, April 26, 2017.

fatal blow after Unite the Right. Brad Griffin (writing as Hunter Wallace) explained:

> Charlottesville was the watershed event that divided the populists from the conservatives who had joined the Alt-Right. The populists who were seeing things clearly were already angry about Donald Trump's steady betrayal of his campaign promises and began to break with him completely after that event... In the aftermath of Charlottesville, the only question that seemed to matter was how the fallout from the event would affect Donald Trump, which was itself a symptom of the rising lawlessness due to the failure of his Justice Department to prosecute and convict Antifa that had begun at his Inauguration. The people who went to Charlottesville, who played by the rules and got a federal court order and who had done nothing that day except show up to voice their opinions were viciously attacked [by Trump-supporting conservatives] as "bad optics." James Fields, Jr. went to prison for half a millennium. The Rise Above Movement was prosecuted by Trump's Justice Department. The guys who were ambushed by DeAndre Harris while returning to their cars went to prison and Antifa got away with it and Donald Trump and the GOP did nothing about it... Over the course of the next three years, there were dozens, if not hundreds of events involving groups like the Proud Boys which played out like Charlottesville although the Alt-Right was never again present at any of them.[10]

The Alt-Right had learned their lessons: That freedom of speech and assembly are no longer protected rights in the United States. That even under a Republican administration, right-wingers would be zealously prosecuted for defending themselves against left-wing

---

10 Hunter Wallace, "What We Have Just Experienced," OccidentalDissent. com, Jan. 19, 2021.

violence. That Trump was capable of being treacherously disloyal to his own supporters.

The "White supremacists and Nazis love Trump" meme was always based on hysteria, not fact. The truth is, in large part because of Charlottesville, the far right saw Trump for what he really was long before any of his other supporters.

CHAPTER 17

PEACEKEEPERS AND PATRIOTS

"They're trying to throw us under the bus."

A NUMBER OF MILITIAS and self-described "patriot" groups were present in Charlottesville the day of Unite the Right. The diverse groups shared a similar purpose for the day: to provide neutral peace-keeping services for the event. Wearing full camouflage, Christian Yingling spoke with a documentary crew the morning of Unite the Right. "I am the commander of the Pennsylvania Lightfoot Militia. All the militia members - some are militia, some are Three-Percenters, some are just patriots - we came out here to make sure that things stay kind of peaceful. A lot of these rallies and stuff that are happening lately, law enforcement is greatly outnumbered."[1]

The sight of heavily armed militia, many dressed in military camouflage, was comforting to some and fearsome to others. During an informational presentation about Unite the Right George Lindbeck, MD, who was in charge of Emergency Medical Services for the Unite the Right, showed a picture of a militia group on patrol, and remarked, "You can see how that would make an impression. They behaved well that day. I am not aware of any significant interactions between the militia groups and protesters on either side... but that's a lot of firepower coming down the street."[2]

---

1   National Geographic, "Violence in Charlottesville," YouTube..

2   Jason Kessler, "Head EMT at Charlottesville Rally" BitChute.com.

On October 12, 2017, the City of Charlottesville, along with a handful of local businesses and neighborhood associations brought a suit against numerous militias – both left and right-wing - who had been present during Unite the Right, seeking to enjoin them from future public gatherings with firearms, claiming that their actions were unlawful and that they terrified local residents. These parties included the Pennsylvania Lightfoot Militia, the New York Lightfoot Militia, the III% People's Militia of Maryland, the American Warrior Revolution, Redneck Revolt, Socialist Rifle Association, and the Virginia Minutemen Militia. Some other non-militia parties associated with Unite the Right such as Jason Kessler, Elliot Kline, Matthew Heimbach, Vanguard America, the National Socialist Movement, and the League of the South, were also named in the suit. They all settled eventually. The last holdouts were Jason Kessler and Redneck Revolt, but by July 2018, all involved parties had signed the consent decrees.

Following are the perspectives of some of the militias on the events of Unite the Right.

The Lightfoot Militia

On October, 22, members of the Lightfoot Militia, which had been present in Charlottesville for Unite the Right, returned to the city to speak with residents. The militia, along with a number of other individuals and political organizations, had recently been served with a lawsuit by the City of Charlottesville and some business owners which sought to prevent them from ever demonstrating in the city again.

Militia members mingled with Charlottesville citizens outside before the meeting began. They received a mostly warm reception from the crowd, made up of many left-leaning people who had been counter-protesters. (One less-than warm attendee was Emily Gorcenski, who was, prior to the meeting, debating with a militiaman whether the militia's tactics had shown partiality to the Unite the Right attendees rather than the counter protesters.)

The meet-up had been arranged by Charlottesville anti-racism activist Tanesha Hudson who warmly greeted the Commanding

Officer of the Pennsylvania Lightfoot Militia, Christian Yingling, with hugs and kisses. She spoke of her appreciation for their service on the day of Unite the Right, describing them as "the only ones who helped us that day."

"The good people of Charlottesville want to thank y'all for protecting us that day. Me especially when the police failed to provide equal protection. If it wasn't for you guys, then you know, it probably would have been a million times worse... Had they did their job and not stood down and not have taken orders, what the police fail to understand is that they're not immune from protections when in uniform. If they felt that you guys were doing something out of line, why didn't they step in that day? As a citizen of Charlottesville, I say that they basically filed a lawsuit to point blame at you guys to move the blame off themselves."

Once inside, Christian Yingling stood at the front of the meeting room and addressed the crowd. Wearing a suit and tie, Yingling was poised, professional, and calm.

"My name is Christian Yingling, I'm the commanding officer of the Pennsylvania Lightfoot Militia. I'm notorious for being quiet when I speak so if I start to get quieter and quieter just let me know. I'll try to keep my voice up so everybody can hear me."

He continued, "A lot of things have been addressed to day with relation to what the militia was doing here on August 12th. A lot of things have been brought up about the lawsuit. I'm not really gonna touch on all that other than to say that we will meet the lawsuit."

"This is not our first dance. We've done this many times before and we've done very good at keeping records. That being said, what I do want to address is some of the questions that people have given to us, especially residents of Charlottesville," he gestured to the audience, "people who, and people even outside of Charlottesville who don't know who we are, don't know what we do, or why we exist."

"The gentleman back there brought up about the statement that the Pennsylvania Lightfoot doesn't have a good reputation. The reason we don't have a good reputation is that reputations don't get ratings."

"Myself, George, Francis, a few others, we're extremely prominent in the Patriot community, especially with the militia. And the media would seek to make that go away because what we represent as a militia is the people. And I really have to stress that point because one of the biggest reasons people fear the militia, is because when people see the militia gathered together, what that is, is that is a microcosm of what would happen if this country gathered together. Because we gather together and we say, 'look, we are not gonna put up with this, we are not gonna put up with that.'"

Yingling motioned towards a man in the audience. "You made a statement. You said something along the lines of the fact that you know if Trump violates the constitution will we stand up to him? Well, I'm here to tell you, when BLM under President Obama was trying to run the Bundys off their land out in Nevada, I was one of the people that stood against it. So yes, we would. We truly stand for the Constitution. When the government violates that Constitution, we will stand against them. That being said..."

(At this point, another militia member interrupted to clarify that the BLM to which Yingling referred was the Bureau of Land Management, not Black Lives Matter. There was some chuckling in the room about the confusion.)

After the clarification was made, Yingling continued to speak. "But in all seriousness, we are a misunderstood lot. And I don't want us to come here and - a lot of these guys came with pre-prepared statements - I've done a lot of public speaking in my life. I never prepare a statement. Never. Because if I prepare a statement, I feel that's not genuine. It's not from my heart. What you're hearing coming out of my mouth right now is 100% off my hip and from my heart. So it's the God's honest truth. I have nothing to lie about. I don't hide anything. The gentlemen here who stand with me regularly will tell you that."

At that point, an audience member inquired whether Yingling was a soldier, to which he replied, "Yes. I'm a veteran. Yes ma'am. I'm ex-Navy."

He proceeded to explain to the leftist crowd that his organization was impartial, treating the protesters and counter-protesters equally. "To continue with what I was saying, we in the militia are a misunderstood lot. Nobody really likes us because nobody really knows who we are. We saw it. We saw that first hand here on the 12th. Because we had these Alt-Right people who thought we were there to protect them, walking behind us, thanking us, until they realized that when they're taking pokes at Antifa, that we're turning around going, 'Hey that's not going to happen. We're not gonna let you do that.' And we made it clear to everybody. We initiate conversations when we go to these rallies to let people know that. And that is a problem for us to find a way - and that's something we will be addressing - to find a way we can address the community in some form before we come to something like this. We do make multiple efforts to deal with law enforcement, local government before we show up at these things."

"The question of 'would you defend, say, Richard Spencer, versus somebody on the left, you know, a Saul Alinsky type, would you support this person, would you support that person. It's not a matter of who we support. It's never been. It's never been. And one thing that I demand of all my people, the minute we step out on the field, is that regardless of what your political views are, they are left at home. When we step out on that field, we are truly a neutral third party."

"It doesn't matter if I support Trump or I dislike Trump. It's irrelevant. When I step out on the field, when these guys step out on the field, we were there solely for the reason to make sure that just people could say what they wanted to say without getting violent. Without getting violent. We don't support people getting violent. We didn't support those guys with flagpoles or Antifa bringing any of the stuff that they threw. We didn't support any of that."

"What we do support and what we do encourage is healthy conversation. And we go through very painstaking measures to initiate those conversations when other people don't want to have them. Because if we initiate them, then maybe more people will have them."

"I tell my guys all the time, 'don't expect to change the world. If you're gonna change the world, you're gonna change it one conversation at a time.' And that's what we seek to do. When we speak to people, we talk to them one on one. I don't speak to them as the Pennsylvania Lightfoot, I speak to them as Christian Yingling. I'm not an organization, I'm a person. And the people in my organization who serve under me are all good people, I assure you, 100%."

"Like George [Curbelo] said, 'don't buy into the media frenzy just because it gets ratings. You know, go by what you see with your own eyes. Engage these people, know what I mean? You don't know who I am, feel free to come up and talk to me and I will talk with you for hours. And I wanna hear about where you come from and I wanna hear about what you believe, and I wanna tell you what I believe. And at the end of the day if you don't believe what I believe, well then, maybe we do both believe about this. And we can work on that. And then we'll build outward from there. When we get way out here - guess what? All of a sudden we're working on things we never would have worked on before. That's what the militia is. That's what the militia is. That's what we stand for. That's what all the groups who stood with us that day stand for. And that's what all the people should stand for. "

"We don't want you guys to be afraid of us. We want you guys to welcome us. We want you guys to be more like us. Because when the people come together as a whole, just like Tanisha said, you know, Richard Spencer and Kessler and their cronies, they can gather up here in the park and run their mouths, but if the entire city of Charlottesville shows up and says hey, you're outta here, there ain't gonna be nothing the police or anybody else can do to stop ya. And that's what you gotta do. That's what you gotta do."

"And that's why a lot of police departments are very skeptical of us. Because we represent that. We represent that coming together of people. So we try to put out a message that look the people need to get together. People need to stand together. And if you don't want those guys in your city, then you've gotta come together as a people."

"What we did, what we did that day, all we did was planted a seed. You guys gotta make it grow. Right, left, it doesn't matter, you guys have gotta come together in this city, in cities across the nation, and say look we're not gonna tolerate this. We are just not gonna tolerate this kind of talk. I don't care if it's from the right or the left. Because at the end of the day we're all brothers and sisters."

"In closing I wanna say I commanded those guys out there that day, regardless of what happens with this lawsuit I accept full responsibility for what we did. I'm not ashamed of what we did. I'm proud of each and every guy that stood here, because these guys risked their lives for you with no payment, with no thanks, and a whole bunch of heartache."[3]

George Curbelo the Commanding Officer for the New York Lightfoot Militia stepped forward to speak to the crowd. Like Yingling, his demeanor was professional, but also personal and genuine. He began by addressing the lawsuit against the militia and other groups.

"First is this lawsuit. I want you to know that this lawsuit, even though the 32 militia members that were out on the street that day are named in that lawsuit are named, some of us individually, some of us through the groups that were there, we are determined to win this lawsuit. We are determined to win this lawsuit because it has to do with everybody's constitutional rights. It removes us from the equation when your constitutional rights are going to be violated. Because that's what's gonna happen with this lawsuit."

"They've made it very clear that this is not just about us, and limiting us from forming to protect your community again, it's not just about us. What they want to do is they want to take this, and they want it to become case law so they can now have it as an example for the rest of the country. What does that sound like to you? Some of you have said you were statists. We call them tyrants. To us, that's tyranny. Once you begin to lose your freedoms, and your constitutional rights go away, we have a statist country. We have a tyrannical country. And for that reason, the second amendment is not only for self-defense. A couple of you said earlier. Do some research. Do some research. Read the Federalist papers. Understand what that second amendment is in place for.

---

3 News2Share, "Militia Groups Return to Charlottesville," YouTube video, posted October 21, 2017.

It's truly in place to defend the citizenry, fellow Americans against a tyrannical government. That's what it's in place for. So, we're gonna fight this lawsuit. We're gonna fight for everybody. We're gonna fight for everybody across this country because, as a constitutional militia, that is our job."

"Now we can't talk about any of the specifics of the case. But I have to point something out to you. In the pre-op, or the pre-event planning for every event that we've been to, the New York Lightfoot militia has been in Harrisburg Pennsylvania, Gettysburg Pennsylvania, Boston Massachusetts, Albany New York, Syracuse New York. Every single one of those events, plus other events, the pre-planning for those events, plus the way we manage ourselves at those events, have always kept those events peaceful. Our track record was stellar."

"There was something different about the pre-planning for Charlottesville. There was something that concerned me about the preplanning for Charlottesville. And those pre-planning irregularities will come out in court. And I can guarantee you that embarrassment is in order. So, yes, we're here to tell you about the lawsuit and what were our intentions, but I have to say this also... ."

"The way we look at this lawsuit is that it's not just about us. This is a constitutional violation, a restriction that they're trying to enforce against the general public. So, that's why we're here."

Tanisha Hudson, the organizer of the meetup, interjects, "There's lawsuits from every direction. We want to be as transparent as possible. I don't think anybody from the clergy team is gonna hold the militia responsible because we know that they were the only people out there helping us that day, and that does make a difference."

Hudson continued to praise the militia "There was 20 of them, and there was 200 cops, and there was cops in armor gear, that should have been in the middle of the street, and after going to court and realizing that Zone Five, which was Market Street, was supposed to be covered by the police and it wasn't, that says a lot about 'why are you suing these men?' when they are the only protection in Zone Five. None of the police were in Zone Five. So there's a lot of unanswered questions that needs to be discussed."

When Curbelo resumed speaking, he was emotional, almost tearful, expressing regret about what happened in Charlottesville. "We want to apologize to the community. We're sorry that we could not do more for you. All of us, when we drove away, there was very, very little conversation in the cars, in the caravan cars, that left this area. We were horrified when we heard that there was a state of emergency declared. And then we were horrified when we heard about the monster that mowed down the people here in Charlottesville. Horrified. We apologize to you for not being able to do more."

An audience member, a middle-aged Black woman, spoke up. "You don't owe us an apology."

Another offered, "It wasn't your fault. It was their fault. If y'all hadn't been there, there would've been a whole lot more deaths."

Visibly moved, Curbelo replied, "I appreciate you saying that."

Hudson spoke up again. "The city continues to blame everybody except themselves. And if this group wasn't there, standing on the wall outside of Emancipation Park, I need everybody to think about what would have happened when you have police hiding behind pens."

With that, lengthy applause erupted in the room.[4]

The Patriots

The evening of Unite the Right, a dozen or so members of self-described "patriot" groups piled into a Charlottesville hotel room to tell their story on video. The group included members of American Warrior Revolution, led by Ace Baker (real name Joshua Shoaff) and members of another group called the Hiwaymen led by Billy Sessions (real name Billy Helton). The groups' members were of various ages. Most of the men had full beards and wore t-shirts and baseball caps with patriotic emblems. There were a few women in the crowd, one wearing a shoulder-revealing white t-shirt and a baseball cap. Unlike the professional and reserved

---

4 News2Share, "George Curbelo Speaks to Charlottesville Community," YouTube video, posted October 21, 2017.

Lightfoot representatives, this group was rowdy and spoke boldly and without restraint.

The main speaker for the video was Baker, a muscular man with tattooed arms and a thick, dark beard, who wore a green t-shirt with the word "FREEDOM" printed in large white letters. Beside him was Sessions, who wore a yellow shirt with "The Hiwaymen" logo and a white baseball cap with an American flag.

Sessions began, "Y'all, share this video everywhere, cause we're gonna tell you the truth about Charlottesville... Share it to every damn patriot group you've got. Because people, they need to hear the truth. They're basically demonizing the patriot community. They're trying to throw us under the bus over the Charlottesville event. So Ace, lead it off, man."

Baker took the floor. "This is probably one of the biggest videos we've ever done, one of the most important videos for the patriot movement as a community that we've ever done... What happened today in Charlottesville needs to be heard. But what really happened in Charlottesville, not what Fox News is telling you. Not what all of the other propaganda news, mainstream machine is telling you. We're gonna tell you what happened in Charlottesville today, we're gonna tell you why we were really here, what our mission was, why we came all of this way from all over the country to be a part of what happened today... Let everyone know that this is the truth. Fox news, shame on you. CNN, shame on you. Mayor of Charlottesville Virginia, shame on you. Police chief of Charlottesville Virginia, I don't even know you. I care so little about you I don't even know your name. But I promise you on Monday the world will know your name. Mark my words."

Others in the room chimed in loudly with words of agreement.

"This is my first time to come to Charlottesville, but I can assure you of one thing, this will not be our last. The people that we brought to Charlottesville this time is a fraction of what you will see in the future. We came to Charlottesville... The patriot movement is built on the Constitution. It's built on the ability for you and I to disagree on a topic, BUT, agree that you and I have the right to disagree. You understand."

"There was an event today in Charlottesville Virginia called Unite the Right. I don't know of anybody in this room that was either for or against the event Unite the Right. That has no bearing on why we were here. Whether we agree on the topics of Unite the Right or the speakers, or what they had to say, we agree with their right, or their ability, or their God-given right and constitutionally protected right to have that freedom of speech. You understand."

"So, whether you're Black Lives Matter - I will tell you right now there isn't a single topic I agree with Black Lives Matter. What I do agree with is Black Lives Matter's God-given right, and constitutionally protected ability to be able to believe that way."

"So the reason that we as a patriot community came to Charlottesville today from all over the country - we didn't come here because we thought, hey let's go stay at a Motel 8 or whatever the fuck we're staying in," the group erupted in laughter, "right, and let's get together and... just come and party it up. We didn't spend our own money, we didn't spend our own time away from our families... this isn't a vacation for us."

Other members of the group chime in "No, it's not!"

Baker continued, "We came to Charlottesville Virginia to tell both sides, the far right and the far left: Listen, whether we agree with what you have to say or not, we agree with your right to say it without being in fear of being assaulted by the other group. I will tell you right now, [League of the South President] Michael Hill, I don't agree with a fucking thing that comes out of your mouth, but I agree with your right to say it, and I think you should be allowed to say it without physically being assaulted for saying it."

The group agrees with Baker. "That's right!"

"Black Lives Matter, I don't agree with a fucking thing that comes out of your mouth, but I agree with your right to say it. And I would stand there and defend you if you were being assaulted or in fear of being assaulted for those things that I don't agree with."

Sessions interjects, "Those damn cops didn't defend us, did they?"

The group responds "No!"

Baker explained, "We're gonna talk plenty about the cops as this video continues. Continue to share this video, because what we're going to tell you is going to blow your freaking mind. I can't even... Look, Fox News, you should be fucking ashamed of yourselves."

Members of the group added on.

"Yes!!" said one.

"You should be ashamed of yourselves!" agreed another.

A third added, "CNN too! Local news media!"

Baker interrupted himself to note that "CNN... Did you guys know CNN now rates below Nick at Night?"

The group erupted with loud laughter, hooting, and whistling.

Baker responded, "I'm dead serious. That's for real. I will tell you this. There is not a man or a woman inside of this room that is a racist."

The group chimed in "No, no!"

"There's not a man or woman inside of this room that is anything that we were called today."

The woman in the white t-shirt raised her fist and proclaimed, "I'm not a Nazi!"

Baker told viewers, "There's not a man or woman inside of this room that is here for any other reason than to defend both of the parties, both of the extreme sides of what happened today in Charlottesville."

As he continued to speak, Baker's passion and anger became increasingly apparent. "What happened when we came here? We were the ones that were assaulted. We're the ones that are on the fucking mainstream propaganda news machine, being called out by the Mayor, by the Chief of Police, you fucking coward, we're the ones that are being assaulted for coming here to defend your constitutional rights to say the bullshit that comes out of your fucking mouths."

The group cheered. "Right! That's right!"

Sessions interjected, "That's right! The conservatives out there need to get behind us on this one. This is bullshit. Everything they're saying is bullshit. The cops caused this shit. They did." He nodded vigorously.

A man in the back of the room wearing a Black t-shirt spoke up for first time on the video. "On TV there's no color. It's all White. That's bullshit."

Baker added to his observation. "We have men that are with our organizations today that are Black. The color of your skin has no bearing - if you believe in the Constitution, that is all that is required to be a part of our groups. That you believe in standing up and defending the U.S. Constitution, that is the only thing we care about. I will tell you this. Charlottesville Virginia isn't the first city we've been to. You guys have watched our videos. You know that we've been from sea to shining sea and that will continue. The things that happened today, the things that are being said on the mainstream propaganda news machine, you fucking pieces of shit, the things that you are spewing out of your mouths for ratings are going to burn you down."

The group chimed in with agreement. "Yes!"

Baker went on, "It's not going to deter us. It's not going to keep us from going to other cities. It's not going to keep us from doing what we do, and it's damn sure not going to keep us from coming back to Charlottesville Virginia again.

Sessions proclaimed, "We'll come back if we need to. We'll come back."

A different man in a tan cap spoke up. "That's the funny thing about these leftist cities that we go to. We keep having to come back."

Baker then contrasted events in Charlottesville with a recent event in Portland, Oregon. "The funny thing is what happened in Charlottesville was worse than what happened a couple of days ago. Let me tell you why. In Portland, there was one police officer that was present in the entire park. Mayhem ensued. People were assaulted with skateboards. People were beat up with sticks and rocks."

As he spoke, a Black man in a yellow "Hiwaymen" t-shirt and camouflage baseball cap walked into the video frame. Baker joked, "Oh look, there's a Black guy in here! Oh my God!"

The group burst into laughter as the Black man turned and smiled at the camera.

Baker picked up his train of thought. "What happened in Charlottesville, Virginia is a lot different than what happened in Portland because the cops were present today."

Sessions fumed. "They let the shit take place. We actually sat back and watched them let Black Lives Matter attack patriots. We got attacked. They set the shit up for to take place."

The woman in the white shirt gestured angrily with her hand as she recounted, "I was assaulted with sticks with them standing right there and they did nothing."

The Black man in the yellow shirt described his experience. "I'm over here blinded from pepper spray, blinded from mace, and we're getting attacked by Antifa. I jumped over the police barricade. What did the police say? They said you need to get outta here before you get arrested. And did they help? I said, 'I can't see. I need to get this stuff out of my eyes so I can see.' 'I don't care, you're gonna get arrested. You're gonna get arrested.' They came in and the rest of my guys helped pull us over... Arrest me when I say I need help. I reached out to them for help. Did they help?"

Sessions went on, "The cops set back, folks, and watched us get pummeled with rocks with water mixed with some kind of acid. They were throwing everything at us. Some of our guys got sticks broke over 'em." [Note: This testimony of assault is corroborated by drone footage which shows the Hiwaymen "...snaking their way around a parked Charlottesville police car as they are shoved and otherwise abused by hostile anti-Lee protesters... you can see the last in line of the Hiwaymen is picked off by someone in the crowd and violently shoved to the ground."][5]

A man in the back of the room interjected, "They funneled us in."

---

5   Ben Wetmore, "Never-Before-Seen Drone Footage from Charlottesville," TheGatewayPundit.com.

Sessions spoke, "They set us up. They let 'em attack us."

Another person in back of the room added, "They were throwing smoke bombs and tear gas."

Baker continued. "With what happened to us and our group, the cops were standing less than thirty feet from us when we were having bricks thrown at us. A man was hit in the head over his ear, has three, four, five, six stitches. They stood there and watched it and allowed it to occur. When I asked the police officers for a medic, for an ambulance to respond and help than man, I was told that they couldn't help us. They weren't there to help us. There was nothing that we could do to carry on. When we asked for an escort - 'you're on your own.' When we asked for can you get us to our vehicles so we can leave - 'you're on your own.'"

Speaking with force, Baker looked into the camera and addressed the police. "If you are a police officer in Charlottesville Virginia and you believe in the U.S. constitution, I ask that you go Monday morning and turn your badge and your gun in."

The group murmured with agreement. "Amen!" said one.

Baker attempted to continue speaking but had to pause several times because the group continued to cheer.

When he was finally able to resume speaking, he forcefully pointed a finger towards the camera. "You find a police department that's actually going to stand up and defend the U.S. Constitution. You took out an oath. You raised your right hand and you swore out an oath. Today you did the fucking opposite. Shame on you. Your kids should be fucking ashamed of you."

Sessions agreed. "That's true. I watched people coming through the streets, I mean, with blood all over 'em... big ol gashes in 'em. I mean, some of my guys got it rough. They got shit broke over their heads. They got thrown on the ground, stomped, and the police did not do shit. They stood right there with their arms crossed like this. They did not do shit."

Baker went on, angrily stabbing a finger at the camera with each sentence. "We are here to hold you accountable. Chief of Police of Charlottesville, Virginia, we are here to hold you accountable. Mayor of Charlottesville, Virginia, these things that have happened over and over and over inside of your city. It is your fucking fault. You are responsible for not protecting the citizens of this community. You should be held reliable, and you are a fucking piece of shit. That's Ace Baker telling you that."

The others in the group cheer. "Yes!"

Sessions addressed why they were in Charlottesville. "We come here for many reasons today. We got the Tennessee Rifles. They come here to stand up for, basically Lee monument and the First Amendment. The Hiwaymen, we come here for all the reasons. To stand up for the First Amendment, come to support our Southern Heritage. Folks, we didn't come to hate on anybody."

The group cried "No! No way!"

Sessions concluded, "We come here basically because it was the right thing to do."

Another man added, "We came here to respect law enforcement and the military. And they fucked us!"

He was met with a chorus of "Amen!" from the group.

Baker agreed. "The one group, out of all the groups that was here in Charlottesville Virginia today, the one group, the patriot community, that stands up and defends constitutional law enforcement, you shit on us... Today, the Charlottesville Police Department, shame on you."[6]

---

6   Vonveezil2, "Charlottesville Aftermath. The Truth on What Happened," YouTube video, posted August 12, 2017.

CHAPTER 17 QUICK LINKS:

 Charlottesville Drone Footage, URL: qrs.ly/96cwsuo
[QR Code: Drone Footage]

 National Geographic, "See the Sparks That Set Off Violence in Charlottesville," video, Aug 19, 2017. URL: qrs.ly/6ocvtgu

 News2Share, "Militia Groups Return to Charlottesville," video, October 21, 2017. URL: qrs.ly/eacvtow
https://youtu.be/lJNbUKfYMgo

 News2Share, "George Curbelo Speaks to Charlottesville Community," video, October 21, 2017. URL: qrs.ly/ehcvtox

 Vonveezil2, "Charlottesville Aftermath. The Truth on What Happened," video, August 12, 2017. URL: qrs.ly/kycvtp1

CHAPTER 18

BACKLASH: DOXING, DE-PLATFORMING, AND CENSORSHIP

"They're doing one-sided prosecution."

De-platforming

ONE OF THE IMMEDIATE RESULTS of Unite the Right was the diminished online presence of parties that were involved with planning and promoting it. Kessler explains, "Heyer's death was used to stoke a moral panic about the boogeyman of 'White supremacy,' which has led to an unprecedented, un-American wave of political censorship against right-wing political dissidents and immigration patriots."[1]

The internet purge was indeed unprecedented. "I can't think of another incident to which the backlash has been nearly so widespread," said Mark Pitcavage of the Anti-Defamation League.[2]

---

1 Jason Kessler, "Don't Compare the George Floyd Riots to Charlottesville! (Oh, On Second Thought, Antifa Was Guilty There Too)," VDare.com, June 1, 2020.

2 Allegra Kirkland, " Airbnb boots white nationalists headed to 'Unite the Right' rally in Charlottesville" *Talking Points Memo*, Aug. 18, 2017.

There was already evidence of this trend before Unite the Right even took place. In the preceding weeks, lodging marketplace service Airbnb had cancelled the accounts of people who they believed were using the service to make arrangements to attend the rally. Kessler complained to the press, "This is outrageous and should be grounds for a lawsuit... It's the racial targeting of White people for their ethnic advocacy... Would Airbnb cancel the service of Black nationalists or Black Lives Matter activists for their social media activity? Of course not!"[3]

Immediately after Unite the Right, there was a barrage of bannings from all kinds of services.

One observer referred to it as "The night of the digital knives," explaining that the events in Charlottesville "have given leftist-run sites the excuse they need to ideologically cleanse their websites."[4]

The provocateurs at the *Daily Stormer* were first on the chopping block when an article published the day after the rally sparked outrage. In response to complaints about the article by Andrew Anglin, entitled "Heather Heyer: Woman Killed in Road Rage Accident was a Fat, Childless, 32-year-old Slut," their domain registrar, GoDaddy, immediately posted a tweet stating, "We informed the *Daily Stormer* that they have 24 hours to move the domain to another service provider, as they have violated our terms of service."[5] The *Daily Stormer* used a quick, automated process to move its site to Google, which in turn shut down the site - and the *Daily Stormer* YouTube account - within hours.[6]

Over the following days, the site bounced around the internet, cycling through domain registrars based in various places all over the world. It now exists on the dark web and may be accessed only

3   Kyle Swenson, "Airbnb boots White nationalists headed to 'Unite the Right' rally in Charlottesville," *Washington Post*, Aug. 8, 2017.

4   Matt Forney, "Night of the Digital Knives: Silicon Valley Launches Biggest Internet Censorship Purge in History," ReturnofKings.com, Aug, 18, 2017.

5   S. Shah, "GoDaddy dumps White supremacist site 'Daily Stormer,'" Endgadget.com, Aug. 14, 2017.

6   Jon Fingas, "Google cancels neo-Nazi site's registration in a matter of hours," Endgadget.com, Aug. 14, 2017.

through the Tor Project's browser. (The Tor Project has said that it was "disgusted, angered and appalled" by the site's content, but would not censor it.[7])

A writer for *Red Ice* remarked on the banishment of the *Daily Stormer*. "We're entering uncharted territory. Anglin's case is evidence that one can essentially be banned from the Internet for having the wrong opinions – something previously unheard of. The battle against politically motivated censorship – both online and offline – has been kicked into overdrive."[8]

Many other right-wing groups faced the "ban hammer" in the days after Unite the Right. Facebook removed the "Charlottesville's Unite the Right" event page. They also removed Christopher Cantwell's profile and banned Vanguard America, the group with whom James Fields had been pictured, as well as a number of other right-wing groups who they said were in violation of "hate speech" policies. Reddit banned a right-wing subreddit known as r/Physical_Removal.[9]

The gaming chat app Discord, which had been used ahead of Unite the Right for planning purposes, shut down multiple accounts associated with events in Charlottesville as well as the altright.com chat server. The company explained that Discord intended to take action against "all forms of hate."[10]

Within a few days of Unite the Right, Twitter banned Baked Alaska permanently. They also paused their "verification" process for review. (Though verification is meant to do what it says – verify that an account belongs to the person it purports to, rather than an impostor – some view the blue check as a sign of honor or an implicit endorsement of the user's content.) When controversy flared after

---

7 Dominique Mosbergen, "Neo-Nazi Site Daily Stormer Retreats To The Dark Web," HuffPost.com, Aug. 21, 2017.

8 "The Mysterious Death of Heather Heyer," RedIce.tv, Sept. 6, 2017.

9 Morgan Little and Sean Hollister, "Reddit, Facebook bans neo-Nazi groups after Charlottesville attack," CNET.com, Aug. 15, 2017.

10 Jon Fingas, "Gaming chat app Discord starts shutting down racist accounts: It's cracking down on hate in the wake of Charlottesville," Engadget.com, Aug. 14, 2017.

Unite the Right about "Nazis" being verified, Twitter addressed it in an apologetic statement. "Verification has long been perceived as an endorsement. We gave verified accounts visual prominence on the service which deepened this perception. We should have addressed this earlier..." The platform instituted new rules, and on November 15th, removed the "verified" status from Richard Spencer, James Allsup, and Jason Kessler. At the same time, Twitter also unverified the accounts of other conservative influencers - like Laura Loomer and Tommy Robinson - who had nothing to do with the events of Charlottesville.[11] The founder of free-speech dedicated social media site Gab, Andrew Torba, reported that Gab received thousands of new users in the immediate aftermath of these actions by Twitter.[12]

The banning trend was not limited to social media. James Allsup was banned from the ride-hailing service Uber. (He and Baked Alaska had been abruptly ejected from a ride in Washington D.C. by their driver, a Black female, the day before the rally for unclear reasons.)[13] The same week, music-streaming service Spotify announced that it had identified and purged White supremacist content.[14]

According to Enrique Tarrio, Charlottesville "was the first time I'd ever been banned off something besides social media." He had an Airbnb account he had never used closed down. "I don't know how the hell they figured out it was me. Much later, it started ramping up more."

Crowd-funding and payment services purged Charlottesville-associated accounts as well. In the following days, PayPal accounts for the National Policy Institute, Identity Evropa, Radical Agenda and the Revolutionary Conservative were closed. The crowd-funding

---

11 Julia Carrie Wong, "Richard Spencer and others lose Twitter verified status under new guidelines," *The Guardian*, Nov 15, 2017.

12 Kerry Flynn, "Inside the reckoning of the Alt-Right on Twitter," Mashable. com, Nov 16, 2017.

13 Caroline O'Donovan, "Uber Bans Racists Too," BuzzFeedNews.com, Aug. 21, 2017.

14 Kerry Flynn, "Spotify is now pulling White supremacy music off its service," Mashable.com, Aug 16, 2017.

site GoFundMe closed down several pages meant to raise money for James Fields, the man accused of crashing his car into a crowd.[15]

This is by no means an exhaustive list of de-platformings and account bannings, but it gives you an idea of the online reckoning faced by right-wingers in the aftermath of Unite the Right.

A Cottage Industry

Kessler was among those whose online life was immediately impacted in the aftermath of the rally. He remembers that over the next few days, "I was trying to move away from some of the social media companies because they were de-platforming me all over the place. I got banned from Coinbase, the bitcoin exchange. I got banned from PayPal. My website was taken down... And I lost everything. I didn't have any way to create a data file and a new website. It was really a shame." (He has since secured a different domain for his website, but his previous work is only available in a stripped-down version on a web archive.) The *Daily Caller* site also deleted his entire archive of work.

"Of course I've been banned from many other places since then and a lot of them happened around the time of the second rally, basically from organizations and enemies who've built up their entire profile and just attacking my social media presence and the social media presence of other people, saying that it supports violence or terrorism or whatever, even though, like, in the aftermath of UTR, I was horrified by the amount of violence that had taken place when the police stood down and people clashed. So I spent, like, all of my time on YouTube denouncing violence, and yet they still de-platformed me."[16]

Kessler explains the process behind the de-platforming trend. There are groups that "manipulate our language and they lie about the things that we're saying, like, omitting things that have to do with the self-defense aspect of what happened. And then they go

---

15 Kaya Yurieff, "PayPal is quietly cracking down on White supremacist accounts," CNN, Aug. 16, 2017.

16 "Jason Kessler," Podcast on DissidentMama.net.

to Uber and they go to PayPal and they go to all these different companies in Silicon Valley and they're giving lectures as if they're authorities, and as if their case has been proven. They're doing one-sided prosecution with these tech companies and that's part of why people are being de-platformed. They don't realize that a cottage industry has sprung up around the aftermath of the Unite the Right rally. And that cottage industry has sown the seeds of what people are seeing [after the D.C. Stop the Steal rally to contest the 2020 election results] on January 6. Because all of it works together. There is just so much hatred around political dissidents right now and partly, it is these people sowing the seeds, saying 'these are all terrorists.'"

"Then the second that something goes even slightly wrong like with the January 6 thing you have the media saying 'These are terrorists! Didn't you heed the warning?' And the tech companies who have been like, mildly, tepidly defending the free speech of dissidents say 'Holy shit! We don't want to be involved in terrorism!' so they kick everybody off the platform. And that's growing larger and larger and larger, the number of people that were political dissidents capable of being silenced. So now it's all the way up to the President of the United States."[17]

Kessler is referring to the culmination of the politically-motivated de-platforming trend. On January 6, 2021, a demonstration of Donald Trump supporters went awry when a number of people protesting what they believed to be an unfair election process stormed the U.S. Capitol Building. Shortly thereafter, the then-sitting President of the United States was banned from posting on Twitter, which had been a favorite platform for communicating with the public. Soon his online presence was purged from other services like PayPal, Shopify, and Facebook as well. A number of Trump's prominent political allies and supportive social-media influencers were banned from major sites around the same time, as were a bevy of pages and sites favored by his citizen supporters.

How might things have been different if Trump and other conservatives had stood up to the wave of censorship that took

17 *Ibid.*

place after Unite the Right by passing legislation to protect the ability of dissidents to access online public forums? Unfortunately, most of them - weak-willed, short-sighted, and unwilling to be associated with the pariahs of Charlottesville - ignored or even applauded the purge.

The Doxing Machine

In the internet age, the practice of "doxing" has become a common tactic of political activists. For those unfamiliar with the term, the online "Urban Dictionary" defines doxing as "Using private information gleaned from the internet to attack someone with whom you disagree, often by publishing their personal info, opening them to abuse and possibly, danger."

There was a copious amount of video on the internet of the events surrounding Unite the Right, and leftist activists salivated at the opportunity to scrutinize the images and identify targets for doxing. One Charlottesville activist put it this way, "... a lot of those fascists came there unmasked and very clearly showed their faces, which leaves an opportunity to expose them to those who have access to online research tools, and that way we can prevent them from organizing any further."[18]

Andy Ngo explains the serious threat of Antifa's doxing practices.

I don't believe violence is all we should be worrying about. In fact, the overfocus on violence, which ebbs and flows, causes us to neglect the other half of the picture: the threat they pose to the public and the republic through entirely nonviolent means. In fact, this is the domain where they are most able to advance their goals...

From my initial exposure to Antifa in late 2016, I was stunned at how fast and effective they are at identifying their enemies and releasing all the "research" in the form of doxes. In fact, one way

---

18 Kessler, "Antifa Comms Director," BitChute.com.

Antifa gain street cred is through their ability to gather counterintelligence.

Indeed, on Twitter, groups like Rose City Antifa release long threads identifying attendees of right-wing public rallies, where they work, to whom they're married, with whom they're friends, what kind of car they drive, and so on. From there, the threads are shared hundreds or thousands of times where they're able to crowdsource additional personal information.

Through going to dozens of Antifa protests and riots, I learned that they expend significant resources on reconnaissance... Antifa use their images explicitly to harm targets. The point is not to document reality but to gather intel to get someone assaulted, fired, or stalked. For this reason, they do not photograph their comrades, who are often engaging in criminal activities...

While the information Antifa groups release on social media is usually obtained through public and open sources, they share it with a community of extremist vigilantes... Most of Antifa's doxing and intimidation tactics skirt the line on criminality... Driven by intense hatred, Antifa want their targets to fear living a normal life. This is their terrorism without violence.[19]

Within days, or some cases, hours, Unite the Right attendees were doxed and their identities widely publicized. National news outlets amplified and celebrated the public shamings. "A Twitter account identified this Unite the Right participant. Now his family's disowning him," gloated Vox.com in an article dated two days after the rally. The article reports that "[t]he protester's

---

19   Ngo, *Unmasked*, p. 160.

father says their family loudly repudiates his son's 'vile, hateful and racist rhetoric and actions.'"[20]

"White nationalists are being outed on Twitter— and one lost his job," shared the *New York Post*, noting that the rally attendee "was axed from his restaurant position in Berkeley on Sunday just hours after being publicly identified by a Twitter account known as 'Yes, you're racist.'" The article noted that another man whose photo had been shared by the same account had gone on local news in his hometown in an attempt to clear his name.[21]

Invictus estimates that "hundreds of people" lost jobs or became estranged from their families because of their attendance at Unite the Right. One man reached out to Invictus, who is an attorney, for legal advice after being doxed and reported to his local Child Protective Services by Antifa who attempted to have his children removed from his home.

Andrew Dodson

The potential harm of doxing cannot be overstated.

Andrew Dodson was a graduate of Clemson University with a degree in electrical engineering and mathematics. He also studied at the University of Arkansas. He was using his expertise to work on developing clean-energy technology.

From a video taken of Dodson at Lee Park on the day of Unite the Right, we can learn something of his views. "The real war here is not fought with sticks and fists and pepper spray. The real war here," he explains, pounding his fist in the air for emphasis, "...is over who truly loves."

"One side says that your family doesn't matter, that your culture doesn't matter, and that all things are going to be brought together and equal, and we must, like, give to everyone... disregarding the duty that we have to our own family. If you do not have a strong

---

20   Abbey White, "A Twitter account identified this Unite the Right participant. Now his family's disowning him," Vox.com, Aug. 14, 2017.

21   Chris Perez, "White nationalists are being outed on Twitter— and one lost his job," *New York Post*, Aug. 13, 2017.

house, how can you love your neighbor? If you can't feed yourself, how are you going to feed someone else? How can these 'Christians' over here sing songs to Jesus, and they're wearing symbols of someone who has murdered a hundred thousand conservative, God-fearing poor Christian farmers in Europe?"

His choice of attire for Unite the Right displayed a quirky style. He wore a white suit adorned with a decal of a Trump-hair topped "Pepe the Frog." Atop his head was a Tea-Party style, red tri-corner hat with "Make America Great Again" embossed on the side. With his unique choice of outfit and a beard of bright red hair, he was sure to stand out in the crowd. In Dodson's case, being noticed had tragic consequences.

Activist Logan James, operating a Twitter account with the handle @YesYoureRacist, posted pictures of Dodson for his followers with the message, "Anybody have a name for this dope at the end of the Baked Alaska video in the ill-fitting White suit, tri-corner hat, and Pepe lapel pin?"

James's followers started digging, and soon found pictures of Dodson wearing a University of Arkansas t-shirt at the previous nights' torch light parade. Several people associated with the University who fit Dodson's general description were incorrectly identified as the Unite the Right attendee, and they were quickly beset by angry online mobs. A man of honor, Dodson stepped forward to protect those falsely accused from receiving further harassment. Speaking with an Arkansas news outlet, Dodson explained "There's a couple of guys in Fayetteville that have been misidentified as me... It's not those guys, it's not them. It's me... I'm so sorry, I would never want to hurt you and your family. If they want my T-shirt back, I'll send it to them..."

While expressing an interest in White identity politics, he could not bear to be associated with a "hate" movement. "I learned so much from these [engineering] guys. It breaks my heart that they're going to think I'm a Nazi, or a KKK, or a White supremacist."

Dodson went on to explain that at Unite the Right, there were people "trying to instigate racial violence — people on both sides —

as an excuse to stop us from having our free speech. Because I want to talk about the money that is corrupting our systems."[22]

The man responsible for doxing Dodson soon appeared on NBC news above a chyron reading "Naming and Shaming: Activists Go Online to shame Charlottesville marchers." James confidently justified his actions to the interviewer. "If they're really so proud to stand shoulder-to-shoulder with White supremacists and Neo-Nazis, then I think that their communities need to know who these people are and what they're trying to do to our nation."

This tactic exemplifies one of Saul Alinsky's *Rules for Radicals*: "Rule 12: Pick the target, freeze it, personalize it, and polarize it. Cut off the support network and isolate the target from sympathy. Go after people and not institutions; people hurt faster than institutions. (This is cruel, but very effective. Direct, personalized criticism and ridicule works.)"

Cruel, but effective, indeed. Dodson committed suicide on March 9, 2018.

Even in death, the mob pursued. "Anti-racists" trolled a memorial web page set up in his honor.

The plight of Dodson was the subject of an article in the *New Republic* entitled "To Dox a Racist: How a dead White supremacist sparked a debate over the tactics used against the extreme right." In the article, another activist who utilizes the practice, Daryle Lamont Jenkins, shrugs off his death. "He most certainly didn't care about Heather Heyer, so why should we care for him?"[23]

The article concedes that "[d]oxing, even in the most extreme cases, is fraught with ethical complications... it can be an ugly and indiscriminate weapon, even when used in the fight against White supremacy." However, they argue that using the tactic against the right is more morally justifiable. "The threats of violence leveled at female, Jewish, and African American journalists and activists

---

22   Jacob Rosenberg, "Arkansas-linked Charlottesville marcher identified, apologizes to those misidentified," *Arkansas Times*, Aug. 16, 2017.

23   Vegas Tenold, "To Dox a Racist: How a dead White supremacist sparked a debate over the tactics used against the extreme right," *New Republic*, July 26, 2018.

are not matched by anything experienced by White people on the fringe right."

Indeed, there is no comparison. Of those mentioned, only White people on the "fringe right" can be condemned on national television without evidence, then denied a platform to refute the accusations.

Ethan Zuckerman, director of the Center for Civic Media at MIT, expresses qualified defense of the practice of doxing as well. He says that "he doesn't want to see anyone being harassed, but that doxing could be effective against people who are just beginning to explore White nationalist ideas... I hope it will be a successful tactic in helping filter people out of this movement who are exploring the identity, but who may not understand just what a hateful and horrible thing they're doing," [24]

None of those who support doxing appear to have questioned whether Dodson's attendance at Unite the Right was proof of his "White supremacy" or his evil intentions. Followers of James's Twitter account didn't even bother to make sure they had identified the right person before unleashing their righteous fury.

Dodson described the experience like this: "It's a fascinating machine to see in progress. These are very hardworking people that are using these social media platforms to scrub the internet for all the data on someone. It's like a giant artificial intelligence or something. This swarm of human beings, Googling, in an attempt to destroy someone."[25]

Dodson's compatriot, known online as Millennial Matt, describes Andrew and what happened to him. "I met Andrew Dodson on numerous different occasions, and he was one of the friendliest, funniest, and most intelligent people. I first met him before the Trump election protesting the Federal Reserve with some of his friends. What was done to him and his family is unforgivable... Andrew Dodson was the victim of a mass campaign

---

24 Corinne Segal, "White supremacists once wore hoods. Now, an internet mob won't let them stay anonymous," *PBS News Hour*, Aug. 20, 2017.

25 *Ibid.*

of harassment led by an account on Twitter called @YesYou'reRacist who is endorsed by NBC. [He] started receiving thousands of death threats. His school, his family, his friends. He lost his job. He was excommunicated from society. It ultimately led to Andrew taking his own life... This particular person did not go to Charlottesville because he hated people. He went to Charlottesville because he loved people."

Was he really loving? It certainly seems so. Additional Lee Park video shows Dodson staggering backwards into the arms of bystanders while screaming in pain after having been pepper-sprayed in the face. "He got me right in the eyes! Oh fuck!"

Moments later, a shirtless, red-eyed Dodson confronted his attacker. Stabbing an index finger towards the man with force, he told him, "I forgive you. I love you. And I would rather suffer this way now than for your families and children to die in the future."[26]

This is the man thoughtlessly condemned by thousands as evil and deserving of severe punishment for his beliefs. A kind, conscientious and gifted man with nuanced, morally sound convictions. A man who, within minutes of a violent and painful attack, told the perpetrator "I forgive you. I love you."

The anti-hate crowd was not nearly so merciful.

---

26 DanTheOracle, "In Memory of Andrew Dodson by Red Ice," BitChute video, posted April 28, 2019.

CHAPTER 18 QUICK LINKS:

 "Dissident Mama, episode 27 – Jason Kessler," Jan. 22, 2021. URL: qrs. ly/cycvto9

 Jason Kessler, "Antifa Comms Director Luis Oyola on Charlottesville Conspiracy," video, June 19, 2020. URL: qrs.ly/4acvtbm

 DanTheOracle, "In Memory of Andrew Dodson by Red Ice," video, April 28, 2019. URL: qrs.ly/2ycvtp4

CHAPTER 19

THE VISITORS - GOING HOME

"What have you done?"

LUKE DROVE BACK TO RICHMOND the day of Unite the Right. When he got home, he turned on Fox News and heard about the car crash and helicopter crash and realized "things had gone really south really quickly." He was in a state of shock. "How can this happen in the modern U.S. where mayhem is allowed to ensue?"

He knew that the deaths from that day would be "the bloody shirt the left would hang out to condemn the right, especially those who are outside the lines of conventional political beliefs." He reflects that "Unite the Right caused a lot of bad things to happen to good people," who lost jobs and were ostracized from friends and family members. Luke says his attendance at Unite the Right didn't cost him any friendships because his friends were confident about what kind of person he was, though he did have one relative write him off for good.

Nathaniel's family and friends had been aware he was going to Virginia for a political rally. When he arrived home, he was confronted with questions from his alarmed relatives who heard about Unite the Right on the news. "What have you done!?" they wanted to know. They were convinced he had gotten involved with some kind of dangerous hate movement.

He tried his best to reassure them. It took a few months for them to realize "I'm not some monster."

Some people at work had also known he was going to Unite the Right. He had gotten what he described as "a ridiculous haircut" before going, and after returning to work, he wore a hat to cover it up because he was worried what people would think. Nobody asked.

As far as lasting impact, "I look back on it fondly. I was one of a thousand people there to defend Robert E Lee and White people. I don't regret that." He does regret involvement with some of the figures there. He does not consider himself to be a national socialist or racial supremacist. He would like to see people of different races get along but is not sure that's realistic.

Jim, who had been arrested for carrying a weapon without a proper permit, spent Saturday evening back at the League of the South campground, then enjoyed visiting with a family member on Sunday. While he was there, an uncle called to tell him that word of his arrest was all over the local news in his hometown.

He returned to the courthouse on Monday, and recalls that it was full of "leftist cuckoos." He found himself seated between an SPLC employee and some "hippie freaks." He waited while other Unite the Right defendants were processed - some of them, including Fields, on closed-circuit TV. When Jim's name was called and he stood up, the SPLC employee seated next to him reacted with shock. He assumed that she had not identified him as a defendant because of his clean-cut and professional appearance. After going through the required legal formalities, Jim got in his car and drove home. While he was on the way home, the CEO of Jim's company called and told him he was fired from his job as a senior director. He stayed on board with the company long enough to help transition his position to a new person but didn't receive severance.

Jim went back and forth to Charlottesville several times over the next few months for legal reasons. He was forced to represent himself in court because he was unable to find an attorney who would agree to represent him, though he searched for one on the internet and through personal contacts. He ended up getting a $500 fine and suspended sentence for the weapons charge.

Jim lived off his savings for about six months, until friends from college were able to help him find a job. Then when his new employer learned he had attended Unite the Right, he was fired on the spot from that job as well. Now he works as a contractor to avoid being directly connected to a company that may find association with him to be problematic.

He lost quite a few friends, and was written off by several family members because of his attendance at Unite the Right. At first, he was naïve enough to believe that he could reason with people when they reacted with horror to the news that he had attended the rally. Eventually he realized that reasoning would not work. "If you were at Unite the Right, you were bad."

His wife's family, who are Southerners and Southern heritage supporters, remained supportive. "They were fantastic."

Despite having lost multiple friends, family members, and jobs, Jim still thinks he made the right decision in attending Unite the Right.

"I don't regret going to Charlottesville. I regret that we didn't think of things more strategically before going. I regret that we didn't realize this was a trap. I don't regret standing up for the South and for the Robert E. Lee statue." He also believes that as a Christian, "I am going to be on the right side of history."

Steve also reveals that several friendships ended because of his attendance at Unite the Right.

He spent the evening after the rally at home in his Charlottesville apartment. He explains that he was "shell-shocked, shaking, nervous, overwhelmed, and trying to make sense of it all. It was too dangerous to go out."

He got online and watched as the news of the day exploded on social media, and the false narrative began to be cemented in the public mind. Based on what he knew to be true, he carefully composed a "restrained, civilized, thorough, and firm" summary of several paragraphs describing his experience, including police complicity, and posted it to Facebook. Immediately, some friends "jumped down my throat" with their "shrill, hysterical leftist narrative" about "White supremacist terrorists!"

Things came to an ugly head with one man in particular who used to be a good friend. The former friend went on an "estrogen fueled rage" in response to Steve's post, telling him that "You are just as guilty as the rest of them." He seemed convinced that anyone that had attended the rally was a bad person, and revealed that he had saved screen shots of Steve's admission that he had been there. Steve tried to be restrained and cautious in his responses, aware that some people had already lost their jobs after being identified as Unite the Right attendees.

His friend's final words to him stung. "You are not somebody that I want my children to grow up knowing."

You can hear the pain in Steve's voice as he tells the story. "That really broke my heart. He had been one of my best friends. It hurts."

He also lost respect for his former friend. "It's hard to understand how he can feel that way and be a man. It is emasculating. I felt bad for him, that he has been reduced to that."

Steve also tried calling the leftist female friend that he had run into downtown that day. He was hopeful that they may still be able to find common ground. He left her a message, but he never heard back from her.

At the time of the rally, Steve had been engaged for less than a month. After seeing the news, his fiancé was concerned. But, after a few tense conversations, they were able to smooth things over.

In addition to the loss of friends, Steve is also grieving the impact of Unite the Right on his hometown, the name of which is now inseparable from this event. He notes that formerly cherished memories are now tarnished. For example, the shop his late grandmother once enjoyed frequenting for lunch will now also be remembered as the scene of the ice-block-throwing melee that took place that day.

He sadly remarks, "I'm so embarrassed that my hometown became synonymous with riots and disaster, with activism gone awry... That place is full of history. That's why we were there! And now the modern generations are going to remember Charlottesville as the Day the Nazis Came to Town. That's horrible to me."

Bill, the pro-monuments activists, says he became depressed in the aftermath of the rally. "It set us back. We lost monuments because of that."

Chris says that he has never told his immediate family, who are typical moderate conservatives, that he attended Unite the Right. He doubts he ever will. "Next thing you know, you're shunned from family and work."

Part Four:
The Battle Continues In Court

CHAPTER 20

THE CRIMINAL CASES

"...nothing less than political prisoners..."

Condemnation And Unequal Justice

THERE WERE QUITE A FEW CRIMINAL cases stemming from Unite the Right. Though the media often claims that White males have an unfair advantage in the United States criminal justice system, this does not seem to have been true for the rally-goers in Charlottesville. Even, or perhaps especially, the Republican-run Department of Justice felt a need to make an example of anyone associated with Unite the Right that they possibly could.

Brad Griffin, writing as Hunter Wallace, fumed, "[The Trump] presidency has unleashed a tidal wave of Antifa violence and instead of prosecuting Antifa or elected officials in Democratic cities like Portland and Charlottesville which issue stand-down orders to police, he has people like Thomas Cullen prosecuting his own supporters for defending themselves from Antifa to 'send a message' to White supremacists... 8 years of President Barack Obama wasn't nearly as bad as 4 years of [Trump]."[1]

---

1 Hunter Wallace, "Washington Post: The Trump Appointee Who Is Putting White Supremacists In Jail," Occidental Dissent.com, Aug. 7, 2019.

Speaking about prosecutions stemming from Unite the Right, Kessler observes, "[I]f you attended the rally they will prosecute you for things that they normally would not have prosecuted you for. And they will also seek much harsher sentences and they're more likely to get the harsher sentences. If you are attacked on the other hand, those people are less likely to be charged with a crime and they're more likely to be able to get away with the crimes. So if you are a dissident and the government really decides they want to go after you they will find something. Everybody has something. And they'll find that weakness and they'll turn it into the biggest thing - you are the most evil person, the most criminal person, whether you are or not."[2]

Attorney Nicholas Stix, who tracked the defendants facing charges stemming from Unite the Right concluded: "The five Alt-Righters, who have been charged with felonies and jailed without bail, are nothing less than political prisoners."[3]

Invictus, who is also an attorney, tried to set up a legal network for the Charlottesville defendants, but laments that he waited too late. He believes now that his efforts should have begun immediately after Unite the Right. Invictus states that the authorities "came down with a hammer on everyone they could." He attempted to assist some of the Charlottesville-related defendants such as the Rise Above Movement [RAM] members and Daniel McMahon (aka Jack Corbin). (Several RAM members who had attended Unite the Right were later convicted of "conspiracy to riot" for actions related to Charlottesville and plans they were making to attend another event. McMahon, who did not attend Unite the Right but did a great deal of research on its leftist perpetrators after the fact, was convicted of threatening a Charlottesville politician.) Invictus explains that these sorts of prosecutions, which he describes as a "total political pony show," are not brought against someone unless they are already hated. He believes what happened to the

---

2 "Jason Kessler," Podcast on DissidentMama.net.

3 Nicholas Stix, "Anarcho-tyranny Update: Mounting proof that Alt-Right Charlottesville Five are Political Prisoners," VDare.com, Sept 29, 2017.

Charlottesville defendants has become the typical treatment of right-wingers. "The government has taken off the mask. They throw the book at them because of politics."

Christopher Cantwell - "I'm a goddamn human being."

One high-profile arrest, that of White nationalist host of the Radical Agenda podcast, Christopher Cantwell, stemmed from the famous torchlight march of August 11, 2017, the eve of Unite the Right.

Cantwell was originally from Long Island New York. As a teen, Cantwell struggled with substance abuse and had numerous brushes with law enforcement. He did his first short stint in prison on misdemeanor charges at the age of 19. While researching for his own legal defense for DUI in 2009, he developed interest in constitutional issues and the overreach of government, which led him to join the Libertarian party. Unlike most Libertarians, Cantwell brazenly talked about the merits of using force to push back against the state, to the point of even openly celebrating the deaths of law enforcement officers. In 2014, Cantwell moved to Keene, New Hampshire, home of the Free State project and a thriving and colorful Libertarian community. He quickly became an incendiary figure there.

As a Unite the Right headliner, Cantwell had agreed to be the subject of a Vice documentary for HBO the weekend of the event. The program, entitled "Charlottesville: Race and Terror," brought a great deal of mainstream name recognition and notoriety to Cantwell.

The afternoon before the torchlight rally, Cantwell and his entourage gathered in McIntire Park. He was wearing a black shirt with a white image of a man falling from a helicopter, an allusion to the darkly humorous Alt-Right "helicopter ride" meme which referenced Pinochet's reported practice of having communists tossed to their deaths from moving helicopters.

Seated at a picnic table across from Cantwell, Vice corresponded Elle Reeve asked him, "When did you get into the racial stuff?"

Cantwell responded, "When the Trayvon Martin case happened, you know, Michael Brown, Tamir Rice, and all these different things happened, every single case, it's some little Black asshole behaving like a savage, and he gets himself in trouble shockingly enough. Whatever problems I might have with my fellow White people, they generally are not inclined to such behavior, and you've gotta kind of take that into consideration when you're thinking about how to organize your society."

When challenged by Reeve about whether White people were also capable of violence, Cantwell replied, "Of course we're capable. I'm carrying a pistol. I go to the gym all the time. I am trying to make myself more capable of violence. I'm here to spread ideas, talk, in the hopes that somebody more capable will come along and do that. Somebody like Donald Trump who does not give his daughter to a Jew."

"So, Donald Trump, but more racist?" inquired Reeve.

"A lot more racist than Donald Trump. I don't that you could feel the way about race that I do and watch that Kushner bastard walk around with that beautiful girl. Okay."

Unsurprisingly, the same unfiltered racist commentary that made him an entertaining podcast host, appealing to his particular subset of mostly young, male, far right-wing listeners, did not play well with the general public.

In the documentary, he also made quite a show of bravado. Later that weekend, Cantwell showed off his considerable stash of arms on camera. As tense music played in the background, as is used when someone in a horror movie is hiding from a killer, he tossed his weapons one by one onto the bed of his hotel room.

"So, I came pretty well prepared for this thing today. Kel-Tec P-3AT, .380 ACP, Glock 19, 9 mm, Ruger LC9, also 9mm. And there's a knife. Well, I actually have another AK in that bag over there. You can lose track of your fucking guns, huh?"

He drew more ire for the comments made in the immediate aftermath of the death of Heather Heyer which appeared to many to be shockingly callous. He remarked that "the fact that nobody on our side died, I'd go ahead and call that points for us. The fact that none of our people killed anybody unjustly is a plus for us."

Asked by Reeve for his interpretation of the fatal car accident, Cantwell explains, "The video appears to show someone striking that vehicle. When these animals attacked him again, and he saw no way to get away from them, except to hit the gas. And sadly, because our rivals are a bunch of stupid animals, and they don't pay attention, they couldn't just get out of the way of his car. And some people got hurt. And it's unfortunate."

Reeve asked, "So you think it was justified?"

"I think it was more than justified. The amount of restraint that our people showed out there, I think was astounding."

When asked what to expect from the next Alt-Right protest, Cantwell, beaming with a broad smile, replied, "I say it's gonna be really tough to top, but we're up to the challenge."[4]

His cheerful disposition would not last.

Cantwell soon learned that activists Emily Gorcenski and Kristopher Goad, who had counter-protested the torchlight march the night of August 11th, had sworn out a felony warrant with the University of Virginia Police against him for his use of pepper spray during the disturbance. Sympathetically portrayed by the news, Gorcenski claimed to have been in mortal fear. "I thought I was going to die that Friday night when we were surrounded. I assumed that I would not walk out of that."[5]

In response to news of the warrant, from an undisclosed location, a tearful Cantwell posted a video to the internet. "I contacted the local police. I called the Charlottesville PD, and I asked them, I said, I have been told that there's a warrant out for my arrest. And they said that they wouldn't confirm it but I could find this

---

4 Vice News, "Charlottesville: Race and Terror," YouTube.

5 TODAY, "White Nationalist Facing Felony Charges over Charlottesville violence," YouTube video posted Aug. 23, 2017.

out... I want to be peaceful. I want to be law abiding. That was the whole entire point of this. And I'm watching CNN talk about this as 'violent White nationalist protest.' We have done everything in our power to keep this peaceful. I know we talk a lot of shit on the internet, but I mean literally, Jason Kessler applied for a permit months ago for this."

He offered to surrender himself to the police peacefully. "I do not want violence with you. I'm terrified. I'm afraid you're gonna kill me. I really am."

In the immediate wake of his boldly racist remarks and show of bravado, Cantwell's display of fear and vulnerability was delicious to his enemies. The online mockery was immediate and brutal. "Mmmm delicious Nazi tears!" taunted one random tweeter. "Leave Britney alone!" mocked another, comparing Cantwell to the teen whose histrionic pleas on behalf of Britney Spears had become an internet meme. Cantwell was quickly dubbed "The Crying Nazi" by the press – a name which has followed him ever since.

Cantwell turned himself in to the authorities on August 24th. Speaking with the Daily Beast from Albemarle-Charlottesville Regional Jail, Cantwell defended his emotional reaction. "When I came down here for a permitted demonstration, championed by the ACLU, where the police are supposed to be clearing our enemies from our path, and then I find myself involved in a riot facing 20 years in prison, I got emotional, shockingly enough... One minute I'm a fucking White supremacist terrorist and the next minute I'm a fucking crybaby? I'm a goddamn human being."

Cantwell admitted that he employed pepper spray – a viral photo taken that evening clearly showed him spraying it in a man's face – but claimed that it was used only in self-defense as the counter-protesters lunged towards him. "That guy is coming directly at me, and I'm spraying him directly in the face. I used the least amount of force possible to prevent that man from harming me in a brawl that my enemies started." (In the same article, they made a point to note that he referred to Gorcenski as a "fucking tranny" and blamed "kikes" for organizing the counter-protest.)

"I got assaulted twice in as many days, and now I'm facing 20 years in prison, which I think is pretty fucked up... If I wanted to go there to harm people, we would not be talking about pepper spray charges... I came there with my keychain — I did not go there with a riot can like the fucking communists did."[6]

Some who have heard Cantwell's free-swearing, slur-laced, aggressive rhetoric may be surprised to learn that he was a voice of caution and restraint on the night of the torchlight rally. Kessler told an interviewer, "Actually, the guy who got arrested, Chris Cantwell, he suggested, 'Look, you need to tell the cops, and make sure that they're in on it, so they can keep the peace.' He did everything by the book."[7]

Invictus confirms, "Cantwell refused to participate unless the police were notified," and complains about the injustice of his having been arrested. "I had everything on camera and they still arrested him."

Cantwell was at first granted bond, but the bond was later denied after the Commonwealth attorney, Robert Tracci, made the unusual move of appealing the granting of that bond to a new judge. The new judge, after being presented portions of Cantwell's Radical Agenda podcast, decided that his "hate speech" (something that is not an actual legal concept in the United States) made him a danger to society.[8] Though he remained incarcerated, he was, with outside assistance, able to continue to broadcast Radical Agenda during the months he was behind bars.

At a preliminary hearing on November 9, 2017, "Defense attorney [Elmer] Woodard opened up the proceedings like a man on fire," reported Kessler. "Prosecutor Tracci wanted a brief session in which the judge certified the three felony charges against Cantwell... [h]owever based on his theory that the charges were

---

6 Hawes Spencer, "Crying Nazi Christopher Cantwell Says He's Just a 'Goddamn Human Being," The DailyBeast.com, Aug. 31, 2017.

7 Nicholas Stix, "Doing Everything by the Book: The Jason Kessler VDARE Interview, Part V," NicholasStixUncensored.Blogspot.com, Sept. 22, 2017.

8 Jason Kessler, "Complete Cantwell Preliminary Trial Rundown," Jason Kessler.u s, Nov. 11, 2017.

politically motivated and based on false testimony, Woodard dragged it out into a 6-hour trial on whether there was even probable cause to allow charges to go to trial."[9] (The reporter from the Vice documentary about Cantwell, Elle Reeve, was in attendance at the hearing, but was ejected for using her phone in the court room.)

Cantwell's accusers Gorcenski and Goad had a history of displaying extreme hostility towards Whites and pro-White causes. For example, Gorcenski has posted messages to social media such as "White genocide is good" and "Good night White pride." Similarly, Goad has described Caucasians as "White trash" and posted musings such as "Perhaps today is a good day to White genocide."

Gorcenski and Goad claimed to have been affected by gas, but Woodard argued that there were multiple individuals releasing pepper spray in the area at the time, and evidence clearly showed that neither was the direct target of Cantwell's spray. Woodard provided evidence that a different man - who, unlike Cantwell, was not a political enemy - was the one whose spray had affected Goad. During the hearing, Prosecutor Robert Tracci tried to invalidate the testimony of one witness who balked at using Gorenski's preferred gender pronouns. Tracci was also reprimanded by the judge for attempting to put Cantwell's politics on trial. By the end of the day, two of the felony charges Cantwell was facing were tossed out, and he faced only one remaining charge for the illegal use of gas.[10]

After crowd-sourced fundraising efforts, Cantwell was released on bail in December, 2017. In July 2018, Cantwell pled guilty to two counts of misdemeanor assault stemming from his actions as the torchlight rally, and agreed to stay out of Virginia for five years. He promptly filed a million-dollar lawsuit against Gorcenski and Goad for malicious prosecution.[11] The parties later signed a mutual release of all claims to avoid liability.

9 Ibid.

10 Ibid.

11 Lauren Berg, "Cantwell files $1M suit against Aug. 11 accusers," Charlottesville Daily Progress, Jan. 4, 2018.

Subsequent to his release, Cantwell has continued to use speech characterized by threatening language towards journalists and other political enemies. He is currently in prison following a conviction for extortion and threats stemming from a dispute with members of the Bowl Patrol, a group who admire mass murderer Dylann Roof.

Hannah Zarski did not know Cantwell prior to Unite the Right, but she took an interest in him as one of the Charlottesville defendants, all of whom she had reached out to with offers of assistance. Zarski had appeared on Cantwell's podcasts after his release to provide updates about the status of Unite the Right-related court cases, and notes that when she was a guest on his show, Cantwell behaved in a professional manner and refrained from using slurs and aggressive language. Zarski has kept in touch with Cantwell and followed his continuing legal battles closely, and maintains that "Cantwell is a choir boy compared to the Bowl Patrol."

Corey Long And Richard Preston

One arrest and conviction of a Unite the Right attendee was for firing a warning shot in response to the deployment of a homemade flamethrower.

The Heaphy Report describes the incident:

> Most of the Unite the Right groups left Emancipation Park through the southwest stairs. As the VSP field force pushed the crowd south onto Market Street, it forced the demonstrators into the angry crowd of counter-protesters. Predictably, several violent acts ensued. The most notorious incident from those tense moments involved a homemade flamethrower and a gunshot. As Alt-Right demonstrators left the park and turned right to move west down Market Street, they passed by counter-protester Corey Long. Video taken by a bystander shows Long igniting the spray from an aerosol canister and pointing the flames at passing demonstrators. Richard Wilson

Preston, a Ku Klux Klan leader from Maryland, saw this as he exited the park. He drew his handgun and pointed it at Long while screaming at him to stop. Preston loaded a round into the chamber of his gun then fired a single shot at the ground next to Long. He holstered his gun and walked away. VSP troopers, identified by their neon yellow vests, stood in a line behind two barricades about twenty feet away. None appeared to react.[12]

At the trial, Preston's attorney Elmer Woodard showed a video clip of Corey Long and his friend DeAndre Harris near the Lee Park stairwell through which Unite the Right attendees were forced to exit. Woodard presented four witnesses who said they had felt threatened by Long's flamethrower. One man, Jonathan Howe, testified that he had been doused by Long with "some kind of paint thinner... This was a very surreal moment... I had a flammable substance on my hand and someone running around with a flamethrower." He feared he could become a "human torch."

Another witness, David Fowler, testified that he had been blinded by pepper spray and was being assisted out of the park when he heard the whoosh of Long's aerosol can. "As far as I'm concerned, [Preston] is a hero... We shouldn't be here."[13]

Another Unite the Right attendee, Gregory Scott Woods testified about his encounter with Long. "I'm right here getting attacked by this guy with a flamethrower... I saw this guy flick this thing three times. Then he sprayed it in my face. I felt the heat." Woods stated he was trapped on the park steps, feeling the heat of the flame, until Preston fired his gun.[14]

---

12 Heaphy Report, p. 136

13 Lisa Provence, "Preston's plea: Imperial wizard says no contest to firing gun," C-ville.com, May 9, 2018.

14 Lisa Provence, "KKK support group: Gun-firer and alleged Harris attackers remain in jail," C-ville.com, Oct. 17, 2017.

Other witnesses included former Charlottesville mayor Frank Buck, and Daryl Davis, a Black musician who lived near Preston in the Baltimore area. Davis is known for befriending Klansmen in the hopes of changing their views about race. "I'm testifying because he's my friend... He's in trouble and I'm trying to help." He had put up 50 percent of Preston's bond.[15]

Notably, Long and Harris did not testify. Kessler, who attended the trial, reported that, "Deandre Harris, who participated with Corey Long in burning Confederate flags with the improvised flamethrower, ducked a subpoena and failed to appear in court. Corey Long himself has disappeared and could not be subpoenaed."[16]

At his sentencing hearing a few months later, Preston apologized but also defended his actions. "I am sorry," he said. "I only had second to figure it out... I didn't want to hurt anybody."

The judge seemed unimpressed. "What he did was aggravating... It was stupid... You're just fortunate this didn't turn into a gun battle," Judge Rick Moore said. "You come and take your stand for a right... You don't defend yourself if you stand for a right."

After being sentenced to four years in prison, Preston touched his heart and mouthed to his family, "I love you."[17]

For his apparent attempt to set his ideological opponents on fire, Long was celebrated by numerous media outlets. A writer for the New Yorker described Long as "[a] graceful man [who] has appropriated not only the flames of White supremacist bigotry but also the debauched, rhetorical fire of Trump..."[18] An article for The Root entitled, "How Corey Long Fought White Supremacy with Fire," celebrated the "iconic photo" of him wielding the flamethrower. Long told The Root, "I went out to voice my opinion. To have my freedom of speech. Just like the racist Nazis who took

15 Lisa Provence, "Preston's plea," C-ville.com.

16 Jason Kessler, "Sentencing for Charlottesville Warning Shot Defendant Richard Preston Deferred Until August 21," VDare.com, May 9, 2018.

17 Brett Barrouquere, "Klan leader Richard Preston sentenced to four years in prison for firing gun at 'Unite the Right'," SPLCCenter.org, Aug. 22, 2018.

18 Jenny Jarvie, "Black man who wielded flamethrower during White nationalist rally in Charlottesville is arrested," *Los Angeles Times*, Oct. 14, 2017.

over my town." The article claims that Long was trying to defend himself and other counter-protesters from White supremacist violence, and falsely implies that the gunshot preceded his use of the flamethrower. It does not explain why Long chose to employ a flamethrower rather than simply remove himself from the exit path into which the rally attendees were being forced.[19] There is clear video evidence that Long was not a hapless bystander on the day of Unite the Right. Drone footage exposes Long during other parts of the day "...shirtless with a white t-shirt around his neck, violently throwing projectiles at the departing pro-Lee protesters."[20]

Long was eventually sentenced to 20 days in prison for disorderly conduct. The local Black Lives Matter chapter stated they were "outraged that Corey Long has been convicted for simply asserting his humanity in the face of White supremacist violence." [21]

Kessler commented on the light sentence of Long for deploying a flamethrower into a crowd "... it further shows the civil rights abuses happen in Charlottesville because we have something called the Fourteenth Amendment, and the reason they implemented the Fourteenth Amendment was because after the Reconstruction, they said that a Black man should not be hung for something that a White man would not be hung for. In Charlottesville it's the opposite. A White man will be hung for something a Black man would not be hung for. [He] fired a flamethrower at my crowd of people... Corey Long, Deandre Harris' friend fired a flamethrower at a crowd of people. If I had done that I would be in prison for the rest of my life. But he got a disorderly conduct."[22]

---

19 Yesha Callahan, "Interview: How Corey Long Fought White Supremacy With Fire," TheRoot.com, Aug 14, 2017.

20 Ben Wetmore, "Never-Before-Seen Drone Footage from Charlottesville," TheGatewayPundit.com.

21 Benjamin Fearnow, "Charlottesville Protester Who Used Aerosol Flamethrower in Iconic Image Sentenced to Jail," Newsweek, June 11, 2018.

22 News2Share, "Jason Kessler's Full Speech at 'Unite the Right 2,'" YouTube video posted Aug. 13, 2018.

The Garage Attack And Deandre Harris

The antics of Long and Harris did not end after the flamethrower incident in Lee Park. Most Americans have seen photos of what happened next, which was perhaps one of the most mischaracterized incidents of the whole day: the beating of DeAndre Harris. This incident resulted in the arrest and conviction of four Unite the Right attendees. A viral photo from Unite the Right depicted of a group of White men holding weapons and standing over a Black man, Harris, as he lay on the ground. This photo, usually provided with no context whatsoever, was exploited by the media to help contribute to the public impression that Unite the Right attendees were violent racists on a rampage, looking to brutalize any non-Whites in sight.

But what happened in the moments before the photo was taken?

Brad Griffin, Public Affairs Director for the League of the South, writes under the pen name Hunter Wallace for his site Occidental Dissent. Wallace reported on the altercation involving some members of the League of the South. "After the flamethrower incident, Corey Long, DeAndre Harris and group of Black males affiliated with Black Lives Matter followed, stalked and menaced a group of our people who were returning to their cars in the parking garage. They were armed with sticks, baseball bats and a Maglite."

Drawing from a massive amount of visual data gathered from the internet in the hours and days following Unite the Right, Griffin compiled a series of videos which reconstructed exactly what happened. The following is his description of a series of videos embedded on his site.

> Here is DeAndre Harris following our people to the parking garage. His friends are screaming "appreciate the bat" and "do something." When DeAndre Harris arrived at the parking garage, he attacked with Corey Long and the Black male in the pink shirt. Corey Long attempts to steal a Confederate flag and DeAndre Harris hits Harold Crews over the head with his mag lite. The Black male in the pink shirt swung a stick

and was pepper sprayed. As they are forced back into the parking garage, a Black male in a blue shirt runs up from behind one of our members, clubs him and knocks him unconscious. He continues to beat him with another Black male. THIS provokes the parking garage fight... DeAndre Harris swings his mag lite and hits Harold Crews. After the parking garage fight, you can see another assault on a League of the South member returning to the parking garage in the video above.

The fake news was only interested in Deandre Harris because he was Black and could be portrayed as a 'victim' of 'White supremacists.' They ignored the White kid who was bludgeoned with the club in the parking garage by DeAndre Harris's friends which provoked others to rush to his defense... Dan Borden and Alex Michael Ramos came to the aid of a League of the South member who had been clubbed and knocked unconscious in the parking garage... What do the Charlottesville Police do? They issued warrants for the arrest Dan Borden and Alex Michael Ramos. Not only did they FAIL to do their jobs and through their criminal negligence put all of our lives in danger on August 12th, they charged people who were forced to defend others.[23]

Rally attendee Gene personally witnessed part of the Harris incident and concurs with Griffin. "[Harris] clubbed one of our people and took off running... They didn't pick him out because he was Black. They picked him out because he ambushed someone from behind."

Griffin expresses his disgust with the media portrayal of the Harris incident:

---

23 Hunter Wallace, "Anarcho-Tyranny: The Corruption of Charlottesville, VA," OccidentalDissent.com, Aug. 27, 2017.

The fake news deliberately took the so-called beating of Deandre Harris out of context in order to push a false narrative that he was a victim of "White supremacists" when in reality he was part of a group of Black Lives Matter thugs who attacked our people returning to their cars in the parking garage. Shaun King and other race-baiting bottom-feeders pushed this narrative and as a result DeAndre Harris was able to raise over $166,000 in donations for aggravated assault through GoFundMe.

Charlottesville is the ultimate example of what Sam Francis once called "anarcho-tyranny..." The police in Charlottesville... deliberately ceded the streets to violent Antifa. When they attacked and we were forced to defend ourselves, the Charlottesville police charged us with crimes. There isn't a better example of this than the DeAndre Harris incident. We were complying with the 'state of emergency' and were dispersing to return to our vehicles. We were stalked, followed, menaced and attacked by a gang of violent Black thugs and were punished by the state for defending ourselves.[24]

Kessler expressed similar sentiments about the Harris incident:

Deandre Harris was a miscarriage of justice. Deandre Harris attacked an innocent man, and that is clear. Deandre Harris was with a group of people who, look, these were Black guys who were taken advantage of by racist liberals because these Antifa, what they did was come equipped with weapons like Maglites, and portable flame throwers, and they gave it to these Black guys so they would attack people. That's what Deandre Harris and Corey Long said when they were in court. Deandre Harris and Corey Long were attacking people with Confederate flags. They were

---

24 *Ibid.*

stealing them and lighting them on fire with portable flame throwers. Deandre Harris took a Maglite, and while Deandre Harris' friend grabbed a Confederate flag out of this hand, Deandre Harris whacked an innocent protester across the face with a Maglite.

I'm not saying that the violence done to Deandre was proportional, but it was clear that Deandre started the violence in that parking garage incident and it would not have happened were he not a violent individual himself... He got a little slap on the wrist... I don't condone the violence that was done to Deandre Harris, but I think he had a GoFundMe, and he did very well off that. He got himself some new sneakers and a rap video, so good for him. He got something out of it. He attacked one of my guys, so it's a little hard for me to have sympathy for him. But look, I don't condone political violence. I disavow political violence. I'm sorry that Mr. Harris got hurt. I'm sorry Mr. Harris' victim got hurt.[25]

The fact that Antifa provided riot supplies to Long and Harris is worth emphasizing. This is an Antifa tactic that has been observed elsewhere. Journalist Drew Hernandez reported to Andy Ngo that in Kenosha, Wisconsin, "Antifa militants enticed Black youth to participate in violence by giving them supplies to start fires."[26]

Griffin tried mightily to correct the mainstream narrative of the Harris incident that permeated the legacy media, but found no outlets interested in providing the whole story to the public. "I contacted The Daily Progress and NBC 29 about the video. I sent it to detectives at the Charlottesville Police Department. I told the Associated Press what really happened in Charlottesville. I played the video in person on my smartphone for a news crew from Atlanta that was interviewing me about the arrest of Alex Michael Ramos. We bombarded reporters with the video of DeAndre Harris

---

25 News2Share, "Jason Kessler's Full Speech at 'Unite the Right 2,'" YouTube video posted Aug. 13, 2018.

26 Ngo, *Unmasked*, p. 29.

attacking with the MagLite on Twitter. No one was interested in investigating or reporting the truth... The media refused to report on it after gleefully showing the out of context video."[27]

Griffin also reported that Charlottesville police officers witnessed the attacks in progress, but declined to intervene or make arrests. Griffin sent the compiled video evidence to the Charlottesville Police Department and the FBI, but after two months of inaction on the part of law enforcement, attack victim Crews took the initiative to press charges.[28]

In an interview with The Root, Harris describes being attacked. There is no mention in the article of his own violent behavior which instigated the fight. "Me and about five of my friends were out protesting. We thought [the racists] left, but at one point they came back. Everyone was exchanging words with the group, but then the KKK and White supremacists just rushed us..." Harris complained that the rally should not have taken place, "I think for them to be allowed to come here and protest is really crazy. How do you expect the KKK to come to your city to protest, and them not be violent? I understand everyone is entitled to their freedom of speech, but the government and the mayor made a bad business move. It's only caused havoc in your own city. It's crazier that people have the hatred in their heart to want to kill Black people."[29]

Links to Harris' GoFundMe page were shared far and wide across social media, and the twenty-year-old educational assistant and aspiring hip-hop artist within 10 days raised over $166,000.[30] Harris' message on the fundraising page stated that donated money would be used for medical bills. Coincidentally, about a month later,

---

27 Hunter Wallace, "The DeAndre Harris Race Hoax Exposed," Occidental Dissent.com, Oct. 10, 2017.

28 Hunter Wallace, "Political Correctness Distorts DeAndre Harris Arrest Media Coverage," OccidentalDissent.com, Oct. 11, 2017.

29 Yesha Callahan, "Interview: 20-Year-Old Deandre Harris Speaks Out About Being Assaulted by White Supremacists in Charlottesville, Va.," TheRoot.com, Aug. 13, 2017.

30 "I Was Beaten By White Supremacists," Aug. 22, 2017, GoFundMe.com .

Harris released a professionally-produced music video starring himself in which he was driving a Mercedes Benz and sporting a $2,000 pair of Nike Air Jordan Retros.[31]

After his arrest, Harris' lawyer claimed that by being charged for attacking Harold Crews, he was being "re-victimized" by "White supremacists."[32] Harris was later acquitted for hitting Crews with a metal flashlight by a judge who accepted his claim that he had only intended to hit the flagpole, not Crews.

The Defendants

Four men ended up serving time for the beating of Deandre Harris: Jacob Goodwin, Alex Michael Ramos, Daniel Borden, and Tyler Watkins Davis. Goodwin, Ramos, and Borden were all held without bail while awaiting trial. Davis was released to house arrest.

Charlottesville resident Hannah Zarski had chosen not to attend Unite the Right in person, because in the weeks prior, she had been monitoring counter-protesters' social media and decided the risks for her as the mother of a nursing infant were too great. However, she was watching live stream of the event and saw the altercation between Harris and Crews occur in real time, so she rejected the media narrative about the fight. "I knew exactly what happened. I knew the claims were bullshit. Harris got the swift street justice that he deserved."

Because Zarski believed the arrests for the Harris beating were unjust, she took a keen interest in the trials of the defendants. She showed up to their court cases and told their attorneys, "Look, I want to help you." She provided assistance with jury selection and the filing of documents. She also opened her home as lodging to the out-of-state families of the defendants during their legal proceedings. "I wanted to provide Southern hospitality to them when they have to come back to this place that has treated them so horribly."

31 Hunter Wallace, "The DeAndre Harris Race Hoax Exposed," Occidental Dissent.com, Oct. 10, 2017.

32 Eric Levenson and Amanda Watts, "Man beaten by White supremacists in Charlottesville is arrested," CNN.com, Oct. 13, 2017.

Daniel Borden, an Ohio 18-year-old with no criminal history, was sentenced to six years for his role in the beating of Harris. According to trial testimony from Borden's father, Borden had been separated from his friends when the order to disperse from Lee Park was issued. As he joined other Alt-Righters in walking towards the parking garage, he picked up a stick he found for protection.

Daniel's father Rick defended him unreservedly. "I absolutely don't think my son did anything wrong," he declared, citing research he had done on the violent tendencies of the counter-protest groups. He explained that Daniel had "tunnel vision" during the attack, and that "Dan has no recollection of anybody even around him. He was that full of fear and anxiety." Borden had been wearing a hat with the words "commie killer," which his father explained was a reference to the film "Full Metal Jacket."

In his own statement, Borden explained "I did not know how overwhelmingly against the statues Charlottesville was. If I did, I would have thought twice about coming." He said he had cried when he saw the pictures of the beating on the news, and made an apology to Harris. "You did not deserve that." He added an apology to the city of Charlottesville, "I'm truly sorry this has happened to your town." [33]

Jacob Goodwin was a 23-year-old from Arkansas who wore Black tactical gear and a pin with the logo of the Traditionalist Workers Party and another with the number "88," (sometimes meant to signify "Heil Hitler") during the attack.

Prior to his trial, attorney Elmer Woodard asked for a change of venue based on, among other things, the fact that the parking garage which would be the likely place for jurors to park was also the scene of the altercation at issue. Other concerns were that "sleeper activists" might be seated on the jury, or that local coverage of Unite the Right would sway jurors. In his opening argument for the motion, Woodard only voiced every other word to his opening

---

33 "Parental Influence: Borden Gets Nearly Four Years for Garage Attack," C-ville.com, Jan. 8, 2019.

statement in order to make the point that surveillance video of the fight only captured fifteen frames per second, and could therefore create a misleading impression.[34]

Prosecution implied that he had arrived to the rally looking for a fight, "outfitted for battle... He's got large goggles, boots. He's got a full body shield."

Many members of the public who viewed photos of Unite the Right attendees outfitted with shields, sticks, and helmets made similar assumptions about their intentions. That assumption is not necessarily correct, argues one attendee writing under the moniker "Charlottesville Survivor." He explains, "[T]he reason many Unite The Right demonstrators arrived with helmets and shields: Antifa are known for tactics such as throwing hard projectiles, hitting people on the head with poles, and using stabbing weapons. In other words, UTR demonstrators were assuming police would not protect them. This assumption was proven correct. Carrying a shield while attending a lawful demonstration is inherently less aggressive than showing up to disrupt it while carrying offensive weapons (for example, a flame thrower)." [35]

Lawyer Elmer Woodard also addressed the fact that Goodwin had been wearing tactical gear. "Body armor's a defensive thing. Nobody ever got beaten to death with body armor... If it's raining, you put on a raincoat. If there's fighting, you put on a helmet."

Goodwin testified that he had been fearful that he was under attack himself at the time. "To be honest, I was terrified."

"They want you to convict this man because he's a White man and DeAndre's a Black man," Woodard argued, also pointing out that Goodwin was not responsible for the most serious of Harris' injuries.

Goodwin and his mother mouthed "I love you" to each other as his guilty verdict for malicious wounding was announced in court.

---

34 Samantha Baars, "Judge takes parking under advisement in August 12 case," C-ville.com, March 28, 2018.

35 Charlottesville Survivor, "Charlottesvile vs AMREN – Anarcho-Tyranny vs Rule of Law? Guess White MSM Wants?," Vdare.com, May 3, 2018.

At his sentencing hearing, Goodwin apologized. "I'm truly, genuinely sorry. I can't even imagine the aftermath of what happened—how this has affected [Harris'] life." He was sentenced to eight years in prison for his role in the assault as his mother collapsed into sobs.[36]

Tyler Watkins Davis, a fifty-year old from Florida, also had no criminal record. His attorney argued that Davis had only struck Harris when he attempted to get up, not when he was lying on the ground. "He was responding to what he perceived to be a threat... He reacted reasonably and proportionately to what Harris had done."

During his bond hearing, "Davis' wife of 25 years, Holly, testified that her husband is a nice, honest and hardworking man who is the primary breadwinner for the family. Since his February arrest, she said, Davis has lost his job at Comcast and can no longer provide medical coverage or income for his family, including their 17-year-old son, who is on the autism spectrum."[37]

Davis struck a single blow to Harris with a stick which resulted in him needing staples in his scalp. He entered a plea and was sentenced to a little over two years in prison. Before sentencing, Davis stated to the judge, "I know [Harris] suffered... I regret ever coming to Charlottesville, and I regret my actions in the parking garage. I was... raging, barely functioning... hated life." He explained that alcoholism played a role in his having been drawn into "negative websites... By day, I was a cable tech, but by night, I was a crusading defender of my people." He said that after about a year of house arrest, he had been rehabilitated and withdrawn from the League of the South.[38]

Alex Michael Ramos from Georgia, 34, was wearing a red MAGA hat when he threw a single punch at Harris. Ramos was denied bail because he had no ties to the Charlottesville community.

---

36 Samantha Baars, "'Just evil:' Men sentenced in August 12 parking garage beating," C-ville.com, Aug. 28, 2018.

37 Lauren Berg, "Man accused of participating in Aug. 12 garage beating granted bond; charge certified to grand jury," *DailyProgress.com*, April 12, 2018.

38 Ian Shapira, "Fourth attacker sentenced in Charlottesville parking garage beating of Black man," *Washington Post*, Aug. 27, 2019.

Zarski tried to persuade a court to allow Ramos to stay in her home with her husband and five children, but the request was not granted. Ramos had celebrated his role in the brawl on social media. "We stomped some ass. Getting some was fucking fun," he posted. This apparent lack of remorse contributed to his being denied bond.

Ramos did not appear to have any family members present during his trial, though Zarski and Kessler were in attendance. He apologized for his actions at his sentencing hearing. "I made a wrong judgment call... I feel pretty bad. I kinda wish I could apologize to Mr. Harris... I am really sorry."[39]

He received a six-year prison sentence.

Zarski shares her reaction to the sentencing of the Unite the Right defendants. "The fallout has been a smack in the face as far as viewing our justice system."

Unequal Justice

Deandre Harris was eventually arrested after the man he struck with a Maglite, League of the South member Harold Crews, became weary of waiting after two months of law enforcement inaction on the matter and took the initiative to press charges. Harris was found not guilty of misdemeanor assault and battery for his role in the altercation.

Kessler wrote about what he believes was racially-motivated injustice with regards to the Harris brawl prosecutions,

> My view, having attended both trials: Goodwin and Ramos arguably did use disproportional force once Harris was on the ground, although nothing that would have attracted attention in a trailer park brawl. Nevertheless, they did not receive a fair trial, due in large part to repeated false testimony by the alleged victim Deandre Harris. This false testimony was materially significant to how seriously they should

---

39 Samantha Baars, "'Just evil:' Men sentenced in August 12 parking garage beating," C-ville.com, Aug. 28, 2018.

be charged and how much time they should serve. Additionally, they were clearly prosecuted more harshly because they were White men (Ramos is actually Puerto Rican) involved in a racially-charged incident... Harris's repeated false statements on the stand have denied these men due process. So has the Charlottesville Commonwealth Attorney's office, which reduced charges against Harris not for any legal reason, but because their Leftist sensibilities were offended that a Black man should be charged with equivalent crimes to Whites... Charlottesville prosecutors made a conscious decision to prosecute the White men more harshly than the Black man because they didn't want to be accused of "White supremacism" by their fanatical Alt-Left constituency. They sacrificed Equal Justice for Public Relations.[40]

Harris' false statements detailed by Kessler include his claim that he had been provoked by balloons full of noxious substances being thrown towards his party. His attorneys presented no evidence to support this claim, and available video footage seems to prove the opposite was true – projectiles were being thrown INTO the area occupied by the permit holders.

To further question the narrative about Harris attending the rally to protest peacefully, Kessler also notes that Harris had been wearing a surgical mask while at the rally. (Note: Unite the Right took place several years before concerns about Covid made mask-wearing an everyday activity; in fact, there were prohibitions in place against wearing masks in public at the time.) Kessler asks, "[I]f masks were so necessary because of pepper spray why were none of the lawful Unite The Right demonstrators wearing them? And isn't that a convenient excuse to legally justify the notorious Antifa tactic of wearing masks?" With regards to Harris' mask, Kessler points out that lawyers made issue of the defensive gear worn by Ramos and Goodwin in order to make inferences about their intentions.

---

40 Jason Kessler, "Charlottesville Anarcho-Tyranny Update: Goodwin, Ramos Convicted By Blatantly False Testimony—Will Appeal," Vdare.com, May 8, 2018.

"Besides the fact that many journalists and counter-demonstrators also wore goggles, helmets, etc. for their safety, it's important to note that Harris also came 'dressed for war'—but a different kind of war. Antifa don't use the same tactics as the Right. They go for guile and deception over strength. They wear masks to disguise their identities and conceal their weapons."

Harris also made a false statement about the large metal flashlight he carried around the day of Unite the Right. Kessler writes, "Ramos' attorney Jake Joyce asked Deandre how he held the mag light: gripped at the end or in the middle, etc. Whether Deandre was walking around holding the mag light like a club prior to the incident would show whether he had premeditated intent to use it as a weapon. He testified under oath that he was holding it "in the middle" (aka not as a weapon)." Kessler posted photos taken shortly before the garage brawl which seem to indicate this is not true.

Kessler reports that Harris contradicted himself during testimony about verbal taunts that took place right before the fight. "Harris, Long, Donald Blakney and a number of other Blacks, along with Antifa, followed demonstrators as they withdrew to the parking lot where their cars were, shaking clubs and other weapons at them. Deandre testified under oath that he was shouting at the White men, 'Yeeeaaah!', 'Let's f—king go, nigga!' and 'We got that flag!' Deandre only admitted to these taunts during the Goodwin trial but said, 'That wasn't me' during the Ramos trial a couple of days later."

During trial, Harris claimed that he had been surprised to see his friend Long struggling with Crews over the flag, and swung his flashlight to break up the fight. However, he admitted to shouting, "We got that flag," and it is known that Harris and Long had been stealing and burning flags throughout the day.

Harris also repeatedly stated in court that he hit Crews' flag pole, not his face. However, photo evidence show that Crews had a face injury prior to a later scuffle with a White Antifa, which Harris' team tried to blame for Crews's injuries. Also, a police officer testified in Ramos' trial that the garage altercation began when "A Caucasian man was struck and stumbled back." It is noteworthy that by the time of the Goodwin and Ramos trials, Harris had already been found legally not guilty of his own role in the events of the day, so he had no motive to lie to protect himself. Kessler concludes, "He lied to deny Goodwin and Ramos any semblance of a fair trial."

In a final and important point, Kessler explains that injustice resulted because the beating of Harris was presented as an isolated incident rather than in its full context.

> There was violence all around as part of a larger melee, not just a one-side beat down as prosecutors claim. A White man in a helmet was tackled by a Black man in a teal shirt. Black and White men were brawling all around. It was in this context that Harris was kicked, punched and clobbered with sticks which left him with a broken wrist and a gash on his head. While violence was certainly inflicted on Harris, it should have been viewed in context. He was a very serious threat. He was with a gang of Black men, all armed with weapons, shaking them at White people and shouting racial abuse. Harris' ally had been shooting a flamethrower into a crowd of Whites. Harris obviously did not object to that behavior and leave. On the contrary, he followed and participated with him in further acts of violence...

> Note also that the severe injuries which the "wounding" charge requires weren't necessarily caused by either Goodwin or Ramos... But Judge Rick Moore ruled that the "Concert of Action" clause was in effect and each man could be found guilty of the most serious crimes done by other men in the group. Clearly without Concert of Action both Goodwin and Ramos would only have been charged with misdemeanor assault.

> As I've said repeatedly, I do believe the White men committed crimes during the parking garage incident, but they are being prosecuted savagely while the Black men are under-prosecuted. Despite volumes

of evidence regarding violence by counter-protestors at Unite the Right, not a single one of them has been punished for their role in what ensued. WHY?! [41]

Kessler's Arrests

Kessler is no stranger to criminal court himself.

Kessler was convicted of assault for punching Jay Taylor while collecting petition signatures in January 2017 to remove Vice-Mayor Wes Bellamy from City Council. After pleading guilty, he was given a 30-day suspended jail sentence and 50 hours of community service. "I'll admit that what I did was not legal. I was having a bad day. I've never done anything like this before, and it will never happen again."[42]

He was charged with disorderly conduct for a clash that occurred at May 2017 protest, but the prosecutor stated that his actions amounted to protected free speech and declined to pursue the case. (A counter-protester who was part of the mob that surrounded him was found guilty of disorderly conduct and required to pay a fine. The special prosecutor remarked that Kessler had "exhibited decorum" during the conflict.)[43]

He was later charged with felony perjury for testimony during that case, which could have meant ten years in prison if he had been convicted. After the charge was dismissed, Prosecutor Robert Tracci sought to retry him for the same incident, arguing that retrying him was justified based on a procedural matter. Kessler complained to reporters that he was being subjected to double jeopardy because of a desire "to punish critics of the Charlottesville government."[44]

---

41 Ibid.

42 Justin Wm. Moyer, "Organizer of Unite the Right rally in Charlottesville arrested again," *Washington Post*, Oct. 17, 2017.

43 Samantha Baars, "Four more down: Kessler-related hearings reach verdict," C-ville.com, Feb. 2, 2018.

44 Andrew Blake, "Virginia seeks new perjury case against Jason Kessler, 'Unite the Right' organizer," *The Washington Times*, April 4, 2018.

He was arrested again after local activist Emily Gorcenski filed charges against him for online harassment, claiming he controlled an account that had tweeted out personal information about "her." As with the complaint Gorcenski filed against Christopher Cantwell after the torchlight march, the claims fell apart when subjected to scrutiny. "This is just the latest in a series of unsubstantiated political prosecutions meant to drag my name through the mud," he told reporters after the charges were dropped.[45]

45 Lisa Provence, "Kessler harassment charge dropped," C-ville.com, Jan. 22, 2018.

CHAPTER 20 QUICK LINKS:

Charlottesville Drone Footage, URL: qrs.ly/96cwsuo

"Dissident Mama, episode 27 – Jason Kessler," Jan. 22, 2021. URL: qrs.ly/cycvto9

Vice News, "Charlottesville: Race and Terror," video, Aug. 14, 2017. URL: qrs.ly/sacvtjp

TODAY, "White Nationalist Facing Felony Charges over Charlottesville violence," video, Aug. 23, 2017. URL: qrs.ly/r9cvtpd

Heaphy Report. URL: qrs.ly/dpcvtcb

News2Share, "Jason Kessler's Full Speech at 'Unite the Right 2,'" video, Aug. 13, 2018. URL: qrs.ly/chcvtpq

CHAPTER 21

JAMES ALEX FIELDS, JR.

*"There's video of him running
his car into the crowd."*

After The Crash

JAMES FIELDS' MOTHER, Samantha Bloom, learned of the fatal crash for which her son was ultimately convicted from a group of AP reporters who approached her while she was outside her Maumee, Ohio apartment. A video released by the AP captured the encounter with Bloom, an attractive, petite, middle-aged woman in a wheelchair, as she returned from dinner the evening of Saturday August 12th. The reporter explained to Bloom that her son was suspected of being responsible for the fatal accident. "He is currently just accused of running into the crowd in Charlottesville as part of the Alt-Right march that was happening there. I don't know if you've heard about this?"

Bloom inquired, "I thought it was Virginia or something, right?"

"Yeah, Charlottesville Virginia," replied the reporter.

Looking intently towards the reporter, Bloom made a face and shook her head as if confused. She then leaned forward with interest as he explained, "Again, right now he's just accused, but there's video of him running his car into the crowd."

Bloom's eyes briefly popped wide with shock, then she furrowed her brows, carefully enunciating the reporter's words back to him as if to clarify. "Running his car into a crowd? Of people? Did it hurt anybody?"

"Yeah, there's one fatality," responded the reporter, "And I'd say twenty or more people have been injured."

Another reporter asked with surprise, "You haven't been notified at all about this?"

"No," replied Bloom.

"So this is the first you're learning of it?" he asked. Bloom appeared to be absorbing the shock of the terrible news. She quietly nodded her head.

The reporter reacted to her change in emotion. "I'm so sorry," he said. Bloom began to turn her chair away as if to leave.

"Was there any indication that this might be where he was going?" pressed the reporter.

Bloom sounded uncertain and spoke less confidently than before. "I just knew he was going to a rally. I try to stay out of his political views." She laughed nervously. "We don't, um, you know, I don't really get too involved. He moved out to his own apartment. I'm watching his cat... Like I said I don't really talk to him about his, you know, political views. I mean, So I don't really understand what the rally was about or anything, so..." She shook her head. "I just know there was, he did mention Al Bright? Albright? What is it?"

The reporter suggested, "Alt-Right?"

"Albright?" asked Bloom.

"Alt-Right," the reporter explained. "It's like alternative right. It's the ultraconservative, White supremacist organizations."

Bloom looked puzzled. "I didn't know it was White Supremacist. I thought that it had something to do with Trump. Trump's not a supremacist." She also seemed bewildered that they considered her son to be a White supremacist. "I mean, he had an African American friend. I mean, so..." She laughed nervously.

The reporter inferred, "So this is surprising to you then?"

Bloom replied, "Yeah, that he would run his car into a group of people who were... I'm really not clear on?"

Police would later arrive to block reporters and other non-resident traffic from driving into Bloom's apartment complex. Local law enforcement had no record of interactions with Fields other than having issued him a citation earlier in the year for driving with expired plates. Shortly thereafter, Bloom would be interviewed by the FBI, who had taken over the case from local authorities.

Early Life

Fields was born on April 26, 1997, in Kenton, Kentucky, to Samantha Lea Bloom. James Alex Fields' father died before he was born. Jay Fields, who had worked as a bouncer, was killed in December 1996 in a drunk driving accident. The other occupants of the crashed vehicle left the senior Fields for dead, and were found later that evening in a bar. The car's driver, David Landsdale, was charged with murder.

Fields was described as quiet and kept to himself as a child and teenager. Some of Bloom's struggles with her son were serious enough that she had filed reports with the police. "Florence Police Department records show Samantha Bloom, Mr. Fields' wheelchair-bound mother, told police in 2011 that her son threatened her by standing behind her wielding a 12-inch knife. In another incident in 2010, Ms. Bloom said her son smacked her in the head and locked her in the bathroom after she told him to stop playing video games. Ms. Bloom told officers that Mr. Fields was on medication to control his temper."[1]

---

1 Andrea Noble, "Man accused of ramming car into Charlottesville protesters held without bond," *Washington Times*, Aug. 14, 2017.

A friend and former neighbor said of Bloom, "She had struggled with him during his teen years but he came around towards the end of school... She was always trying to do the best for her son." [2]

After news of the Charlottesville crash was known, former classmates and teachers shared their impressions of Fields. One high school teacher, Derek Weimer, remembered from conversations with Fields that he was interested in military history, and Nazi Germany in particular. "A lot of boys get interested in the Germans and Nazis because they're interested in World War II, but James took it to another level," adding that Fields was "a very bright kid but very misguided and disillusioned."[3] According to Weimer, "Once you talked to James for a while, you would start to see that sympathy toward Nazism, that idolization of Hitler, that belief in White supremacy... It would start to creep out." Weimer said that Fields had also confided to him that he had been diagnosed with schizophrenia and had been prescribed psychiatric medication.[4] (At a hearing after his conviction in 2019, Fields would tell a judge that he had been treated for mental health issues since he was six years old and that he was on medication for bipolar disorder, depression, anxiety, schizoid disorder, explosive onset disorder and ADHD.[5])

One classmate described Fields as "just a normal dude" who made dark jokes sometimes. "He had friends, he had people who would chat with him, it wasn't like he was an outcast." The classmate recalled that during a class trip to Europe, Fields referred to Germany as "the Fatherland."[6] Another classmate had a very

---

2 Jonah Engel Bromwich and Alan Blinder, "What We Know About James Alex Fields, Driver Charged in Charlottesville Killing," New York Times, Aug. 13, 2017.

3 Alan Blinder, "Suspect in Charlottesville Attack Had Displayed Troubling Behavior," New York Times, Aug. 13, 2017.

4 "Classmate: Fields referred to Germany as 'the Fatherland,'" AP, Aug. 14, 2017.

5 Denise Lavoie, "Guilty plea to hate crimes in deadly car attack at rally," AP, March 27, 2019.

6 "Classmate: Fields referred to Germany as 'the Fatherland,'" AP, Aug. 14, 2017.

different memory of Fields. "On many occasions there were times he would scream obscenities, whether it be about Hitler or racial slurs... [He was] exceptionally odd and an outcast to be sure." [7]

Fields entered the Army on Aug. 18, 2015, but was released a few months later for failing to meet training standards. At the time of the crash, he was making a modest salary working for a security company. Fields asked for a public defender for his trial, but the Public Defender's office reported to the judge that a relative of someone who worked there had been injured in the crash, so the judge instead appointed local attorney Charles Weber.[8] Weber was soon removed due to conflict of interest when it was revealed that he was a plaintiff in a case against the city about the removal of the Robert E. Lee statue. Denise Lunsford was then appointed to represent Fields.[9] Running as a Democrat, Lunsford had been elected to serve as Albemarle County Commonwealth's Attorney in 2007 and served until 2015.

Fields had been photographed during Unite the Right amongst a group of men wearing white polos and carrying a shield bearing the emblem of nationalist group Vanguard America. The day of Unite the Right, after the photos had spread on social media, Vanguard America released a statement: "The driver of the vehicle that hit counter-protesters today was, in no way, a member of Vanguard America. All our members had been safely evacuated by the time of the incident. The shields seen do not denote membership, nor does the white shirt. The shirts were freely handed out to anyone in attendance."

The following Monday, August 14, 2017, dozens of reporters and other onlookers milled about the street outside the General District Court where bond hearings for Fields and other Unite the Right arrestees were taking place. Matt Heimbach of the Traditionalist Workers' Party took the opportunity to make a statement about the events of the weekend. Standing in the street outside the court

7   Alan Blinder, "Suspect Had Displayed Troubling Behavior."

8   "Classmate: Fields referred to Germany as 'the Fatherland,'" AP, Aug. 14, 2017.

9   "Former Albemarle prosecutor Lunsford appointed to Fields case," Charlottesville Daily Progress, Aug. 16, 2017.

house, he began to speak. "The blood is on Wes Bellamy's hands. This is on Charlottesville, the police department." As he spoke, dozens of reporters and onlookers encircled him. Some hecklers began to shout. He continued, "We had a permit for this event. We had every right to be here. The police department did absolutely nothing to enforce a legal permit. We defended ourselves. We brought helmets and shields, while the Antifa improvised flamethrowers, while they brought bleach, while they brought paint, while they brought sticks and they brought knives."

Attempting to be heard over the jeering crowd, Heimbach spoke with even more force as he continued. "The nationalist community defended ourselves against thugs in a battle that was brought by this city that wanted a blood bath. The police were given a stand-down order as we were trying to exercise our legal, constitutional right to have a permit. This is on the hands of the city government, on the police, and the radical left."

A reporter asked, "Is there any accountability for you?"

"Not at all," Heimbach declared. "These radical leftists are the ones who brought violence. They are the ones that were preparing for violence. They said in their chants, 'Kill the Nazis. Kill the fascists.' They came prepared for war. They're the ones that tried to kill us. What happened was an attack on the nationalist community here. Also on reporters, as you are lying. As the media is lying about what happened. The media were attacked."

One woman had been repeatedly shouting "Asshole!" at Heimbach as he spoke, while flipping him off with both hands. She began to chant, "Nazi, go home!" She repeated the chant while following Heimbach as he walked away. A growing crowd joined in following and robotically chanting, "Nazis go home! Nazis go home! Nazis go home! Nazis go home!" A small group of police officers held them back as Heimbach was escorted away to safety.

An activist named Heather Cronk took the same opportunity to address the gathering of reporters outside the court house. Her voice shaking, she delivered a delusional screed about the supposed evil intentions of Unite the Right participants and suggested that their actions were being directed by President Trump. "These guys are not amateurs. They are professional hit men who are out to murder people of color, Jewish folks, LGBTQ folks. This isn't a one-time story. They are coming back to Charlottesville. They've already filed for a permit in Richmond. This is going to keep continuing until folks intercede. This is the moment for folks across the country to look at what's happening in Charlottesville as something that could happen in your community. The folks of Charlottesville are rising up in opposition to Nazis and White Supremacists and White Nationalists who are coming into this community for fueling hatred and violence and who are getting their instructions from folks who live and work inside the White House."[10]

Fields, who had no ties to Charlottesville, was denied bond. Fields was assaulted in jail while awaiting trial by a man named Timothy Ray Brown, Jr., who was reportedly in the crowd near Heyer when Fields' car plunged into it. Fields did not suffer any severe injuries from this assault.[11]

The Trial

Long before Fields set foot in a courtroom, he had essentially been convicted for the death of Heather Heyer.

On August 14, two days after Unite the Right, President Donald Trump spoke as though it was a given that Fields' actions behind the wheel were intentional and malicious, and labeled him a murderer. "Well, I think the driver of the car is a disgrace to himself, his family, and this country. And that is — you can call it terrorism. You can call it murder. You can call it whatever you want... The driver of the car is a murderer. And what he did was a horrible, horrible, inexcusable thing."

A month later, he was declared to be a domestic terrorist by the US Senate. On September 17, 2017 the US Senate passed a resolution "condemning the violence and domestic terrorist attack that took place during events between August 11 and August 12,

---

10 Ruptly, "USA: Charlottesville violence an 'attack on nationalist community' - far right leader," YouTube Video posted Aug. 14, 2017.

11 "Officials say Charlottesville suspect assaulted in jail," AP, Oct. 26, 2018.

2017, in Charlottesville, Virginia... rejecting White nationalists, White supremacists, the Ku Klux Klan, neo-Nazis, and other hate groups..."[12] (It is also worth noting that the Senate only condemned right-wing groups associated with Unite the Right, and not any of the many violent, racially antagonistic counter-protest groups like Antifa or Black Lives Matter).

What happened to the presumption of innocence? ("Waiting for facts is now the 'Nazi' position," quipped Ann Coulter.[13]) Fields was convicted (formally and informally) by the highest-level national office holders, and his jury pool was inundated for over a year with coverage by a hostile media. Is there any chance Fields could have received a fair trial?

Opening statements for Fields' formal trial took place on November 29, 2018 in the United States District Court for the Western District of Virginia, before Chief Judge Michael F. Urbanski.

There was no dispute at trial about whether Fields had driven his car into the crowd of protesters. At issue was whether the crash was intentional and malicious, or a fearful reaction to a high-stress situation. The prosecution made the claim that Fields was angry when he drove his car into the crowd, presenting as evidence the fact that he had twice posted a meme on his Instagram account depicting a car running into a crowd of protesters. They claimed he had come to Charlottesville with the intention of acting on his rage. The defense offered testimony from other rally attendees whom Fields had assisted by driving them to their cars after the dispersal order. They claimed that he seemed calm at the time. The prosecution painted a picture of the post-dispersal streets as benign, presenting police officers that said the counter-protesters seemed "joyful." By contrast, the defense emphasized the violent clashes between protesters and counter protesters in the hours and moments before the crash.

---

12 "S.J.Res.49," Congress.gov, https://www.congress.gov/bill/115th-congress/senate-joint-resolution/49.

13 Ann Coulter, "When Liberals Club People, It's With Love In Their Hearts," Ann Coulter.com, Aug. 16, 2017.

One rally attendee who observed the trial reacted to the description of the counter-protesters. "What was truly striking were the outright lies told in the courtroom. The crowd of leftist protesters was described as 'joyful' - astonishing given that even leftist journalists were being attacked by Antifa that day. But I was there. I saw the hate in the crowds. I narrowly escaped physical harm at several points... I find it nothing less than horrifying to see how casually people go along with what they know to be a lie... Video shows other cars being set upon by protesters. Yet somehow the myth of a peaceful crowd was still allowed to stand."[14]

Police body camera footage shown during the trial shows Fields' reaction to the crash. When an officer apprehended him about a mile away, he said he was sorry. "I didn't want to hurt people... I thought they were attacking me." He reportedly sobbed and hyperventilated when he learned during an interrogation that he'd killed someone.

Despite initially seeming remorseful, a recording of a jailhouse phone call with his mother that was played during the trial revealed a harsher attitude. He referred to the counter-protesters as "a violent group of terrorists," and the mother of the woman who was killed as "one of those anti-White communists."

"She lost her daughter," Fields' mother replied.

"It doesn't fucking matter," Fields said. "She's a communist."

"Stop talking like that," Bloom said.

"It isn't up for questioning," Fields said. "She's the enemy, Mother."[15]

What do we really know about Heyer?

Heather Danielle Heyer, the daughter of Mark Heyer and Susan Bro, grew up in Ruckersville, Virginia. The high school graduate had previously been a waitress and bartender. She was working as a paralegal in the bankruptcy division at the Miller Law Group in Charlottesville at the time of her death at age 32.

---

14 Charlottesville Survivor, "Unequal Justice in Fields' Charlottesville Trial – And Increasingly Throughout the Left's America," Vdare.com, Dec. 14, 2018.

15 Tess Owen, "James Fields told his mom it "doesn't fucking matter" Heather Heyer died in Charlottesville," Vice, Dec. 5, 2018.

The crash victim has been beatified in the national media. Heyer's mother, Susan Bro, has created a foundation in her name. The foundation's site describes Heyer as "a young woman with a big heart and a passion for equity for all individuals regardless of race, ethnicity, religion, gender identity or preference... Heather was a young woman deeply involved in taking a stand against injustice." Bro, who is venerated as "one of the revered survivors of the trauma still shrouding the city,"[16] frequently speaks about the dangers of White supremacy and carrying on Heyer's work on issues of racial equity.

Just a few days after the crash, Bro visited the site of Heyer's death. In a statement that contributed to public confusion about the fatality, a tearful Bro told reporters that Heyer had died of a heart attack. "She died pretty instantly. She didn't suffer. She, um, died of a heart attack right away at the scene. They revived her briefly and then- not consciously, just got her heart beating again - and then her heart just stopped. So I don't feel like she suffered. That's been a blessing."[17] Bro's statement attributing Heyer's death to a heart attack caused some to speculate that Heyer was not killed by the car crash at all. Theories swirled that Heyer, a 4-foot, 11-inch-tall, 330-pound, smoker who had been walking around for hours in intense summer heat, died of natural causes which were merely exacerbated by the stress of being at the crash scene. However, the cause of death was ruled by medical examiners to be "blunt force injury."[18]

Most are reluctant to speak ill of the dead, and the tendency to view a deceased person as a martyr or saint is natural and understandable. I have no wish to be disrespectful or cause pain to anyone who has suffered loss. However, Unite the Right is a significant historic event with a lingering impact on the nation, and it is important that the

---

16 Mike Valerio, "Heather Heyer's mom says move past her daughter's death, focus on the work left after Charlottesville," wUSA9.com, Aug. 11, 2020.

17 "Heather Heyer's Mother's Warns White Nationalists: Karma is a 'You Know What,'" NBC News, Aug 19, 2017.

18 Daily Progress Staff, "Heather Heyer's cause of death ruled as blunt force injury," Charlottesville ; Daily Progress, Oct 17, 2017.

facts from all sources be fully considered. Below, witness testimony from multiple sources is presented so that the reader may draw their own conclusions about what really happened.

Below is a portion of the Heaphy Report detailing a conflict between some militia members and a group of counter-protesters that occurred shortly before the car crash. The investigation confirms militia members were attempting to leave, and being pursued and assaulted by counter-protesters, who sometimes attacked their cars. (*Note:* Several patriot groups and militias attended Unite the Right in a neutral peacekeeping capacity. Their members - mostly White, and wearing clothing and symbols associated with traditional America and conservative beliefs - were frequently mistaken by counter-protesters for Alt-Right rally attendees. My emphasis below.)

Incidents south of the mall occurred as counter-protesters pursued members of the militia that were parked along Water Street. Video posted to social media shows one militia group called American Revolutionary Warrior gathering at 1st and Water Streets after passing by the VSP mobile field force lines across the mall. The militia group then patrolled west along Water Street to "locate individuals being infringed upon" to protect their rights. They circled back east by the Omni Hotel, crossed the Downtown Mall at Old Preston Avenue, and walked through a parking lot to arrive back on Market Street. They walked east, where they passed by a large group of counter-protesters who had gathered at the southeast corner of McGuffey Park, near 2nd Street NE and Market Street.

The militia group approached the CPD mobile field force line that was stationed at 2nd Street NW and Market Street, preventing pedestrian access to Emancipation Park. They spoke with Lieutenant Hatter, who advised them that everyone was remaining calm at that time and they did not want any more altercations. Lieutenant O'Donnell told us that Christian Yingling, the commander of the Pennsylvania Lightfoot Militia, was with the militia group that approached the CPD field force line. He told Yingling that the militia's presence was a "lightning rod" and encouraged them to leave. The militia group complied and walked back toward the Downtown Mall.

After their encounter with CPD, the militia group decided to leave the area. They walked across Water Street and entered the surface lot near 1st Street SE. **As the militia members attempted to enter their vehicles, a group of counter-protesters followed and yelled at them.** CPD received word of a disorder in the area, so United Command deployed the combined CPD/VSP field force units that had taken up a position in the alley near the police station.

After one militia member experienced difficulty getting into his car and exiting the lot, the other members opted not to get in their vehicles. Instead, they continued to walk east, away from the crowd of counter-protesters. When they reached the intersection of South Street and 2nd Street SE, they turned right, moving across the train tracks. **The counter-protesters followed. By that time, the police field forces had started to arrive along Water Street, but they chose not to follow.** Lieutenant Gore later explained in his after-action report that he did not want to chase the angry groups farther away from law enforcement units on the mall that could provide backup.

Witness Richard Goodin followed the group of counter-protesters that pursued the militia to Garrett Street. He told us that **he saw young men picking up and throwing rocks at the militia** as they crossed the railroad tracks near Garrett Street. Video provided to us confirms the rock-throwing, as does the open source video showing the militia's perspective. When one of the militia members was hit in the head with a rock, they took up a position along the wall near the Sultan Kebab restaurant at the corner of Garrett and 2nd Street SE. **The militia members apparently did not realize that they had stopped directly across the street from Friendship Court, a predominantly African-American public housing complex.** Mr. Goodin told us that the counter-protesters continued to yell at the militia to leave, to which the militia members responded that they were not being allowed to leave. Someone approached the police and advised them that someone was injured. As the CPD forces started to move towards the crowd, it dissipated, and the militia members made their way back towards the parking lot on Water Street.

At 1:05 p.m., CPD requested medics to respond to the Water Street parking lot. In addition to the militia member who had been hit by a rock, a woman apparently tripped and hit her head on the ground. The combined field forces formed a semicircular wall to separate the militia on one side from the counter-protesters on the other. Street medics cared for the woman who hit her head until the ambulance arrived. At that point, the field force escorted the militia to the western lot on Water Street. The ambulance left, and the police departed and headed towards City Space to hydrate. **The militia got in their cars and prepared to leave the area. Aerial footage shows that one of their cars accelerated to flee the counter-protesters, nearly running one of them over. The crowd of counter-protesters reacted angrily, kicking and swinging objects at the car. The car sped around South Street, then 2nd Street, then west on Water Street, with counter-protesters chasing on foot.**

Unbeknownst to the police, the counter-protesters who had followed the militia across the parking lot believed that they were intentionally headed towards Friendship Court to harass residents. The call went out through their communications channels that Friendship Court was under attack. Large groups at Justice and McGuffey Parks began to mobilize.

VSP helicopter footage shows a group of more than 100 counter-protesters leaving Justice Park around 1:20 p.m., walking south on 4th Street. **As they passed through the intersection at Market Street, there was no officer present and they passed the small plastic sawhorse that stood to prevent southbound traffic.** They crossed the Downtown Mall and Water Street, went under the railroad tracks, then arrived at Garrett Street. Dan Haig, who was with the group from Justice Park, told us that when they arrived someone from the community ran out to tell them that everything was safe and they should stop shouting. The group stopped for a moment to regroup. At 1:30 p.m., the group continued west down Garrett Street, then turned right on 2nd Street SE and moved back towards Water Street.[19]

The above scenario overlaps with information compiled about Heyer's last moments. Brad Griffin, who writes under the name Hunter Wallace at his website Occidental Dissent, combed through an enormous amount of video from Unite the Right in order to collect documentation of Heather Heyer's actions shortly before the infamous car crash. Heyer appears sporadically on camera throughout the lengthy footage, with her hair pulled back tightly into a braid and wearing black from head to toe, consistent with the black bloc style often employed by left-wing protesters. Wikipedia explains, "A black bloc is a tactic used by protesters who wear black clothing, ski masks, scarves, sunglasses, motorcycle helmets with padding, or other face-concealing and face-protecting

---

19 Heaphy Report, pp. 140-141.

items. The clothing is used to conceal wearers' identities and hinder criminal prosecution by making it difficult to distinguish between participants...The tactic allows the group to appear as one large unified mass. black bloc participants are often associated with anarchism, anarcho-communism, communism, libertarian socialism, antifascism, or the anti-globalization movement."

Much of Wallace's information comes from cell phone video taken by Courtney Commander, a friend of Heather Heyer. Commander had taken video at the KKK rally in July, and at the previous night's torchlight parade, during which she confronted police officers for their inaction. "Are you guys going to wind up doing something about this?" she asked. "I'm really not trying to criticize you, but are we allowed to have torches out here?" Reportedly Heyer was not planning to protest Unite the Right because she feared it would be too dangerous, but she became determined to do so after viewing Commander's video of the August 11th torchlight parade.[20]

The following comments are compiled from descriptions of videos shared on Griffin's website. My emphasis below:

> [Heyer] arrived with Courtney Commander, Marcus Martin and Marissa Blair after UTR had been cancelled shortly before 1 PM. This is about 1 hour and 30 minutes into the 'state of emergency.' They start out in a parking lot across from the South Street Brewery. People are leaving the area. The crowd is taunting them. The Patriot group American Warrior Revolution is there. Courtney Commander argues with them without realizing they are a neutral party. Courtney Commander says on video that people are complaining about their cars being blocked. They're trying to go home. She doesn't "believe that bullshit" though. **The riot police are standing around in the parking lot doing nothing. BLM agitators are ranting and raving.** Heather Heyer seen at 1:59:30 in

---

20 McAuliffe, *Beyond Charlottesville*, p. 81.

the Ruptly livestream. After walking away from the parking lot, Courtney Commander says **"this is really about to get dangerous."**

At this point, Courtney Commander, Heather Heyer, Marcus Martin and Marissa Blair leave the parking lot across from the South Street Brewery. They follow the mob that is chasing a group of Patriots. Faith Goldy and Ruptly also follow the mob who pin the Patriots behind the Sultan Kebab at the corner of Garrett and 2nd St. SE. The crowd is extremely hostile. They find a mob haranguing a Patriot group. Scream "go home mother****ers." Heather Heyer is with them. The trapped Patriot group being taunted by Commander and Heyer was American Warrior Revolution. I recognize Ace Baker. The mob is screaming at American Warrior Revolution and throwing rocks at them. This is also captured in the Ruptly Livestream between 2:00:00 and 2:10:00. Parading through the street with Heyer, Commander says **"this is really, really dangerous."**

Heather Heyer is captured on the Courtney Commander videos. This is when the mob is chasing American Warrior Revolution back to the parking lot across from the South Street Brewery. Faith Goldy and Ruptly are in front of them filming the entire incident... The Virginia State Police separate the two groups.

Courtney Commander is standing with Black Lives Matter and can be seen in the crowd from Faith Goldy's perspective. They're pursuing and haranguing a Patriot group. Cops are standing around doing nothing. Faith Goldy is in front of them. Courtney Commander is wearing the red backpack. Commander is heard saying, "F*** that White bitch." Presumably, the "White bitch" here is either Faith Goldy or one of the women with American Warrior Revolution. There are no other options.

In the Ruptly Livestream, **the mob in the parking lot across from the South Street Brewery chase down and try to attack cars leaving the area. Between 9:24 and 12:00 in this video, you can see the mob attacking the cars leaving the parking lot across from the South Street Brewery.** They return to the parking lot across from South Street Brewery. The riot police are there with the shields. [The protesters are] not told go home. "That man himself looks like he is half Black. He's out here with the Alt-Right." This is one of the Patriots.

Heather Heyer has been relatively quiet during all of this, but the Black Lives Matter mob she is traveling with is extremely hostile. There is a moment when Heather engages a woman in red helmet in a brief conversation. The woman tells her that she doesn't have an argument. Heather is talking to some young woman in a helmet who is either Alt-Right or a Patriot. Likely the latter. Heather pulls out the Newports.

Courtney Commander, Faith Goldy and Ruptly are all following the mob. It leaves the parking lot across from the South Street Brewery. Commander is excited because "dem n****s are goin to Garrett" because "there's about to be a war." For the record, this is Corey Long and friends who are responsible for the flamethrower incident, the parking garage incident, another exchange in the South Street Brewery parking lot and attacking American Warrior Revolution with rocks.

Basically, Commander and Heather Heyer go from place to place looking for trouble during the "state of emergency."

In the course of the next 15 minutes, they meet up with the Antifa mob parading down Water Street. This is the end when [Heyer] turns down Fourth Street with Marissa Blair, Marcus Martin and Courtney Commander. They had been parading through traffic for an hour looking for trouble when this happened. Commander even said several times that what they were doing was "really, really dangerous." It was also foolish and illegal and **the Charlottesville Police, Virginia State Police and National Guard made no effort to deter them** even though under their orders they were supposed to be "providing for the safe movement of traffic and pedestrians." They were incapable of even closing the intersection of Fourth Street and Market Street which was supposed to be closed until 7 PM.

In the final video, Courtney Commander is with the mob screaming "Whose Streets, Our Streets" as they pass parked Charlottesville Police patrol cars. She screams and says "it feels like a revolution" and "this shit feels unbelievable" and "it feels like a nightmare, yo." The mob is chanting "anti anti Antifa-ista." Three minutes before the car crash, Commander says, "this is so liberating." She screams in joy while chanting "No Nazis, No KKK, No Fascist USA." The mob is having a great time screaming "Whose Streets, Our Streets" and "Black Lives Matter." Finally, we hear "Go Left, Go Left." BOOM.

This is the best frame we have of the wreck. Heather tumbles to the ground on the right side of the Challenger while another dude takes the direct hit. It is possible her legs could have been scraped or injured, but she is blown to the side of the street like everyone else. Heather Is Given CPR. RIP Heather Heyer.

There are plenty of gaps left to be filled in this timeline. I'm confident Heather Heyer, Commander, Blair and Martin were captured on video in the vicinity of Garrett Street and Water Street. The reckless actions of this group who were seeking out conflict really comes across in the full timeline. They knew that what they were doing was "really, really dangerous" and did it anyway.[21]

Eyewitness testimony has accounted for one of the gaps in the timeline. The witness in this case, Enrique Tarrio, is a controversial figure who draws criticism from the political right and left. Condemned by the left as the leader of an SPLC- designated "hate group" the Proud Boys, Tarrio became an object of suspicion to many on the right as well when he was identified in January 2021 as a "prolific federal informant" who had, after a felony conviction for fraud in 2013, assisted law enforcement by providing "substantial assistance" in securing the prosecution of 13 others in exchange for a reduced sentence for himself.[22]

As Tarrio was leaving Unite the Right with a small group of friends, they were surrounded by a group of what he took to be BLM counter-protesters. He and his party surrounded his friend's new car as he drove through the parking area to protect it from the menacing crowd. Though he was not filming at the time, ("I was trying not to get fucking mobbed," he explains), Tarrio, who is Afro-Cuban, discloses that a White female counter-protester wearing all black, called him a "nigger" and a "coon." Tarrio and his friends walked the car away from the mob and drove away. A few months later, while doing research about Unite the Right, Tarrio says he found a video from the YouTube channel of Courtney Commander and recognized the woman who had hurled slurs at him. He says it was Heather Heyer.

---

21 Hunter Wallace, "Charlottesville: Reconstructing Heather Heyer's Movements," Occidental Dissent, Sept. 7, 2017.

22 Aram Roston, " Exclusive: Proud Boys leader was 'prolific' informer for law enforcement," Reuters, January 27, 2021.

Preventable Chaos

It is important to ask why droves of protesters were out marching when James Fields turned down Market Street. Hunter Wallace writes,

> The #UniteTheRight protesters had come from all over the United States to participate in a legally permitted rally in Lee Park. After the "unlawful assembly" and "state of emergency" was declared though after 11:06 AM, we were ordered to disperse or be arrested... Antifa were still parading through the streets of Charlottesville nearly three hours into the "state of emergency." The car crash happened around 1:46 PM by which time there should have been no unlawful assemblies in Charlottesville... The Charlottesville Police should have told Heather Heyer to disperse and go home. There has to be a reason why they didn't do this and why a state of anarchy still existed in the streets of Charlottesville nearly three hours into the "state of emergency."[23]

It is clear to anyone who examines the video closely and with an honest eye that the media has whitewashed the reality of the counter-protesters' mob with their descriptions of peaceful, happy, and loving anti-racists. Members of Heyer's entourage willingly entered and participated in what they knew to be a hostile and potentially violent situation. Flagrantly disregarding the state of emergency that had been declared, they marched through the streets in eager pursuit of conflict with their enemies. Do those who chose to break the law and inflame a combative situation, and the authorities who allowed them to do so, not bear at least some responsibility for their role in the tragic turn of events?

---

23   Hunter Wallace, "Heather Heyer Was Allowed To Commit Crimes," Occidental Dissent, Sept. 6, 2017.

Mitigating Factors

Evidence unheard by most of the public suggests that Fields did not have malicious intentions when he drove his car into the crowd, but was rather afraid for his life. For example, Fields had programmed his home address into his GPS moments before the crash, but found each of its suggested routes impassable in the chaotic aftermath of the rally dispersal. Furthermore, there is clear evidence that Fields was threatened with a firearm mere moments before the crash.

The person wielding the firearm at issue was UNC cultural anthropology professor and Redneck Revolt leader Dwayne Dixon. The mainstream press often uses the benign label "anti-racist activist" to describe Dixon, a descriptor which belies the extreme nature of his affiliations and activities. Antifa reporter Andy Ngo paints a more menacing portrait of Dixon's militia. "Redneck Revolt is an Antifa militia-style group that is closely linked with its Pacific Northwest offshoot, the John Brown Gun Club... Its members wear military-style gear and open-carry pistols and semiautomatic rifles. They're unapologetic about intimidating opponents. They call themselves anti-fascist, anti-capitalist, anti-nation-state, and pro-gun. They see themselves as revolutionaries. In other words, they are armed Antifa who have the training to kill."[24]

In the wake of Unite the Right, Dixon posted a picture of his rifle to Facebook with the text, "I take a perverse pleasure in having carried this Spike's lower in the defense of Justice Park on August 12th. I used this rifle to chase off James Fields from our block of 4th Street before he attacked the marchers to the south. Spike's needs a good lesson in ethics and Antifascism."[25] Dixon would later describe these actions publicly at a seminar. "So James Fields, driving his Charger, slow-rolled our western perimeters. So that was Fourth

---

24 Ngo, *Unmasked*, p. 165.

25 Gregory Conte, "Today's Testimony of Military Rifle Toting Antifa Enforcer Dwayne Dixon Should Gravely Damage Charlottesville Prosecution," UnzReview.com, Dec. 6, 2018.

Street. Several times. One time he paused right in front of me. And I waved him off with my rifle. At his last pass he accelerated a block away and he killed Heather."[26]

Dixon clearly does not shy away from violence. At another public event, Dixon elaborated on his activities at Unite the Right, and alluded to physical altercations in which he was involved. "Like, let's ask the people who were rescued by people like me, others, all of us, fighting, like physically fighting, kicking, striking, bloodying, cracking heads, I mean, bloody ugly things that I would never wish. But I'm not, I just, I can't... We need people who have this moral clarity and this determination to preserve that..." [27]

With these facts in mind, is it possible, or even likely, that Dixon intimidated Fields, and contributed to a fearful state of mind for him in the moments before the car crash?

Gregory Conte, a Unite the Right attendee and attorney who was present in the courtroom during Fields' trial, described Dixon's testimony:

> The defense called Dwayne Dixon, an "anti-racist activist," to testify about his actions that day, and about a Facebook post, in which Dixon claimed that he had used an AR-15 rifle 'to chase off James fields from our block... before he attacked the marchers.'
>
> Dixon said that he came to Charlottesville with 18-19 members of the leftist militia group Redneck Revolt 'to join others to protest against White supremacy and fascism.' According to Dixon, between 12:40 PM and 1:15 PM, he saw a "silver muscle car with tinted windows" pass his location multiple times before it crashed into a crowd two to three blocks south of him at 1:42 PM.

---

26 "WATCH — Leftist Professor Dwayne Dixon Brags To Class: I Waved A Rifle at Charlottesville Driver Before Crash," BigLeaguePolitics.com, March 6, 2018.

27 Jason Kessler, "Dwayne Dixon Describes 'Kicking, Punching, Cracking Heads' of Unite the Right Protesters," BitChute video posted Feb. 21, 2021.

He also testified that he brought two magazines, but that he kept his rifle slung across his chest. When Fields' car passed, shouted 'Get the fuck out of here.' He also said he saw a number of vehicles with "White nationalist insignia," but that Fields' Challenger did not have any such markings.

Dixon is a key piece of the defense's case. They must argue that Fields had no other route out of Charlottesville than to go through the Antifa mob that was moving toward him, and that Dixon was instrumental in preventing him from his only other course of action.

Another key defense witness, Philip Depue, testified yesterday. Depue, a digital forensic scientist said that, based on his analysis of data extracted from Fields' phone, Fields had entered his Ohio hometown into Google Maps less than three minutes before the crash. The app presented Fields with two routes out of town, neither of which included heading south on 4th street, the route he would eventually take.

The app suggested that Fields continue west on E. Market Street or turn around and head east. However, the first route would mean making an illegal u-turn and heading back into an area where Dixon had been loitering. The second route was likely obstructed by a roadblock, as can be seen from police helicopter footage from approximately 15 minutes before Fields came to the intersection.

Fields' only other options would have been to make an illegal right turn, going the wrong way up the one-way 4th street, or turn left onto 4th street. Fields made the left, and was faced with a crowd of hundreds marching toward him. At that point he backed up and, according to Depue's testimony, checked Google maps again.

Trapped, he attempted to drive through the crowd at 17 miles per hour. But when he came within meters of the crowd's main body, his car was hit hard by two people with sticks.

He then accelerated, and hit Heyer at 23 mph, while simultaneously hitting a stopped car in front of him. He then switched into reverse, and several of the crowd attacked the back of his car with sticks and bats. He reversed a block and a half and fled.[28]

Attorney Nicholas Stix has examined the facts of the case, and believes Fields' legal defense was inadequate. He wrote after Fields' conviction: "I don't believe James Alex Fields Jr., 22, got justice from the U.S. court system, and I certainly don't expect he will get mercy. And I further believe that, to a considerable extent, this is the fault of his court-appointed defense attorneys, Denise Lunsford and John Hill."

Stix explains (my emphasis below):

Fields is a victim of a totalitarian campaign uniting a nationwide terrorist organization called Antifa and complicit prosecutors and judges, aided and abetted by Establishment "conservatives." Unite the Right was one of the few groups willing to fight said campaign.

The heart of the defense case: Fields had been "frightened" when he drove into the crowd—and, based on the reports I read, little more. The defense simply stipulated to the prosecution's facts. But it should have questioned or objected to every comma, period, and quotation mark.

(Many of Fields' online defenders have cited the attack on him by racist, Black, aluminum baseball-bat-wielding thugs, who destroyed his Dodge Challenger. Said defense is, however, seemingly specious, as they only attacked Fields after he had

---

28 Gregory Conte, "Today's Testimony" Unz Review.

plowed into them. If he had attacked them, they were only engaged in self-defense—or vengeance. However, the video above also shows he was attacked before he accelerated.)

(Granted, when UTR demonstrators defended themselves against violent assaults by the likes of Corey Long and DeAndre Harris, the Whites were treated like felons, while the Blacks were treated like victims. The photo of Long's attempted mass murder was variously called "iconic" by *Newsweek* and "memorable" by The Grio.)

But nothing in the interim, after Fields' earlier posting of the photo of a car ramming the crowd—a trope of which e.g., Instapundit's Glenn Reynolds was also guilty—connected it to his actions. **He demonstrably sought to avoid such a result on the day of the rally. The Communist and anarchist rioters refused to let him avoid violence...**

[The defense team] had to show that Fields had attempted in vain to escape from Charlottesville before encountering Heather Heyer and her thug friends.

One attempt to leave was thwarted by Antifa activist UNC professor Dwayne Dixon, who allegedly aimed a rifle at him.

A second escape route on Fields' GPS was blocked with a police barricade.

And Fields' last attempt resulted in his being repeatedly attacked by bludgeon-wielding Antifa thugs, just before he hit the gas. (The videos I have seen do not show Fields going into reverse or idling, and then hitting the gas, to run down Heyer.)

The defense team had to establish the key role of armed Antifa UNC professor Dwayne Dixon. Dwayne Dixon testified that he only shouted at Fields with his AR-15 rifle on his shoulder (!), when the latter approached the area Dixon was blocking, and never pointed his rifle at Fields.

However, shortly after Charlottesville, **Dixon bragged to all the world on social media, in statements that he has since scrubbed, that he had aimed his loaded, deadly weapon at Fields, and forced him to turn around.**

It was essential that Lunsford and Hill impeach Dixon's testimony, calling him a liar, who either lied in his declarations on social media, or had just perjured himself in open court. Instead, they accepted Dixon's testimony unchallenged...

Fields' defense team of Denise Lunsford and John Hill were culpable, as far as I can see, of reversible ineffective assistance of counsel. Instead of providing Fields with a vigorous defense, they just phoned it in.[29]

Conte had a similar assessment of Fields' attorneys. "Their cross-examinations have been unaggressive at best. Their examination of Dixon was especially weak... [Lunsford] did not ask "What exactly did you mean by 'I used this rifle to chase off James Fields from our block?'" Nor did she ask if he had ever raised his rifle to the low-ready or pointed its muzzle at Fields or anyone else. She did not ask if he or his group had moved the roadblock. She did not inquire into who gave him the authority to direct traffic, or why his group had failed to disperse well over 2 hours after a state of emergency had been declared."[30]

Another courtroom observer who had attended Unite the Right explained why he believed the murder charge for Fields was excessive. "Fields also did not exactly act like a person trying to run down as many protesters as possible. He immediately slammed the brakes after the collision, did not go onto the sidewalk, and backed up only after being set up on by attackers. At absolute worst, and

---

29 Nicholas Stix, "Neither Justice Nor Mercy For James Fields—And It's His Lawyers' Fault," Vdare.com, June 25, 2019.

30 Gregory Conte, "Today's Testimony," UnzReview.com.

JAMES ALEX FIELDS, JR.

with no evidence to support this interpretation, Fields gave in to a moment of rage at seeing the threatening crowd. More likely he panicked. Either way, first degree murder is insane – but political realities demanded it."[31] There is additional evidence that the Fields car crash may have been misrepresented by the media. Some believe recently released drone footage proves "...there was almost no chance convicted driver James Fields knew that he was turning onto a street with extreme left-wing protesters as a gathering left-wing crowd waited while protesting through the whole city... [this c]ould be critical evidence in the pending appeal by James Fields."[32]

Fields was convicted on December 7, 2018 of first-degree murder, five counts of malicious wounding, three counts of aggravated malicious wounding, and failing to stop at the scene of a crash.

On March 27, 2019, Fields pled guilty to 29 hate crime charges as part of a deal, authorized by U.S. Attorney General William Barr, to avoid the death penalty. Heyer's family supported the plea deal, stating that putting Fields to death "would not bring back Heather."

According to a press release issued by the Department of Justice, "... Fields admitted under oath that he drove into the crowd of counter-protestors because of the actual and perceived race, color, national origin, and religion of its members... Fields also admitted that, prior to Aug. 12, 2017, he used social media accounts to express and promote White supremacist views; to express support for the social and racial policies of Adolf Hitler and Nazi-era Germany, including the Holocaust; and to espouse violence against African Americans, Jewish people, and members of other racial, ethnic, and religious groups he perceived to be non-White."[33]

Ann Coulter wrote in 2018 about the absurdity of adding hate crimes to the charges against Fields:

---

31 Charlottesville Survivor, "Unequal Justice in Fields' Charlottesville Trial – And Increasingly Throughout the Left's America," Vdare.com, Dec. 14, 2018.

32 Ben Wetmore, "Never-Before-Seen Drone Footage from Charlottesville," TheGatewayPundit.com.

33 "Ohio Man Sentenced to Life in Prison for Federal Hate Crimes Related to August 2017 Car Attack at Rally in Charlottesville, Virginia," Justice.gov, June 28, 2019.

Fields has already been charged with murder in state court. (I would think that "hate" would be subsumed by a murder charge.) But the federal "hate crimes" statute allows the feds to skirt the Constitution's ban on double jeopardy — at least for certain kinds of "hate."... To make their case, prosecutors did a deep dive into Fields' social media postings to prove that, yes, while he might have killed a White woman in this particular case, he's still a racist... This is a prosecution of Fields for Bad Thought, utterly oblivious to not only the Constitution's double jeopardy clause, but the free speech clause and also simple common sense. It's like a parody of what serious people feared about criminalizing "hate."... Fields' state of mind was right before he hit the gas pedal is of no consequence compared to his state of mind years earlier, when he was furiously typing hateful posts alone in his bedroom. He could be guilty of "hate."[34]

Sentencing

A sentencing memorandum filed on behalf of Fields read as follows:

"James did not come to Charlottesville with any plan to commit an act of violence. In the space of only a few minutes, caught in circumstances he did not intend to create, he acted in an aggressive and impulsive manner consistent with his mental health history and his age," the memo reads. "In a matter of seconds he caused irreparable harm for which there is no excuse. But this Court can understand his actions, without excusing them, as symptomatic of transient immaturity, and not consider them to be predictive of who he might be in the future with time and medication." The memorandum notes that Fields' grandfather killed his grandmother and then himself, and that his father died in a car accident before Fields was born. His mother was in an accident that left her paraplegic before he was born and raised him as a single

---

34 Ann Coulter, "Sarah Jeong Better Drive Carefully!" AnnCoulter.com, Aug. 8, 2018.

mother. The memo also says he has been taking medication since his imprisonment that has controlled his symptoms. "No amount of punishment imposed on James can repair the damage he caused to dozens of innocent people. But this Court should find that retribution has limits," the memo states."[35]

Fields had already received a life sentence on June 28, 2019, after pleading guilty to the aforementioned federal hate crime charges. Weeks later, on July 15, Fields was sentenced to a second life sentence, plus 419 years, by the state of Virginia for killing Heather Heyer and injuring many others.

When Mr. Fields hit the gas pedal that fateful day, was his heart full of malice, fear, or some combination thereof? No one but Mr. Fields and the Lord can know for certain. But we can know this: If the authorities tasked with guarding public safety in Charlottesville that day had done their jobs, there would have been no opportunity for the crash to have occurred.

---

35 *CNN* Newsource, "Charlottesville car attacker pleads for mercy in sentencing memo," News5Cleveland.com, June 24, 2019.

CHAPTER 21 QUICK LINKS:

 Charlottesville Drone Footage, URL: qrs.ly/96cwsuo

 Ruptly, "USA: Charlottesville violence an 'attack on nationalist community' - far right leader," video, Aug. 14, 2017. URL: qrs.ly/wdcvtpw

 "Senate Joint Resolution 49," URL: qrs.ly/mycvtq4

 Mike Valerio, "Heather Heyer's mom says move past her daughter's death, focus on the work left after Charlottesville," Aug. 11, 2020. URL: qrs.ly/escvtqc

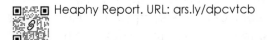 Heaphy Report. URL: qrs.ly/dpcvtcb

Hunter Wallace, "Charlottesville: Reconstructing Heather Heyer's Movements," Occidental Dissent, Sept. 7, 2017. URL: qrs.ly/t1cvtqf

 "WATCH — Leftist Professor Dwayne Dixon Brags To Class: I Waved A Rifle at Charlottesville Driver Before Crash," BigLeaguePolitics.com, March 6, 2018. URL: qrs.ly/9icvtqj

Jason Kessler, "Dwayne Dixon Describes 'Kicking, Punching, Cracking Heads' of Unite the Right Protesters," video, Feb. 21, 2021. URL: qrs.ly/ epcvtqn

CHAPTER 22

LAWYERING UP

"Calling, calling, and calling..."

Finding Representation

DURING THE TIME that Kessler was planning Unite the Right, he had never even considered the fact that he might be personally sued for fallout resulting from the event. But in the subsequent months, he was indeed personally served with multiple lawsuits. He reports that when that happened, "the bottom dropped out of my world."

Kessler had the need for a defense attorney for those lawsuits, and he was also intent on suing the City of Charlottesville for violating his First Amendment rights. However, finding legal representation when one is a pariah is especially challenging. Kessler recalls that he pulled up the attorney listings for his city and called each and every one of them, going from A to Z. He found none of them - not one single law firm - willing to take him on as a client. He became aware of some major law firms that specialized in First Amendment cases, but they were all prohibitively expensive. Still determined, Kessler continued calling, calling, and calling, but to no avail.

Kessler was even thwarted when attempting to do legal research on his own. He visited the law library of his alma mater, the University of Virginia, twice during April 2018, sparking protests and complaints. After being banned from the campus, Kessler wrote on his website, "It's shocking that an allegedly sober and responsible public university would claim something like this just to appease a mob who has no tolerance for political dissent... Lying about 'threats' to ban someone is a cynical and cowardly move on the part of #UVA to cover up the deeper rights violations happening to White dissidents on campus."[1]

A break finally came when one Virginia attorney, Elmer Woodard, had called Kessler to express support for him and his situation. Woodard is a colorful character both in his appearance and his courtroom presence. Sometimes seen sporting mutton chops, a straw hat, and a seersucker suit, Woodard has participated in Civil War reenactments and written a book about some of its battles.

Woodard has served as local council for Kessler's lawsuit against the City of Charlottesville, however, he was unable to represent Kessler in all of his cases. Eventually Matt Parrot of the Traditionalist Workers' Party referred Kessler to an Ohio attorney, James Kolenich, that was representing some of the other parties involved with Unite the Right - not only Parrot and the Traditionalist Workers' Party but also Cantwell, Robert "Azzmador" Ray, Nathan Damingo and Identity Evropa, and American Vanguard. (Some of these parties have since been dropped as clients.)

---

1 Andrew Blake, "Jason Kessler, Charlottesville rally organizer, banned from University of Virginia campus," *The Washington Times*, April 28, 2018.

CHAPTER 23

CIVIL COURT, ON THE OFFENSE: KESSLER V CHARLOTTESVILLE

"I'm motivated by injustice."

Fighters And Flighters

KESSLER DESCRIBES HOW he has dedicated his life to the legal battles ensuing from Unite the Right. "I'm a single-issue guy. I'm focusing on the Charlottesville thing. I think that it's gonna take divine intervention and every ounce of energy I could possibly muster for years of my life to be able to beat this thing, and to beat these lawsuits, these false accusations against us and to hold the city accountable. And so that's my primary focus."[1]

Kessler is indeed a man on a mission. Focused and tenacious, he has dedicated himself for nearly four years to learning everything there is to know about Unite the Right. He has spent countless hours personally studying photos, watching videos, listening to podcasts, scouring legal documents and government records, and combing through the websites and social media posts of everyone involved with the event. He is determined to uncover every bit of available truth about the events of Charlottesville with which his name will forever be linked, and to make that truth known both in the minds

---

1 Kessler Interview, LukeFord.net, Jan. 14, 2021.

of the public and in court. His enemies range from bloodthirsty street thugs who bombard him with death threats to politically-connected power players with bottomless pockets. Most men would have buckled by now under the pressure of the relentless assaults from such daunting foes, cut their losses, and moved on. But thus far, Kessler has unflinchingly met every challenge, and consistently matched his enemies blow for blow. Asked why he is such a fighter, Kessler explains,

> I'm motivated by injustice. I always have been. I was motivated to do the Unite the Right rally because of the double standards with the treatment of racism towards White people versus racism towards other people... I've always been working class. I know what it is to be bullied in school. I know what it is to not be the richest person. I know what it is to not be listened to by the power structure, not be able to get a good job when I need one, all these things. And so, I want to fight back against that. And I hate when the truth doesn't win out, when people suppress the truth, and everyone believes in a lie. And that's what happened at Unite the Right. The truth was lost behind this agenda and these horrible lies are believed by people, and it's a major historical event that people have no idea what the hell really happened. That drives me crazy.

> And there's a personal involvement to that with me, because so many people believe that I'm like some neo-Nazi or something and I'm not. And I hate that, and I want to fight back against that. But I think even more broadly, it's the fact that I can't believe what they did to free speech in this country, you know?... I don't know how it changed so quickly that people need to be destroyed over the words they say... [The rally attendees] were turned into history's biggest scapegoats. And it's totally unacceptable to me, and it's unacceptable that the government clearly set this thing up. And they're not being held accountable. So I

want that to be dealt with. And the ramifications, I see on and on and on, and it frustrates me because I don't see Richard Spencer, or a lot of those other people who attended the event as top billed speakers, ever think deeply about the ramifications of what's happening and how Charlottesville relates. Because I see it.[2]

A fierce advocate for the First Amendment, Kessler was determined to sue the City of Charlottesville for violating his civil rights and the rights of all Unite the Right participants. He sought support for his suit from other people associated with the event, but found most of them either wanted to distance themselves from the residuum of Charlottesville, or were struggling financially and unable to help with legal expenses. Out of everyone involved with Unite the Right, Matt Parrott of the Traditionalist Workers Party is the only other named plaintiff on the lawsuit against the City of Charlottesville.

Kessler and Parrott are both middle-class men working ordinary jobs to make a living and pay their legal bills. After Unite the Right, Kessler had great difficulty finding employment and was living from hand to mouth for a while. Eventually, he moved away from Charlottesville to another city where he was able to make a better living. Parrot has had to sell all his property and his car to pay hundreds of thousands of dollars in legal bills. Others cannot afford to fight at all. "A lot of people have just given up," laments Parrott. (Sometimes they receive donations, but it is challenging to fundraise when one is banned from major social media outlets and mainstream financing options like PayPal and GoFundMe).

Kessler complains about the lack of support from the other high-profile Unite the Right participants for the civil suit. "I've been working my butt off to try and hold these people accountable, and I've really had to do a lot of it in silence because the media never tried to hold the Charlottesville government accountable for what happened. A lot of people who attended UTR, as important as it is, they don't seem to care... I'm sorry if that offends them but there is

---

2 "Jason Kessler," Podcast on DissidentMama.net.

serious work that needs to be done that people have abdicated their responsibilities in my opinion."[3]

Freedom Of Speech And Heckler's Veto

On August 12, 2019, Kessler and Parrot filed a lawsuit against the city of Charlottesville and some named officials; Charlottesville city manager Tarron J. Richardson, Chief of Police Al Thomas, City Manager Maurice Jones, and Virginia State Trooper Lt. Becky Crannis-Curl for violating their First Amendment Rights.

On February 21, 2020, Judge Norman K. Moon of the United States District Court, Charlottesville division dismissed the suit, ruling that law enforcement has no obligation to protect people when other parties attempt to suppress their speech. Kessler explains, "Basically instead of arguing that our rights weren't violated, the presiding Judge Norman Moon tried to argue that there in fact was no such thing as a heckler's veto, and that the police have no duty to protect speakers who are being attacked by a mob, which is a pretty novel ruling. We were floored when we got it."[4]

On March 2, 2021, Kessler's legal team filed an appeals brief to the United States Court of Appeals for the Fourth Circuit.

Though not an attorney, Kessler speaks as one who is well-versed in the legal matters at issue in his lawsuits. The issue in question for Kessler v. Charlottesville is that of the "heckler's veto." He explains, "The heckler's veto has in some ways been established for a long time, then in some ways the details of it need to be fleshed out. The heckler's veto essentially says that the government can't curtail the speech of a controversial speaker because of an expected violent reaction of the crowd." After citing examples of prior heckler's veto cases and the precedents they set, Kessler continues:

Charlottesville is the final frontier of the heckler's veto. Charlottesville is the ultimate representation of a culture that has turned against the First Amendment

---

3 Jason Kessler D-Live live stream, Dlive.tv, April 2, 2021.

4 "Aftermath podcast with Jared Taylor," AmRen.com.

and the consequences of that. Regardless of what they say about the rally - that they were White supremacists, Nazis, or whatever - even if that were true, those types of ideas - and any ideas - should be protected by the First Amendment.

The culture has embraced violence towards people who disagree with what the media is saying and what the elite in our society want people to accept... In Charlottesville you had Antifa who attacked the event. That is beyond dispute. We have voluminous evidence of that. We filed this lawsuit and Judge Moon ruled that police have no duty to protect protesters from hecklers. That right there - he was wrong - but that is something that we need to be decided, and it needs to be decided now because we're facing this epidemic of left-wing agitators attacking people. And it's not just people like me. It's people like Jordan Peterson, Ben Shapiro, and anyone else you can think of... If the police aren't obligated to protect people, the First Amendment is done.

We're already four years in and they're trying to wear us down by wasting our time, wasting our money... Four years in, we're just at the Fourth Circuit. It could be years more before we're done with this. But if - IF - we win, it will establish a clear heckler's veto precedent across the land.

[The significance is] not just with the fact that the government can't abridge speech because of the reaction of hecklers, but that police have to protect you from violence. They have to do something to try to protect you, and that totally changes the dynamic. What happened in Charlottesville was so unfair because average American citizens were forced to defend themselves, and then that opened them up to all kinds of crap from the media and from attorneys who are willfully and maliciously misinterpreting

self-defense against people who are the aggressors...
The people who defended themselves were not the
aggressors and they should not have been put in the
situation by police that they had to defend themselves.

That's what this case is about. Something like
Charlottesville should never, ever happen again.
No one, protesters, counter-protesters, should have
to worry about violence. Those effing cops need to
show up and separate the groups and protect the
First Amendment. It's that simple. And it shouldn't
be up to some left-wing Democrat on city council
to decide whether they are going to honor the First
Amendment or not. So that's what it's about.[5]

Kessler and his legal team are optimistic, believing that their
case is strong despite the controversy surrounding Unite the Right.
They also believe that if they lose at the Appeals Court level, there
is a strong chance the Supreme Court will hear the case due to the
fact that standards on this issue vary in different districts within
the United States.

FOIA

In an effort to uncover as much information as possible about
what the authorities of Charlottesville were doing the day of Unite
the Right, Kessler has filed a series of FOIA (Freedom of Information
Act) lawsuits demanding the release of records. The details of the
Heaphy Report have been useful for helping him identify specific
documents to request. He describes this as "an avenue, like an
Achilles' heel, to attack these people for what they had done, to get
at the truth because they had been stonewalling me on a lot of issues
for a long time." What he learns from one set of documents give
him more information upon which to build the next request. City
officials have not only been less than forthright in responding to his
information requests, they have reported that important records,
critical to his First Amendment suit, have been lost or destroyed.

---

5   Jason Kessler D-Live live stream.

"There is a serious thing that happened at UTR that we need to talk about, and that's the fact that the government broke the law when they destroyed evidence to cover up what they did to engage in this heckler's veto and infringe our First Amendment rights. This is not speculation. It is not a conspiracy theory. It is backed up with evidence. The Charlottesville Independent [Heaphy] review alleges that the former police chief Al Thomas and the Charlottesville PD command staff deleted text messages relevant to their review. In other words, about the rally. Why did they destroy this evidence? They also went in and doctored certain documents to make it seem like they had done certain preparations that they really hadn't done. That is a class one misdemeanor that should, if these people were convicted, bar them from future public service. Of course, the government is not going to police themselves. So who is going to hold them accountable? That's where I come in. I've been filing FOIA requests for the past 3 or 4 years."[6]

When Kessler requested text messages from city manager Maurice Jones, he was told that no messages existed. This assertion was proven false by none other than the former mayor, Mike Signer. In his book about Unite the Right, *Cry Havoc*, Signer provided a detailed accounting of his of exchanging of emails and text messages with Maurice Jones. Kessler, filing pro se to save himself legal expenses, took pages from Signer's book and used them to demand release of the data. Kessler explains why officials' communications in the heat of the moment on August 12th are so critical:

> The record shows that the former Mayor Mike Signer was desperately trying to get into what is called the Unified Command Center on the day of the rally, and that's where the Charlottesville Police Chief, the City Manager, members of the FBI, and some others were basically watching this protest, and where these comments were made to "let them fight." The fact that the police chief and the city manager would not let the mayor into the Command Center - to me it's very highly suspect. There may be involvement from

---

6   Jason Kessler D-Live live stream.

the FBI - they were there - and the Virginia State Police which respond to the orders of then-governor Terry McAuliffe... But it's clear, I think, that the city manager and the police chief were trying to mitigate some of the damage of that conspiracy, to not allow the mayor and some others to know about it. Who knows how much advance notice they made in this plan? But it was clearly a preapproved plan that they were going to declare an unlawful assembly and they were going to allow that violence, which they knew was going to take place, to happen as an excuse.[7]

A week before the FOIA trial was to take place, Kessler received a letter with a link to 1,200 pages of emails, and an apology attributing their late response to their misunderstanding of what he was requesting.

The text messages were another matter. City officials claimed the text messages were lost when Maurice Jones' phone was wiped upon his resignation. Kessler explains why the missing text messages are such a concern: "... the reason the text messages were crucial is number one, you already had people destroying them. So that's a huge red flag. Why would they do that in the context of the review that was going on? The Chief of Police was doing that. But also, the few text messages I do have from those individuals - it's not like a lot of emails where people know that they're subject to FOIA and they are being very careful, saying things that they would only say with a lawyer present or something. In these text messages that were described by the mayor, are, like, passionate. They're angry. They're blaming and finger pointing. They're right in the moment. Like, "why are you allowing people to be beaten in the streets without doing anything?" and "Let me into the Command Center! I'm the mayor, dammit!" That kind of stuff. So I wanted more of that. I wanted to see all of that, and the stuff that they didn't want to put in there. Because they were blaming each other in closed door

---

7 "Aftermath podcast with Jared Taylor," AmRen.com.

meetings after the fact too. So the fact that they destroyed that is very suspect."[8]

Not only is it suspect, it is against the law. "It's illegal to destroy records while lawsuits are pending. A dozen or more lawsuits were tainted by the fact that these scumbags were destroying evidence. And they need to be held accountable,"[9] Kessler fumes. A donor contribution allowed Kessler to hire noted FOIA lawyer Andrew Bodoh, and he fought for an injunction to prevent the city from destroying any more records related to his lawsuit. At a later hearing the city changed their claim that Jones' phone was wiped, instead describing it as damaged, and as a result of Kessler's suit, independent experts are now examining Jones' phone in an effort to extract information from the device. Even some of his enemies have sided with him in his fight for government transparency.

Speaking with passion, Kessler denounces the attempts of the government to evade accountability for their actions by destroying records:

The Virginia public records act says that the city manager communications are never supposed to be destroyed. They're supposed to be kept permanently in agency. Then regardless of what the retention laws are, the law in Virginia says you cannot destroy public records when they are subject to litigation. There are so many people - the Charlottesville government has screwed people over and taken their civil rights from them so many times, so egregiously. When you think about what they did at the rally, just standing down and allowing Antifa to beat the crap out of people, then charging and prosecuting the hell out of people who defended themselves. Then when someone like me goes in and tries to look for the records to see what really happened about us being set up, they destroyed the records. And no one in the media is holding them

---

8 "Jason Kessler," Podcast on DissidentMama.net.

9 Kessler Interview, LukeFord.net, Jan. 14, 2021.

accountable, and even a lot of people who went to the rally are just moving on, like this doesn't matter anymore. It does matter. People were set up. How am I supposed to defend myself against these horrible accusations that people who are suing me make? How am I supposed to prosecute the city government for our civil rights violations when the evidence has been destroyed? It's absolutely unacceptable.

And so that's why we filed this newest lawsuit which is dealing with FOIA and dealing with the Public Records Act this time, and it is to address that letter where they admitted they destroyed evidence. We're trying to set some pretty exciting precedent for open government in Virginia because it's such a murky area where precedent hasn't been set. But we're trying to get a declaration of law saying that these people broke the law by destroying evidence for Unite the Right and that will have ramifications for everybody involved in a court case with Unite the Right. Everybody. Because how can we properly defend ourselves? How can we properly prosecute our rights without the full and complete evidence?

But also we want an injunction to keep them from ever destroying more evidence like this again and we want them to recognize that these text messages are public documents and they need to change their practices forever because of this situation. And then finally, probably the most interesting aspect is that we're going to try to deal with this loophole in the FOIA where you don't have to turn over records if you put them into a paper shredder or delete them off your hard drive. That's crap. So we're asking for the judge to order them to hire an electronic forensics, an e-discovery firm, to basically go over their hard drives, their phones, with a fine tooth comb and reconstitute these destroyed messages so we can find out what the hell it is that they were saying in the first place that they so badly didn't want anybody to see.[10]

The ACLU And Free Speech

The American Civil Liberties Union went to bat for Kessler when the City of Charlottesville wanted to relocate Unite the Right from Lee Park to another location, and succeeded in securing his right to assemble at the original location by the Lee monument. In the heated aftermath of August 12th, they found themselves on the defensive for their support of Kessler. Outraged social media users claimed that the ACLU were White supremacists or had blood on their hands, and called for people to stop donating to them. One member of the Virginia ACLU board, Waldo Jaquith, resigned immediately, explaining on Twitter, "What's legal and what's right are sometimes different. I won't be a fig leaf for Nazis." The Thursday after the rally, the *New York Times* ran an op-ed by UCLA law professor K-Sue Park entitled, "The ACLU Need to Rethink Free Speech." The ACLU was singled out for criticism by Governor Terry McAuliffe for defending the Lee Park location which he claimed made the rally "a powder keg."

ACLU executive director Anthony Romero defended their decision, "Some have argued that we should not be putting resources toward anything that could benefit the voices of White supremacy. But we cannot stand by silently as the government repudiates the principles we have fought for – and won – in the courts when it violates clearly established First Amendment rights."[11] However, Romero did announce that in the future, the ACLU would review legal requests for "White-supremacy protests" more closely and include consideration about whether demonstrations would involve weapons and have the potential to become violent.[12]

---

10 "Jason Kessler," Podcast on DissidentMama.net.

11 Joan Biskupic, "ACLU takes heat for its free-speech defense of White supremacist group," CNN.com, Aug. 17, 2017.

12 Joshua Barajas, "Charlottesville violence prompts ACLU to change policy on hate groups protesting with guns," Aug. 18, 2017.

Though the ACLU initially defended their advocacy for the rally, public pressure was mounting against their principled support of free speech for all. Since then, the ACLU has retreated further from its defense of free speech. In 2018, new guidelines detailed in a leaked internal document were published. In the document it is claimed that "the ACLU is committed to defending speech rights without regard to whether the views expressed are consistent with or opposed to the ACLU's core values, priorities and goals," yet explain that they may decline to defend some cases based upon "the extent to which the speech may assist in advancing the goals of White supremacists or others whose views are contrary to our values." The document states that in the future the ACLU will balance considerations of "impact of the proposed speech and the impact of its suppression."[13]

Kessler bemoans the post-Unite the Right change in the ACLU. "Charlottesville was the death knell for the old ACLU, and now it's really a situation where those rights that they used to champion even for dissident groups are hanging on by a thread. We have to raise our own money. We have to hire our own attorneys - if we can find them - and we have to renew those rights, because new precedents can be created. Those old cases protecting the right to protest for dissident groups free of violence can be overruled as new judges, activist judges, or just through neglect from groups like the ACLU no longer stepping in to defend them."[14]

Parrot complains about the chilling effect on organizing since the ACLU backed down. "The ACLU got federal permission for our rally, then pulled the rug out from under us when the police denied our civil liberties." He has reached out to them, trying to persuade them that devastating consequences that would result from their refusal to defend civil liberties except for specially protected groups. "The ACLU had been the only thing standing in the way of civil liberties eroding for decades."

---

13 Wendy Kaminer, "The ACLU Retreats From Free Expression," *Wall Street Journal*, June 20, 2018.

14 "Aftermath podcast with Jared Taylor," AmRen.com.

CHAPTER 23 QUICK LINKS:

 "Were the Capitol Hill Riots Charlottesville II? A Jason Kessler Interview," LukeFord.net, Jan. 14, 2021. URL: qrs.ly/e1cvtdi

 "Dissident Mama, episode 27 – Jason Kessler," Jan. 22, 2021. URL: qrs. ly/cycvto9

 "Charlottesville — Unite the Right — the Aftermath podcast with Jared Taylor," Podcast, May 13, 2021. URL: qrs.ly/qucvto3

CHAPTER 24

CIVIL COURT, ON THE DEFENSE: SINES V. KESSLER

"We will chase these people around for the rest of their lives."

The Lawyers And The Claims

THE LARGEST AND MOST SERIOUS civil suit aimed at Unite the Right participants is Sines v. Kessler. The suit alleges that the named defendants "conspired to plan, promote, and carry out violent events in Charlottesville... Starting at least as early as the beginning of 2017 and continuing to today, they have joined together for the purpose of inciting violence and instilling fear within the community of Charlottesville and beyond..." The plaintiffs reached as far back as Reconstruction for a legal basis for their claims, alleging violations of the Civil Rights Act of 1866 and Ku Klux Klan Act of 1871. (Though several of the alleged victims were White, the legal protections extend to supporters of non-White victims, so the laws may still be applied).

One of the lead attorneys for Sines v Kessler is Roberta "Robbie" Kaplan. Kaplan is an adjunct professor at Columbia law school, and is celebrated for successfully arguing against the Defense of Marriage Act before the Supreme Court in 2013, paving the way for the legalization of gay marriage. She has represented Uber,

Airbnb, Goldman-Sachs and Wall Street financiers. Kaplan worked on Hillary Clinton's presidential campaign, and had hoped to serve under her in a senior role in the Justice Department. She filed three law suits against President Donald Trump while he was in office, and her firm represents several other parties who are currently suing him for fraud and defamation. This firm, Kaplan Hecker & Fink LLP, has offices that take up an entire floor of the Empire State Building. According to Stephen Gillers, a legal ethics professor at New York University School of Law, "The consensus in the New York legal community is that she's a powerhouse. She's a lawyer that you don't want to see opposing you."[1]

The other lead attorney, Karen Dunn, has been widely honored as a top litigator, and has served as Associate White House Counsel under President Obama and a Senior Advisor to Hillary Clinton.

Soon after viewing the events of Unite the Right, Kaplan phoned her friend Dahlia Lithwick, a legal reporter and Charlottesville resident who was reportedly also a friend of then-Mayor Mike Signer. Lithwick quickly helped Kaplan set up shop in Charlottesville, and within days of the rally, Kaplan had begun interviewing potential clients for her lawsuit. Kaplan soon invited Karen Dunn to join the effort. At the time, Dunn was practicing with Boies Schiller Flexner LLP, the same firm Signer had hired when he was trying to relocate Unite the Right from Lee Park. Boies Schiller Flexner, has also represented Al Gore, the NFL, the New York Times and Harvey Weinstein, and Principal David Boies has been involved in litigation related to Jeffrey Epstein.[2]

When Kaplan interviewed potential clients, she explained to them that a victory in the case would not result in their financial gain. "And when we met with the plaintiffs, we said that we think a lawsuit needs to be brought against the people who actually did this. Um, but many of you have been very injured, and you may have other lawsuits that you want to think about. You may want

1 Erik Larson, "Roberta Kaplan Builds Progressive Firm Suing Trump, Defending Wall Street," Bloomberg.com, May 13, 2021.

2 Jason Kessler, "More Regime Narrative Collapse: Jason Kessler Updates Us On Charlottesville Unite The Right Lawfare," Vdare.com, May 5, 2021.

to think about suing the police department or suing others. And we understand that. And if you do that, that's fine, because many of you may need costs for your medical costs, etcetera. But if you do that, you can't be in our case. And if you're in our case, you're probably not gonna get a lot of money at the end."[3]

Asked what she hoped the outcome of the case would be, Kaplan explained, "We absolutely can and will bankrupt these groups. And then we will chase these people around for the rest of their lives. So if they try to buy a new home, we will put a lien on the home. If they get a new job, we will garnish their wages. The reason to do that is because we want to create a deterrence impact. So we send a message to other people that if you try to do something like this, the same thing will happen to you. And it already has been a deterrence."[4]

The lawsuit is financially supported by Integrity First for America (IFA), whose executive director is Amy Spitalnik. IFA bills itself as "a nonpartisan nonprofit organization dedicated to holding those accountable who threaten longstanding principles of our democracy—including our country's commitment to civil rights and equal justice." The IFA, whose site invites activists to "#SueANazi," brags that the Sines v Kessler case is "is the only current legal effort to take on the vast leadership of the violent White nationalist movement." Integrity First for America boasts donors such as tech billionaires LinkedIn founder Reid Hoffman and CraigsList founder Craig Newmark and actress Natalie Portman.

The Plaintiffs

Elizabeth Sines was a UVA law student at the time of Unite the Right. She and her roommate, fellow law student Leanne Chia, attended the torchlight march on August 11th and were on Market Street at the moment James Fields' car crashed into the crowd. Sines shared videos and her observations of the events in a Facebook post that went viral, and a few days later, Sines and Chia

---

3 Jason Kessler, "Attorney Roberta Kaplan Convinces Clients Not to Sue Police for Charlottesville Stand Down," BitChute video posted Feb. 24, 2021.

4 EllenWexler, "Roberta Kaplan Takes White Supremacy to Court," *Jewish World*, Winter 2020.

shared their story, framed as an inspirational call to oppose hate, with *Glamour* magazine. Sines described her experience of the "Nazi" rally, then contrasted it with that of the counter-protester gathering. "We then regrouped in McGuffey Park, and when I look back on what happened, this is what I will choose to hold onto. As soon as I walked in, it was the first time I felt at peace. There were no Nazi groups or White supremacists on site—just counter-protesters. It was like the resistance camp at the end of the world. There was a soft breeze, a DJ was playing reggae, balloon bouquets were everywhere, someone had made a papier-mâché statue of Sally Hemmings. There was diversity in age, race, gender, and ability."

When the counter-protesters received misinformation that a Black neighborhood was under attack, they began to march. "We got our things together and began marching, but it was still this beautiful, diverse group of people. We started singing and the power radiated from this group. Within minutes, we had tears in our eyes... it felt like we had won: We had taken back our town and protected our people. We were heading toward another nearby park, chanting 'Our streets! Our streets!'—and that was when the car came." [5]

Asked why she joined the lawsuit, Sines explained "I never want anything like this to happen again... I joined the lawsuit because Black lives matter, because antisemitism is on the rise around the world and cannot be left unchecked, and because White supremacy is a disease."[6]

Though she is usually portrayed in the media as a plucky young idealist, Kessler describes Sines as "a very wily political operative. After the rally was over, she went to the home of a fellow law student who actually is one of the law clerks for the judge in our case. We had to file a motion for them to get this guy recused from the case because he's one of her best friends. So her best friends were helping to decide these cases."[7]

---

5 Maggie Mallon, "Elizabeth Sines and Leanne Chia Were in Charlottesville When White Supremacists Descended—This Is What They Saw," Glamour.com, Aug. 18, 2017.

6 Ali Zablocki, "Suing White Supremacists: Elizabeth Sines '19 Takes on August 11-12 Organizers," *Virginia Law Weekly*, Aug. 31, 2018.

7 "Aftermath podcast with Jared Taylor," AmRen.com.

Kessler is referring to the fact that in March, 2020, his attorneys filed a motion for recusal for some of Judge Norman K. Moon's clerks, Hutton Marshall and Joshua Lefebvre, after close connections with Sines were discovered. (It should be mentioned that it is common practice for judicial clerks to write the opinions of the judges they serve.) Kessler found a Facebook photo that had been posted by Marshall of a smiling group of people, including Marshall, Lefebvre, and Sines. Under the photo, Sines had added the comment, "The BEST OF FRIENDS."

Not only was Judge Moon's clerk Marshall "the best of friends" with the main plaintiff in a case against Kessler, but he had also worked at the Office of the New York State Attorney General's Office at the same time as Amy Spitalnik, the director of the organization bankrolling the plaintiffs' case.

Incredibly, Joshua Lefebvre also had a connection to Sines that could possibly cause him to be considered a material witness to the case. An article about Sines' Unite the Right experience states that immediately after witnessing James Fields' car crash, Sines and her friend, "retreated to the home of law student Josh Lefebvre '19 to begin to understand what had happened."[8]

The motion for recusal of Marshall and Lefevbre was granted by Judge Moon on June 18, 2020.

Some of the additional plaintiffs are Marcus Martin and fiancé (now wife) Marissa Blair. Martin and Blair, who appeared on the Ellen Degeneres show to talk about their Unite the Right experience, were injured in the car crash and also claim to suffer residual emotional distress. Natalie Romero, Thomas Baker, and Chelsea Alvarado also suffered injuries resulting from the car crash. April Muniz, who was nearly struck by the car, claims to suffer from acute stress disorder. An African American plaintiff known as John Doe also claims to have been "intimidated, harassed, assaulted, and sprayed with caustic substances" at the August 11th torchlight march.

---

8 Mary Wood, "Standing Up for Charlottesville," UVA Law School website, law.virginia.edu, Aug. 16, 2017.

Another of the plaintiffs is long-time Charlottesville activist Reverend Seth Wispelwey. He was not injured during Unite the Right, but claims to suffer extreme emotional distress due to having been "harassed, intimidated, and assaulted by the defendants and their co-conspirators."

The Defendants

The defendants on the suit as originally filed included not only Kessler, but about two dozen other individuals and groups, including:

- Richard Spencer
- Christopher Cantwell
- Andrew Anglin, Robert "Azzmador" Ray, Moonbase Holdings LLC (which operates the Daily Stormer website)
- Identity Evropa, Nathan Damigo, Elliot Kline (aka Eli Mosley)
- Traditionalist Workers Party, Matthew Heimbach, David Matthew Parrot
- League of the South, Michael Hill, Michael Tubbs
- National Socialist Movement
- Nationalist Front, Jeff Schoep
- Fraternal Order of the Alt-Knights, Augustus Sol Invictus
- Mike "Enoch" Pienovich
- Loyal White Knights of the Ku Klux Klan
- East Coast Knights of the Ku Klux Klan
- Vanguard America
- James Alex Fields, Jr.

It is significant that Fields listed as a defendant, because the plaintiffs mean to tie the death and injuries caused by Fields' car crash to the rally organizers and headliners to prove they were part of a violent conspiracy.

Kessler summarized the case from his point of view,

> So basically it's using civil conspiracy claims, which are very different than criminal conspiracy claims, which require a very high bar of evidence. In civil

court it's a very low bar of evidence. And with the civil claims it can be very nebulous. It's easy to claim so-and-so was conspiring with so-and-so; they were in the same room together, and then you just say they were conspiring to do this or that. And it can get you to a trial, believe it or not, to say that kind of thing.

So for them, they are saying the rally was just a pretext to violently attack counter protesters, specifically racial minorities. Yet they have no evidence of that. They say that we conspired with James Fields, the individual who drove his car into the crowd of people, and yet there is no evidence of that. They've gone through all of our text messages, all of our emails, all of our social media. There's no evidence of that. We have the head investigator with the CPD Steve Young testifying under oath that there is not only no conspiracy in the death of Heather Heyer, but that there was no communication with James Fields whatsoever...

It's a difficult thing, even when they don't have the facts on their side, because they can bring up "here's offensive speech." And we're in this environment where people want to hurt other people who say things that they don't agree with. And you have people saying the most objectionable dissident speech you could possibly imagine, and then on top of that, you have the fact that there were people who were legitimately injured in that incident with James Fields. And that's sad. It's terrible. But we did not have anything to do with that. And they are trying to exploit the situation to attack a political faction.[9]

---

9 "Aftermath podcast with Jared Taylor," AmRen.com.

Weaponized "Justice"

Several defendants maintain that the Sines v. Kessler suit amounts to nothing more than lawfare. In other words, they believe it is a factually baseless attempt to use bad-faith litigation to cripple them reputationally and financially. Kessler has described the tactic as "economic terrorism," and points out that "[i]n nearly four years, IFA haven't proven a single thing except that they can mug and beat down defendants who can't afford attorneys... Many of their opponents can't afford attorneys, and those who do can't afford researchers, expert witnesses, and evidence collection software to defend themselves on the same footing."[10]

Michael Hill, President of League of the South, defends his belief that the suit is illegitimate and meant to place a financial burden on disfavored groups. "So if you have to lie about what actually happened on the ground, then you malign your opponents with accusations of things–racism, anti-Semitism, fascism, historical revisionism–that are not illegal but are meant to destroy a person's reputation and their ability to make a living. This is not only morally wrong and with no legal basis, but it is sheer evil based on a deep hatred of those of us who were there... When such accusations of "wrong-think" become, in part, the basis of a legal suit, then we are treading perilous ground."[11]

Matt Parrot of the Traditionalist Workers Party was required to provide data from social media as part of discovery for the suit. In response, he wrote, "[t]his is part of an ongoing fishing expedition where they're desperately looking for some sort of evidence of a criminal conspiracy to initiate violence in Charlottesville. They'll find nothing here, either... Essentially, they know they don't have a case, but they have unlimited financial resources and they're leveraging them with the hopes that we'll eventually trip ourselves up on a technicality or run out of funds for our legal support... Our

---

10 Jason Kessler, "More Regime Narrative Collapse: Jason Kessler Updates Us On Charlottesville Unite The Right Lawfare," VDare.com, Apr. 5, 2021.

11 Dr. Michael Hill, "Punishing Beliefs," LeagueOfTheSouth.com, June 19, 2019.

movement has always been cash-starved, but is especially cash-starved in the wake of our being systematically driven from using conventional payment processing services." [12]

According to Parrot, Sines is a strategic lawsuit meant to deter disfavored groups from organizing peacefully. "Our communications were clean and clear. The event was an historical preservation rally... I think we'll manage to win, but we've already been destroyed... Their point is the ride."

In April, 2021 Cantwell, who is currently in prison for a conviction unrelated to Unite the Right, filed a motion for dismissal from the Sines case, alleging that the plaintiffs had for fourteen months not been properly serving him on matters relating to the lawsuit. In his request to be dismissed from the suit, he wrote, "This lawsuit survived a motion to dismiss because the Plaintiffs had 'plausibly alleged' that a bunch of complete strangers got together with the plan to commit a bunch of felonies on camera, just because they harbor inexplicable and irrational hatred for a favored handful of demographics. To the Defendants, the cartoonish depiction of us it not at all credible, and the conspiracy theory is absurd on its face..." Even though he believes the claims of the suit are absurd, Cantwell has considered giving up the fight. He explained that he had taken the plea agreement over the clash at the torchlight march "...for the same reason I have contemplated defaulting on this lawsuit: Abuse of process is an effective means of wearing down a man's resistance."

In the motion, Cantwell explained what he believes are the reasons for the groundless suit. "I am so broke I can't even afford bankruptcy... This is purely an exercise of power over the weak for them... I believe the discovery powers are being misused by Plaintiffs to spy on their political opponents. I do not believe that they have any intention of winning this lawsuit on the merits of the case. The whole point was to drag us through the system, bankrupt us, and obtain information."[13]

---

12 Matt Parrott, "Charlottesville Lawfare Circus: Twitter Subpoenaed," OccidentalDissent.com, Feb. 10, 2018.

13 Sines v. Kessler, Defendant's motion to sanction plaintiffs, filed April 12, 2021.

Some of the information used by the plaintiffs was obtained by left-wing journo-activists. According to Kaplan, "We got a break early in the case because someone hacked into the Discord servers that the organizers used."[14]

The Arduous Battle

The Sines v. Kessler lawsuit was filed in October, 2017, and it has been plodding along ever since. The trial has been postponed several times, supposedly due to concerns about Covid. Kessler spoke about the lawsuit defense. "Thankfully we do have two very brave attorneys. We have James Kolenich out of Cincinnati, Ohio and Elmer Woodard out of Blue Ridge, Virginia, who is our local counsel." In addition to Kessler, Kolenich and Woodard also represent Nathan Damigo, Identity Evropa, the Traditionalist Workers Party, and Matt Parrott. Woodard and Kolenich previously represented Cantwell and Ray, but dropped them as clients in July, 2019.

In June, 2019, Cantwell had posted on social media that when Kaplan "loses this fraudulent lawsuit, we're going to have a lot of fucking fun with her."[15] Shortly thereafter, Kolenich and Woodard withdrew as his attorneys, stating, "Mr. Cantwell has rendered Attorney's continued representation of him unreasonably difficult, has created a conflict of interest between himself and Attorney's other clients, and has engaged in conduct Attorney's consider 'repugnant or imprudent.'"

Ray had been in hiding since he was charged with releasing pepper spray after the Unite the Right torchlight march. His attorneys had been communicating with him through an online forum in which they asked him to call when they needed to speak with him. At the time they withdrew as his attorneys, Kolenich and Woodard stated that they had not heard from Ray in over six

---

14 Ellen Wexler, "Roberta Kaplan Takes White Supremacy to Court," *Jewish World*, Winter 2020.

15 Denise Lavoie, "Lawyers ask judge to order White nationalist to stop threats," AP, July 2, 2019.

CIVIL COURT, ON THE DEFENSE: SINES V. KESSLER

weeks.[16] Ray continues to make money through his podcasts while in hiding. In September 2020, an arrest warrant was issued for Ray for contempt charges stemming from Sines v Kessler. [17]

According to Kessler, Woodard and Kolenich are "doing a fantastic job making sure that we catch up with all of our responsibilities to court, making sure that we turn over all of our evidence that we have to in discovery... a lot of folks in the Charlottesville lawsuits have been roughed up really badly by things that no one who hasn't been involved in a major legal battle would know about. Like you think in terms of the case, that you just gather evidence and present it in court. But when you're dealing with something of this nature, especially in the internet age, when so many of us have so many accounts and were sending text messages and all these other things, like if they want to be dicks about it - and they do want to be dicks about it in this case - they'll make you turn over every single thing. And you have to think of every single account you've had where you've ever mentioned the damn rally. And the rally was such a big deal to someone like me, for instance, of course I've said so many things in so many places. So you've got to come up with all of that in discovery. And if you can't do that then you'll lose before the thing even begins."[18]

Several of the defendants in the suit have faced sanctions due to failure to comply with discovery. Others have faced financial obstacles to defending themselves.

Elliot Kline (aka Eli Mosley) has been ordered to pay fines, and was briefly jailed in January, 2020 for contempt of court after plaintiffs complained that he had failed to turn over requested records. (Kline claimed that he did not have the devices in question and that the requested passwords were lost.) His failure to cooperate may result in the judge issuing an "adverse inference" ruling, basically telling

---

16 Kelly Weill, "Charlottesville Lawyers Dump Nazi Clients," TheDailyBeast. com, July 26, 2019.

17 Michael Kunzelman, "Arrest warrant issued for neo-Nazi podcaster in Charlottesville rally lawsuit," AP, Sept. 14, 2020.

18 "Jason Kessler," Podcast on DissidentMama.net.

the jury to assume the plaintiff's assertions about the data that was supposedly on the devices, is true.[19] Kessler complains, "I was harmed by Eli Mosley not turning over his evidence."[20]

Matt Heimbach, Jeff Schoep, and Vanguard America have likewise been sanctioned and ordered to pay attorney's fees for failure to comply with discovery requests.

Heimbach has also caused some to speculate about his true loyalties, and potentially harmed his defense, with displays of erratic behavior since Unite the Right. In March, 2018, Heimbach was arrested on domestic violence charges for an altercation stemming from an alleged affair with Matt Parrott's wife – a dispute which also led to the dissolution of the Traditionalist Workers' Party. For a time, Heimbach was seemingly rebranding himself as a "former extremist," formally renouncing White nationalism.[21] Then in July 2021, he made a bizarre public statement in support of a violent revolution, arguing that "[a]ny violence the proletariat brings [against the capitalist class] is simply in self-defense."[22]

After some initial difficulty securing an attorney, Richard Spencer announced that he would be represented by John DiNucci. However, in June 2020, DiNucci withdrew as counsel, citing unpaid fees and lack of cooperation.[23]

Michael "Enoch" Peinovich was dismissed from the suit when the judge found that while Peinovich had promoted the event, he had not used Discord nor taken part in the violence at Unite the

---

19 Brett Barrouquere, "Former Head of Identity Evropa Taken Into Custody for Contempt of Court," SPLCCenter.org, Jan. 6, 2020.

20 Kessler Interview, LukeFord.net, Jan. 14, 2021.

21 Brett Barrouquere, " Two Prominent Neo-Nazis Recant, but Their Actions Sow Doubts," SPLCCenter.org, May 14, 2020.

22 Mark Greenblatt and Lauren Knapp, "Extremist Heimbach To Relaunch Hate Group, Says He Supports Violence," Newsy.com, July 20, 2021.

23 Michael Kunzelman, "White Nationalist Richard Spencer Loses Lawyer in Lawsuit," AP, June 22, 2020.

Right.[24] Shortly before being dismissed, Peinovich had received assistance from a mystery attorney who chose to remain anonymous due to fear of harassment.[25] Invictus (who, like Peinovich had not participated in the Discord chat used for planning) was likewise removed as a defendant. Invictus explains that he was never properly served so got a default judgement.

In January 2019, defendant Nathan Damigo, founder and former leader of Identity Evropa, filed for bankruptcy. [26]

A different problem arose regarding James Alex Fields, Jr., whose inclusion in the case is critical to the Plaintiffs. His attorneys filed a motion in February, 2021 for a stay in his scheduled deposition pending a psychiatric evaluation, citing concerns that Fields, who has a long history of mental illness, was displaying signs of mental incompetence. They requested the appointment of a Guardian ad Litem. In response, IFA requested sanctions against Fields for his "refusal to testify."

Despite the David-versus-Goliath balance of the case, League of the South President Michael Hill is optimistic. "We are truly outnumbered, outgunned, and out-resourced, but we do have one fundamental advantage on our side: The Truth. And, by God's grace, we shall prevail! [27]

Finally, it is worth noting that even though an immense amount of data is available about the defendants' communications and their activities the weekend of Unite the Right, none of the numerous defendants in the Sines civil suit have been criminally charged with anything remotely resembling a conspiracy to commit violence. If they are guilty as the Sines plaintiffs claim, why not?

---

24 Brett Barrouquere, "Judge upholds bulk of lawsuit against Alt-Righters in Charlottesville after 'Unite the Right,' dismisses Peinovich," SPLCCenter.org, July 10, 2018.

25 Brett Barroquere, "Not alone: Michael 'Enoch' Peinovich has a secret lawyer in the Charlottesville lawsuit," *SPLCCenter.org*, June 28, 2018.

26 Brett Barrouquere, "Nathan Damigo, founder of White nationalist group Identity Evropa, files for bankruptcy protection," *SPLCCenter.org*, Jan. 8, 2019.

27 Dr. Michael Hill, "Lawfare against The League," LeagueOfTheSouth.com, Oct. 29, 2018.

CHAPTER 24 QUICK LINKS:

 Jason Kessler, "Attorney Roberta Kaplan Convinces Clients Not to Sue Police for Charlottesville Stand Down," video, Feb. 24, 2021. URL: qrs. ly/a3cvtqq

 "Charlottesville — Unite the Right — the Aftermath podcast with Jared Taylor," Podcast, May 13, 2021. URL: qrs.ly/qucvto3

 "Were the Capitol Hill Riots Charlottesville II? A Jason Kessler Interview," LukeFord.net, Jan. 14, 2021. URL: qrs.ly/e1cvtdi

 "Dissident Mama, episode 27 – Jason Kessler," Jan. 22, 2021. URL: qrs. ly/cycvto9

Part Five:

Autopsy

CHAPTER 25

HEAPHY SPEAKS

"Protected neither free speech nor public safety..."

THE INDEPENDENT INVESTIGATION of Unite the Right and surrounding events led by Tim Heaphy and performed by his law firm Hunton & Williams was released December 1, 2017.

For creation of the 200-plus page report, the City of Charlottesville paid $350,000. Investigators reviewed hundreds of thousands of documents and electronic communications from the City of Charlottesville and numerous agencies and offices of the Commonwealth of Virginia. They reviewed thousands of photos and hundreds of hours' worth of video footage and audio recordings, some obtained from the internet, some submitted by witnesses, and some obtained from law enforcement sources. They interviewed 150 witnesses including law enforcement personnel; representatives and members of the right-wing protester groups and left-wing counter-protest groups that attended, as well as unaffiliated attendees. They also provided phone and internet tip lines for members of the public to submit information.

The report heavily condemned the Charlottesville Police Department leadership. Police Chief Al Thomas resigned on December 18, 2017.

One observer summarized the damning conclusion of the extensive review: "Heaphy merely corroborates our worst fears about what drives the government at all levels: power, money, ego, politics and ambition."[1]

A Catalog Of Failures

Variations of the word "fail" were used dozens of times in the 200-plus page report. There is a lengthy list of serious deficiencies attributed to the Charlottesville Police Department in particular, including:

Failure in information gathering. Failure to adequately train, equip, and brief law enforcement officers. Failure to coordinate and communicate effectively with Virginia State Police and other law enforcement and public safety entities. Failure to separate hostile groups. Failure to restrict certain items that could be used as weapons. Failure to place protective gear in an area accessible to officers so they would be able to intervene in conflict. Failure to control crowds and manage traffic after the event dispersal in the downtown area where a woman was hit by a car and killed.

The widely-held perception among all those present the day of Unite the Right was that the police had been given a stand-down order for the event. Police refused to intervene in episodes of violence and injury, even in cases where attendees implored them to help. Part of the problem may have been that VSP Ground Commander Lieutenant Becky Crannis-Curl made changes the morning of Unite the Right. Per the Heaphy Report, that morning she decided:

> 'she was going 'off-plan' and was 'not going to send arrest teams into the street'.. We developed substantial additional evidence that suggests that Lieutenant Crannis-Curl's "off-plan" directive had been passed along and adopted by all of the VSP troopers stationed in and around Emancipation [Lee] Park. Lieutenant McKean told us that the VSP sergeant assigned as his

---

1   John Whitehead,"This Is Amerika: Where Fascism, Totalitarianism and Militarism Go Hand In Hand," agovernmentofwolves.com, Aug. 11, 2020.

counterpart in Zone 1 told him he would not send troopers over the barricades to engage the crowd if their safety was compromised. A trooper in Zone 3 told Officer Lisa Best that VSP was "under orders not to go in." Another VSP officer in Zone 3 indicated that troopers had been instructed "not to break up fights... Multiple citizens provided further evidence of the VSP "off-plan" decision to refrain from leaving barricaded areas adjacent to Emancipation [Lee] Park. Several witnesses told us that they directly solicited help from VSP troopers and were told that they were not available to assist.[2]

Though the Heaphy Report did not find that a direct stand-down order had been issued for the entire event, the mismanagement by the police essentially had that effect:

The planning and coordination breakdowns prior to August 12 produced disastrous results. Because of their misalignment and lack of accessible protective gear, officers failed to intervene in physical altercations that took place in areas adjacent to Emancipation Park. VSP directed its officers to remain behind barricades rather than risk injury responding to conflicts between protesters and counter-protesters. CPD commanders similarly instructed their officers not to intervene in all but the most serious physical confrontations. Neither agency deployed available field forces or other units to protect public safety at the locations where violence took place. Instead, command staff prepared to declare an unlawful assembly and disperse the crowd.

These damning statements must not be overlooked: Neither agency deployed available field forces or other units to protect public safety at the locations where violence took place. Command staff prepared to declare an unlawful assembly and disperse the crowd.

---

2 Heaphy Report, pp. 121-122.

Further, the report concludes that, "[I]n contrast to the July 8 [KKK] event, the City of Charlottesville protected neither free expression nor public safety on August 12. The City was unable to protect the right of free expression and facilitate the permit holder's offensive speech. This represents a failure of one of government's core functions—the protection of fundamental rights. Law enforcement also failed to maintain order and protect citizens from harm, injury, and death." [3]

Again, we must reiterate the report's conclusion: The City of Charlottesville protected neither free expression nor public safety on August 12... This represents a failure of one of government's core functions—the protection of fundamental rights.

Chief Thomas - "Let them fight."

Police Chief Al Thomas was singled out for blame for many reasons.

The Heaphy Report describes Chief Thomas' response to reports from the field of increasing violence as "disappointingly passive." Further, it notes that Captain Lewis and Thomas' personal assistant Emily Lantz both reported that at the first signs of open violence on Market Street, Chief Thomas said "Let them fight, it will make it easier to declare an unlawful assembly."

Considering that his fundamental duty was to protect the safety and basic human rights of the public in his jurisdiction, this statement, verified by two witnesses, is absolutely astonishing.

"Let them fight. It will make it easier to declare an unlawful assembly."

The report condemns "Chief Thomas' slow-footed response to violence [which] put the safety of all at risk and created indelible images of this chaotic event."[4]

---

3 Heaphy Report, p 6.

4 Heaphy Report, p. 133.

The report also complained that Thomas impeded the process of investigators in a number of ways:

Chief Al Thomas initially attempted to sequence our review by limiting our access to information about various topics. He directed subordinates to provide us only with information regarding the planning for the protest events, not the events themselves. He later admitted to us in an interview that his goal in this process was to educate our review team in a methodical process which he controlled... Pursuant to the Chief's strategy of controlling the flow of information to our review team, we had several interviews with officers in which they refused to discuss certain topics.

In our interviews with CPD personnel, we learned that Chief Thomas and other CPD command staff deleted text messages that were relevant to our review. Chief Thomas also used a personal e-mail account to conduct some CPD business, then falsely denied using personal e-mail in response to a specific FOIA request. Chief Thomas and the commanders with whom we spoke denied any effort to hide information from our review team.

In addition to limiting our initial access to all relevant information, Chief Thomas directed the creation of various documents that outlined CPD's preparation for these events. For example, Chief Thomas asked his captains to create a "checklist" to document CPD's preparation for each event... Captain Shifflett then went through the various items in the checklist and "checked" each task that had been performed [in preparation for the July 8ᵗʰ Klan event]... Chief Thomas and Captain Shifflett both denied any intent to "back-date" the checklist or any other document. They indicated that the checklist was created as a mechanism to catalogue the preparation that informed the Department's approach to the July 8 event. Chief Thomas acknowledged that the document was designed to be used in advance of these events, though he denied any intention to suggest it had been used in advance of these events.

In addition, Chief Thomas attempted to gather information from CPD personnel about the substance and tenor of our interviews. He questioned his assistant and members of the command staff after interviews occurred, asking about what areas were covered. His attempts to follow our interviews resulted in the City Manager directing all CPD employees to refrain from discussing the substance of our interviews with others.

Chief Thomas's attempts to influence our review illustrate a deeper issue within CPD—a fear of retribution for criticism. Many officers with whom we spoke expressed concern that their truthful provision of critical information about the protest events would result in retaliation from Chief Thomas. They described a culture of conformity within the Department that discourages officers from raising issues and providing feedback. These officers suggested that this hierarchical approach hampered the planning for the July 8 and August 12 events, as lieutenants, sergeants, and line officers were not sufficiently consulted or asked to provide input.

Regardless of these issues, we were able to develop fulsome information from CPD regarding the handling of the protest events. We eventually obtained all requested documents and got access to all CPD personnel with whom we requested to speak. In the face of the culture of conformity described above, many officers were willing to criticize the Department's planning for the rallies and conduct during the events. Some officers provided information without attribution, but others openly provided important details that appear in this report. Without the cooperation of a large number of dedicated professionals within CPD who elevated duty over fear of retaliation, we would not have gotten the truthful information that informs the findings and recommendations below.[5]

Detailed Conclusions

The Charlottesville Police Department was called out for a collection of very serious errors that contributed to the catastrophic turn of events that transpired at Unite the Right.

> *[P]olice planning for August 12 was inadequate and disconnected. CPD commanders did not reach out to officials in other jurisdictions where these groups had clashed previously to seek information and advice. CPD supervisors did not provide adequate training or information to line officers, leaving them uncertain and unprepared for a challenging enforcement environment. CPD planners waited too long to request the assistance of the state agency skilled in emergency response. CPD command staff also received inadequate legal advice and did not implement a prohibition of certain items that could be used as weapons.*

> *CPD devised a flawed Operational Plan for the Unite The Right rally. Constraints on access to private property adjacent to Emancipation Park forced planners to stage particular law enforcement units far from the areas of potential need. The plan did not ensure adequate separation between conflicting groups. Officers were not stationed along routes of ingress and egress to and from Emancipation*

---

5   Heaphy Report, pp 13-14.

Park but rather remained behind barricades in relatively empty zones within the park and around the Command Center. Officers were inadequately equipped to respond to disorders, and tactical gear was not accessible to officers when they needed it.

CPD commanders did not sufficiently coordinate with the Virginia State Police in a unified command on or before August 12. VSP never shared its formal planning document with CPD, a crucial failure that prevented CPD from recognizing the limits of VSP's intended engagement. CPD and VSP personnel were unable to communicate via radio, as their respective systems were not connected despite plans to ensure they were. There was no joint training or all-hands briefing on or before August 12. Chief Thomas did not exercise functional control of VSP forces despite his role as overall incident commander. These failures undercut cohesion and operational effectiveness. CPD and VSP operated largely independently on August 12, a clear failure of unified command.[6]

Though this thorough, independent review condemned the authorities for a litany of failures, the mainstream news either ignored or gave passing mention to their findings. The preferred narrative promulgated by the media and political elites, that the right-wing attendees were dangerous and were the primary parties responsible for the violence, was already ingrained in the public psyche, and was far too politically useful for them to want to upend.

---

6 Heaphy Report, p 5.

CHAPTER 25 QUICK LINKS:

 Heaphy Report. URL: qrs.ly/dpcvtcb

CHAPTER 26

BLAME AND PRAISE

*"A spectacular and utterly preventable
government leadership failure."*

ON THE POLITICAL CESSPOOL podcast the evening of Unite
the Right, co-host Eddie Miller said this: "I think we all agree that
the actions taken by local law enforcement and the government
were in effect fake law. It struck us as unlawful. We had a permit.
We had the permit vindicated in federal court, and observing the
activities that unfolded today, it seemed quite obvious that the
plan by law enforcement from the beginning was not to permit us
to speak, instead to simply corral us into a small area of the park
- which, we had the entire park permitted and they only put us
in a small area. They didn't effectively protect us from protesters
at the beginning, and instead waited to deploy riot police against
us and not the protesters, and when they did so they pushed us
out into the throng. So, they had no intent from the beginning of
honoring the court decision."

During the same show, Henrik Palmgren of the Red Ice
podcast declared what he believed was the cause of the problems.
"Absolutely appalling behaviour by the authorities. I don't know if
it was the City Council or the Mayor, or something, that decided
that this was an unlawful assembly, but when the cops told us all to

disperse, that's when the real issues happened. If they had allowed us to go there, to do the speeches, to hear us out, to make our protest in terms of the attack on our heritage, and get out of there, this would never have happened. People have died today. The lives that have been lost are on the authorities. They should never have done what they did today... They handled it the worst possible way. They should have dispersed the crowds and made sure we could get in and get out without any possible issue but they didn't. At the worst possible time they told us to disperse and leave the park and they sent in the freaking National Guard."

Co-host Eddie Miller agreed, "We have never encountered the duplicity that was encountered by the Unite the Right organizers from the police department or the government of Memphis. Charlottesville hit a new low."

Brad Griffin of the League of the South also spoke of the malfeasance of the authorities on the podcast. "[The police] allowed Antifa to attack us in collusion with the Governor of Virginia. The Governor of Virginia then declared a State of Emergency so we couldn't have a rally anywhere in the state of Virginia... After we had dispersed, we were miles away. I heard someone got ran over. Antifa was rioting. They attacked a car, and someone was run over. I don't know, we were like miles away when that happened, but we heard about it. But this was an absolute clusterfuck, and it's absolutely the fault of the police, because they were afraid the Antifa would accuse them of police brutality, and because they were afraid of being accused of police brutality, the let Antifa riot and attack us."[1]

The same day, Richard Spencer tweeted condemnation of the police. "Trump should not have praised the state and local police. They did the opposite of their job. Total disaster. #Charlottesville"

"The cops just plain set us up," maintains Invictus. "We had all cooperated with the police leading up to the event." Though he agrees city officials bear some blame, that does not excuse the

---

1   The Political Cesspool Radio Show, podcast aired Aug. 12, 2017, www.thepoliticalcesspool.org.

passivity of the police. "They could have done their fucking jobs. They had an obligation to the public."

Enrique Tarrio condemns the police as well. "They failed miserably at their duty of protecting the public... What they should have done - I've been to a million of these things – the street should've been barricaded and the cops in the middle. It's not fucking rocket science."

Though he believes Governor McAuliffe is ultimately responsible, Trace Chiles also assigns the city a portion of the blame. "Wes Bellamy egged it on." He believes that despite any orders to the contrary, the police should have protected the public. "I don't understand how a police officer who took the oath could live with themselves."

Matt Parrot maintains that the authorities planned for the Unite the Right attendees to be beaten up. "They meant to walk us into a trap and let us get the shit beat out of us." But the nationalists had anticipated leftist attacks and come well-prepared. "We were able to completely defend ourselves." Parrot believes that when the stand-down plan failed to result in rally attendees being beaten up, the authorities dispersed the crowds in a way that would create more fighting. "We got out okay, then the car accident happened."

Asked who is to blame for what went wrong at Unite the Right, attendee Luke replies, "I blame the city of Charlottesville, their police, the Virginia police, and the Governor, in that order... The city allowed carnage... When local governments sympathize with Antifa, you get another Charlottesville."

He continues, "My respect for law enforcement is zero at this point." He recalls that at VMI, people had honor system and valued their duties and took their oaths seriously. "To see officers stand down, I lose faith in institutions and people who choose dereliction of duty. You allowed good people to get hurt. They failed to do their duty, and valued their paycheck more than their honor."

Steve, too, blames law enforcement, and he does not mince words. "The Charlottesville Police Department and the Virginia State Police can rot in hell. Screw them."

He explains, "Had leftist demonstrators not provoked and attacked, and had politically motivated politicians not instructed police to act in the way that they did, disaster would not have taken place. It was not the right's fault."

Bill, the monuments advocate, agrees, summarizing it with a colorful metaphor. "When you've got two dogs in a fight, the person that put them together is guilty."

He continues, "The police pushed us into that crap." He contrasts the experience in Charlottesville with that at other events he has attended. "I was in protests at Ole Miss over Confederate monuments this past summer... We marched the campus, and one leftist get in our space, and the police chief put them on the ground. We had no other problems. The police did their job and I thanked them afterwards... [In Charlottesville] they had plenty of police. They chose to use them to push people together... I felt like it was a set up. It could have come off as a peaceful protest. I feel like police forced the trouble. That was deliberate."

Bill also thinks part of the problem is that some of the people involved, like Richard Spencer and Augustus Sol Invictus, "had their own agenda." Though the rally "got hijacked by a couple of groups... There were a lot of good people that came there for the right reasons."

Asked who he believes is to blame for what happened that day, Chris replies, "The police. At the time I blamed Antifa, but looking back I would say the police because they had intel. They knew who would be there." Upon reflection, he is surprised that considering the circumstances, that the violence was not worse.

Gene blames the Mayor of Charlottesville and the Governor of Virginia first, and the Charlottesville Police Department second. "We were foolish enough to think the government and police were going to do something. The government was totally rotten ... They weren't law enforcement. They sided with the criminals."

Jim blames "the Governor on down," including the city government, the local police chief, and the media. He believes the Democratic establishment saw this as an opportunity to hurt Trump. He believes that the rally could have and should have been a safe event. "We weren't there to start a fight. We were there to hear people speak."

Jim specifically exempts Kessler from blame. "He was naive and believed too much that his constitutional rights would be protected... I don't blame Kessler. Anyone who blames him is straight-up wrong. The only thing Kessler is guilty of is naiveté." Jim thinks it is shameful how the other organizers, like Richard Spencer, turned their back on him.

"They should be fighting with him. Some of those guys are charlatans."

Ayla made a similar observation. "A lot of people wanted to blame Jason. I didn't see why they were so angry at him." When she watched Jason address the hostile crowd at City Hall on August 13th, she remembers thinking, "Everyone has abandoned him... Why is no one there? Where is Richard [Spencer]? Where is Nathan [Damigo]?"

She concludes, "I don't blame anyone on our side except for our tendency to wrestle with people when it's really a spiritual battle. There was hyper-focus on earthy things, which led to pride. People thinking they have all the answers. A lot of people walked into Charlottesville feeling like they owned the place."

Asked who is to blame, Tom concludes, "I would say the city of Charlottesville." He has attended lots of political rallies in Tennessee, where law enforcement made it clear that anyone throwing things or being violent would end up in jail. He has been to rallies all over the Southeast over the years, and found that if you do what they ask, usually the cops are cordial and professional.

"We had a permit. We had a right... Maybe the whole state of Virginia was in on it. It was pre-planned for us to fail, I believe." Though never into conspiracy theories until this happened, he has since started to wonder about the plans our elites make behind the scenes.

Nathaniel unapologetically blames the problems at Unite the Right on a "conspiracy" between the governor and the city government of Charlottesville to prevent the rally from occurring because "they don't think we have the right to free speech and assembly."

Unite the Right headliner Pax Dickinson also placed blame squarely on the heads of the authorities.

> My conclusions are that police wanted this to happen. It's clear that VSP had specific orders to drive us out of the park to the south, into the teeth of violent armed Antifa counter-protesters.

> Police could have easily separated the barricades and removed all rally participants to the north, away from Antifa and into empty streets fully controlled by law enforcement. We were driven into a hostile situation intentionally. It's impossible not to believe that the authorities issuing these orders knew exactly what would happen and that they wanted rally attendees to be harmed and possibly killed.

> There was an assumption that police would allow a retreat to the north in the event of a rally cancellation, no one imagined the police would choose to facilitate a clearly violent situation and force the two sides into uncontrolled contact. This looks like it was done with the intent to deny civil rights of a legal protest, in direct defiance of a federal court order. We were set up and trapped, then pushed into a kill zone full of hostile armed enemies. Every injury at this event was due to the nonsensical withdrawal order of the police.

> I got out relatively unscathed, my relatively mild (but still very painful) pepper spraying was my only injury. I was lucky, but many others were not so lucky. Serious questions need to be asked about who gave this order and why the rally participants were not extracted to the north, away from Antifa. The opposing sides could have been kept apart very easily, but police chose not to keep the sides apart.

Governor Terry McAuliffe and the Virginia State Police have blood on their hands, and they must be held to account for that.[2]

Matt Parrot of the Traditionalist Workers' Party agreed. "The media can try to blame nationalists all day long, but just about anybody short of Mother Theresa herself... is going to fight like hell when they've got the fully armed National Guard blocking them from one side and a real-life zombie apocalypse of pissed off degenerates with flamethrowers on the other. This weekend, the media narrative has been all about "Nazi terrorism," pretending we shot down the helicopters, drove into people on purpose like White ISIS, and sucker punched innocent anti-racists who were there to passionately yet peacefully demonstrate their principled opposition... Daryle's naturally running with his necessary narrative in his cable news appearances, that Nazi terrorism has run amok in the New South. But we both know what happened was a spectacular and utterly preventable government leadership failure."

He continues, "[t]he police all appeared angry, frustrated, and confused as I've never seen them before. While I was furious at them at the time, it's clear that they were the victims of an egregious leadership failure which also imperiled them. They were not able to keep up with the entirely unnecessary chaos they had been ordered to unleash and then ordered to deal with. Police don't hire on to enact a maniacal politician's revenge fantasies. They hire on to protect both townies and visitors alike and they were being used."

"With the amount of manpower and firepower at their disposal, the Commonwealth of Virginia could have EASILY and EFFORTLESSLY forced both Antifa and nationalists to sit on picnic blankets and play patty-cake together. Instead, Mayor Signer and Vice-Mayor Bellamy chose to lead the nationalists into a trap, corner us with the help of the fucking military, and stand by as we were beaten to death. It didn't play out like that, but that was clearly the plan."[3]

---

2 Pax Dickinson, "Virginia State Police Facilitated Violence," DailyCaller.com.

3 Matt Parrott, "Catcher in the Reich," Steemit.com.

Hunter Wallace also blames local authorities, pointing out that his group has held many, many prior demonstrations in other jurisdictions without incident. "The mistake that we made in Charlottesville was assuming that it was like other cities in the South. The League of the South has held public demonstrations in Uvalda and Vidalia, GA, New Orleans, LA, Harrison, AR, Tallahassee, FL, Richmond, VA, Shelbyville, TN, Pikeville, KY, Montgomery and Wetumpka, AL, Greenville, SC and many, many other places over the past five years that have been peaceful and uneventful because local law enforcement is competent and capable of doing their jobs. Normally, the police separate our people from counter-protesters as they have most recently done at the 2018 Amren conference in Burns, TN or at the recent NSM rally in Newnan, GA, but that didn't happen in Charlottesville."[4]

In a video statement on August 14th, 2017, Faith Goldy laid blame with the Charlottesville authorities for the event that transpired there specifically, but with the larger culture for creating the climate that allowed it to occur.

> This weekend I intended to report on the facts wherever they led, and there were many that the MSM missed in their own reports, too busy condemning the Alt-Right and accusing me of being one of their ilk. So now, a word to you the corporate media. What happened in Charlottesville was a stark violation of not only everyone's First Amendment rights, but of a federal court order. The police failed to uphold the law that day. They failed to keep the opposing groups separate, even when tensions ran red hot. And they failed to be present in the moments before the scene became deadly. You see, the car attack was not the only horrific scene that day, there were countless instances of illegal deployment of mace, guns drawn, sticks and flag poles used, and from left-wing demonstrators even more often than the right ones.

---

4   Hunter Wallace, "Jacob Goodwin Found Guilty In Charlottesville," OccidentalDissent.com, May 1, 2018.

Alt-left violence is nothing new. We've seen it at countless protests over the past year. And yet, only one group is protected by you the media, not to mention the politicians and some police forces too. Left wing violence at Trump rallies in Chicago, San Jose, Trump's inauguration, Berkeley. Y'all just turn a blind eye. You're happy to loop the B-roll of the handful of idiots with swastika flags, but you don't say a damn thing about the scores of Antifa and BLM donning the emblem associated with even more blood, of the Hammer and Sickle. And then, you try to tie the whole thing to Trump. Well news flash, this isn't Trump's fault. It's the whole damn culture's fault. Decades of identity politics, rammed down the throats of our young in our classrooms now permeates our corporate culture.[5]

It was not only those sympathetic to the right-wing protesters who faulted the authorities for the clashes. Black Lives Matter New York leader Hawk Newsome was questioned by a reporter on the street the day of Unite the Right. Wearing a Black Lives Matter t-shirt and holding a baseball bat on his shoulder, he told the reporter, "I've been protesting in this movement for six years, and the police always form barricades between hostile groups. Today was the first time I didn't see that happen. And that's a fact."

The reporter inquired, "Are you saying groups were hostile?"

Newsome replied, "Everybody was hostile. And they always stand in between hostile groups. But they didn't do that here today. Why? They wanted us to fight each other. They wanted that."[6]

Vegas Tenold is an author and reporter who has spent years covering the far right, often times embedded among its members. Days after Unite the Right, he decisively condemned the police for failure to prevent the mayhem. Tenold wrote that conflict between

---

5 Rebel News "Faith Goldy: Charlottesville, In My Own Words," YouTube video posted Aug. 14, 2017.

6 Jason Kessler, "BLM Leader: 'They wanted us to fight' in Charlottesville," BitChute video uploaded June 23, 2020.

the far right and protesters at rallies usually occurs "all from a safe distance...[I]t is a song and dance that both far-right groups and Antifa understand, and have come to rely on." However, it was different in Charlottesville. "It was no secret that hundreds of armed and angry nationalists were about to rally in the city. They had been given a permit to be there. Antifa had also made it abundantly clear that it had no intention of letting the nationalists rally unchallenged... There are dozens of cities and towns that Charlottesville authorities could have looked to if they needed tips on how to deal with the threat of racist extremists marching in their streets. Yet they chose to do nothing until it was too late. The radicals may have brought violence to Charlottesville, but the police chose to let it loose."[7]

Local Charlottesville news blogger and podcast host Rob Schilling says, "The city is culpable in a lot of ways... there was institutional failure on multiple levels." He singles out some local officials. "Maurice Jones was overpaid and underqualified, which is a provable fact," calling him "a neophyte who didn't know how to manage... the same can be said of Al Thomas." Schilling believes Thomas may have had the skills to succeed in a small-town setting, but when it came to managing a major event in a large city, "he wasn't up to the task." Schilling also denounces the "bumbling city council," and believes that Signer's botched attempt to handle the crisis was "worse than nothing."

Unhailed Restraint

One thing that is seldom considered by those who decry the "violent White Nationalist rally" is the astounding amount of restraint showed by the attendees. Open carry was legal in Virginia, and there were hundreds of militia members and Unite the Right attendees bearing arms that day. Despite hours of being pummeled by hard projectiles and chemical weapons, those hundreds of armed Unite the Right attendees exercised remarkable self-control and restraint by NOT drawing their firearms. Only one shot was fired by a Unite

---

7   Vegas Tenold, "The Cops Dropped the Ball in Charlottesville," *The New Republic*, Aug. 16, 2017.

the Right attendee that day, and it was a warning shot not intended to inflict harm. It was fired towards a counter-protester who was aiming a makeshift flamethrower towards a crowd of people.

Not only did Antifa provoke Unite the Right attendees for hours, law enforcement made the situation even more provocative. Cantwell interpreted the dispersal of rally attendees into the mob as a deliberate attempt to induce them to release gunfire. "They pushed hundreds of armed White nationalists into a crowd of communist rioters who threw rocks and piss and shit and bleach and pepper spray and hit us with clubs and did everything they could to provoke us into shooting them."[8]

Rebecca Dillingham, also known as Dissident Mama, did not attend Unite the Right but has followed the event closely and written about it for years. In her podcast interview with Kessler, she reflected, "It's actually amazing, I think, that there wasn't more violence. So sometimes I try to turn the tables on people and say, 'Wow, I think the Unite the Right people deserve medals because it could have gone so much crazier... really the fact that it wasn't a shoot-out, I think is amazing.' It's almost a testament to how self-controlled the Unite the Right people were, in my opinion."

Kessler replied, "Definitely. In addition to the Alt-Right groups, you had a number of militias, and the MSM constantly uses the images of the people with the AK15s to attack the rally and say, 'Look how prepared for violence they were!' But those militia people, they had enormous restraint. And they didn't have an affinity for the actual protesters. I think they may have provided medical assistance to more of the counter- protesters than the actual protesters. But these people were being attacked. Cars were being attacked. Mobs of people were attacking cars of people who were trying to leave. And still not a single - well, one bullet was fired. There was the guy who fired a warning shot to stop the individual who was shooting an improvised flame thrower at people who were being pushed out of the park. Of course, they prosecuted that guy to the hilt. It was unreal. Technically, firing a warning shot is not legal in Virginia,

---

8 Hawes Spencer, "'Crying Nazi' Christopher Cantwell Says He's Just a 'Goddamn Human Being," TheDailyBeast.com , Aug. 30, 2017.

but I mean within the context that this individual was shooting a flamethrower at people, you'd think they've cut him a bit of slack."[9]

One attendee went even further. "The city fathers should be offering Unite the Right activists tearful tributes for the latter's saint-like restraint in not opening fire despite more than justified provocation."[10]

---

9 "Jason Kessler," Podcast on DissidentMama.net.

10 Charlottesville Survivor, "The System Revealed: Antifa, Virginia Politicians And Police Work Together to Shut Down Unite the Right," Vdare.com, Aug. 12, 2017.

CHAPTER 26 QUICK LINKS:

The Political Cesspool Radio Show, podcast aired Aug. 12, 2017. Hour 1 URL: qrs.ly/r8cvtl5 ; Hour2 URL: qrs.ly/r8cvtm1 ; Hour 3 URL: qrs.ly/9jcvtm3

Rebel News "Faith Goldy: Charlottesville, In My Own Words," video, Aug. 14, 2017. URL: qrs.ly/wmcvtqt

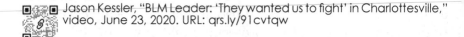

Jason Kessler, "BLM Leader: 'They wanted us to fight' in Charlottesville," video, June 23, 2020. URL: qrs.ly/91cvtqw

"Dissident Mama, episode 27 – Jason Kessler," Jan. 22, 2021. URL: qrs.ly/cycvto9

CHAPTER 27

DEFLECTION AND PROJECTION: THE CARPETBAGGERS

"They're just using this as a vehicle to spew their hatred."

FROM THE BEGINNING, the government of Charlottesville displayed a lack of understanding of the right-wing protesters in their city as well as a grave dearth of self-awareness.

In all the books mentioned below, right-wingers and monument supporters are referred to continuously, and with no justification provided, as "White Supremacists," "White Nationalists," and "Neo-Nazis." They provide no evidence to support their use of these labels, despite the fact that they are explicitly rejected by most of the people to whom they are applied. This must either mean the officeholders are willfully ignorant of the true beliefs of citizens who are their ideological opponents, or that they are deliberately using the most inflammatory terms possible to vilify and dehumanize them. Whether disingenuous or ignorant, this mislabeling is offensive and dangerous.

Wes Bellamy, the City Councilor whose conflict with Kessler precipitated Unite the Right, wrote a book entitled, *Monumental: It Was Never About a Statue,* in which he condemns the city of Charlottesville, saying "racial inequality runs through its blood."[1]

---

1   Bellamy, *Monumental,* p. 1

With regards to his efforts to remove the Lee statue, Bellamy admits, "It wasn't about the statue – it was about changing the culture of the city."[2] Of the monument supporters, he says," The people who came to the press conference were not there to defend the statue. They were there because they felt that there was an attack on their culture and their way of life."[3]

Well, yes. Are leaders meant to represent all the citizens in their jurisdiction, or to foist fundamental changes upon the portion of people for whom they have personal distaste? If, like Bellamy, you view the citizenry as morally flawed and inferior, and yourself as noble and righteous, you would probably choose the latter.

Bellamy interpreted backlash to his efforts at cultural cleansing like this: "Challenging the status quo or even demanding that Black people be treated as equals was seen as an immediate threat... our values were deeply rooted in traditional southern beliefs. Beliefs that meant that people of color, specifically Black people, were seen as inferior."[4] Viewing the issue solely through the lens of Black identity politics, he could not understand the issue from the view of Whites or Southerners who had no desire to subjugate Black people, but merely wanted to preserve symbols of a culture and history they cherished. Even though he was in a position of authority in the city and the instigator of the situation, the devotee of Cultural Marxism perceived himself as the victim.

In *Cry Havoc*, the book by former Mayor Mike Signer about the events surrounding Unite the Right, he recalls,

> I felt [a chill] when I stopped to look at three young men crumpled on the sidewalk along Fourth Street, three hours after Heather Heyer was killed. They wore ragged camouflage and rebel flag garb. The guy in the middle had a gash on his forehead, and blood was trickling down his cheek. They looked stunned

2 Bellamy, p. 31.

3 Bellamy, p. 42

4 Bellamy, p. 47.

– as if they didn't even understand what they had unleashed. I almost shivered.[5]

"They looked stunned – as if they didn't even understand what they had unleashed."

This statement shows an absolutely staggering lack of understanding and responsibility on the part of Signer. Though he held a position of authority in an historic Virginia city, Signer's family hailed from New York and he earned his PhD at Berkeley. He describes himself as having been "[a]larmed by the surge of Trumpism on the national scene,"[6] and states that after Trump won the South Carolina primary in 2016," Wherever I went, a dark, sick feeling followed me like a shadow." [7]

On January 31, 2017, early in the presidency of Donald Trump, Mike Signer held an unscheduled and unpermitted rally on Charlottesville's Downtown Mall in which he declared Charlottesville to be the "Capitol of the Resistance" to Trump's agenda. His speech was so strongly worded that CPD Lieutenant Brian O'Donnell described it as "tantamount to war rhetoric," and feared it would undermine legitimacy in government institutions.[8]

With this admitted revulsion towards American populism, and no real appreciation of the culture or values of the traditional population of Virginia, Signer callously dismissed those who cherished the history of their state. For example, when he referred in his book to "rebel flag-wearing defenders of 'southern heritage,'" he placed the term "southern heritage" in scare quotes.[9] He hailed Nikki Haley's efforts to remove the Confederate flag in South Carolina as a means to "repudiate [Dylann] Roof's twisted, demonic project."[10] Signer wondered, with regards to the Confederate statue

---

5 Signer, *Cry Havoc*, p. 6.

6 Signer, p. 23.

7 Signer, p. 30.

8 Heaphy Report, p. 24.

9 Signer, *Cry Havoc*, p. 39.

10 Signer, p. 43.

issue, how he would feel "as a Jew, if I had to walk by a Statue of Adolf Hitler or Josef Mengele, in Charlottesville. Wouldn't I want them torn down?"[11]

When Virginians and other Southerners came to assemble around the statue of an admired leader whose memory Signer hoped to purge, he failed in his responsibility to protect their right to assemble, leaving them at the mercy of a dangerous mob. When they were injured and reeling from shock because of the failure of the government to perform its most basic duty of protecting citizens, he blamed them – HE BLAMED THEM – people who were reacting to his city's attempted purge of their cultural emblems from the land of their forefathers, for "unleashing" the horrors of the day.

Signer, like the other governmental authority figures in Charlottesville, only viewed Southern and right-wing citizens as a pathology of which society must be cured. That he and his lot vowed to promote inclusion by excluding their own disfavored groups would be laughable were the consequences not so tragic. Through vilification of his own ideological enemies – for example, his bizarre likening of Jason Kessler to Heath Ledger's "horribly twisted" Joker character "who delighted in toying with others, creating pain and destruction for pleasure" – Signer undermined the supposed righteousness of his own motives.

Then-Governor Terry McAuliffe also penned a book about Unite the Right, which makes it clear that he does not understand or respect the historic people of Virginia. He acknowledged that when he thought to run for the highest office in the state, "[e]ven people who liked me as a candidate thought I might have a hard time convincing Virginians I was truly one of them." Though he had grown up in New York he declared, "Virginia was my home, where I paid taxes and sent my children to school."[12]

There was much mention in his book about the historic sins of the state and the duty he felt to rectify them. He spoke about the "deep legacies" of racism, and described Richmond as "the capital

---

11 Signer, p. 46.

12 McAuliffe, *Beyond Charlottesville*, pp. 9-10.

of the Confederacy, spearheading the resistance to freeing slaves in the Civil War."[13]

He wrote at length about his pet issue of restoring voting rights for felons, describing their disenfranchisement as "a legacy of Jim Crow, a variation of the poll tax," adding, "I never whitewashed Virginia's sordid history. In June 2015, I used my executive authority to remove the Confederate flag from Virginia license plates."[14]

He rebuked the words of Robert E. Lee's great-granddaughter who spoke at the dedication of the Charlottesville statue of Lee in 1924, "remembering her ancestor as a man who she said represented the 'moral greatness of the Old South.' For her, the Civil War was not about slavery, it was about differing 'interpretations of our Constitution' and differing 'ideals of democracy.' She was wrong. It was about slavery and it was about treason, pure and simple, and we know the deep and lasting damage that comes from running away from that simple truth." [15]

In the book, McAuliffe also expressed disgust with Charlottesville's "pathetic" permitting process and the city's lack of response to Kessler's permit application which allowed it to be automatically approved. Upon hearing about the permit approval, he admits remarking to a colleague, "This has nothing to do with the Robert E. Lee statue. Most of these idiots don't even know who the hell Robert E. Lee actually was. They're just using this as a vehicle to come spew their hatred." He described Kessler as "clearly delusional," for decrying the purge of White history, and Unite the Right as a "scheme ... to pull White nationalists, neo-Nazis, and other right-wing extremists from all over the country." [16]

Displaying an astounding lack of self-awareness and unintentional irony that most Southerners will find darkly humorous, McAuliffe described Unite the Right attendees as "So

---

13 McAuliffe, p. 8.

14 McAuliffe, p. 26.

15 McAuliffe, p. 50.

16 McAuliffe, p. 56.

many out of state agitators [who] had come in to defile everything we care about. It was disgusting and infuriating."[17]

That sounds just awful, Governor. I can hardly imagine.

17 McAuliffe, p. 85.

CHAPTER 28

THE ALT-RIGHT
AFTER UNITE THE RIGHT

"There was a real busting up of camaraderie."

Effect On The Movement

THE EVENING OF UNITE THE RIGHT, the Political Cesspool podcast host James Edwards made a prediction about what might happen to right-wing activists. "I think you could see a definite crack down on our organizations and on our leaders as a result not just of this, but this will be used as a catalyst perhaps to advance us from mere hate groups to what they will inaccurately call perhaps even domestic terrorist groups, because of course you've seen... the media is of course blaming those who came on our side to peacefully assemble for the entirety of the violence, and the people who were actually of course perpetrating the violence were, as Keith mentioned, held as 'counter-demonstrators' and nothing more or less."[1]

Reflecting on the impact of Charlottesville on the Alt-Right, Ayla recalls that things in the movement had gone fairly well up to that point. "It was growing like wildfire, and it was fun." She explains

---

1 The Political Cesspool Radio Show, podcast aired Aug.12, 2017, www. thepoliticalcesspool.org.

that there was lots of optimism, and people felt they were on the cusp of changing things for the better and had the ear of the country. The new right had momentum after Trump was elected, and the opposition needed to knock the wind out of it. "We miscalculated the enemy. We didn't realize how hard they'd smack us down. A lot of people we thought of as strong leaders crumbled. We weren't strong enough and didn't have the right people in the right places." She notes, "There was a real busting up of camaraderie after that."

In the aftermath, Ayla says, "I lost touch with a lot of people." She was particularly disappointed by Richard Spencer. She had once viewed him as a leader, but lost trust in him after he gave her what she believes was a bad-faith referral to an unscrupulous journalist.

Invictus states that after Charlottesville, the Alt-Right was "destroyed. It splintered everybody." He believes "that was clearly their aim. We were all getting together, getting our ships sailing in the same direction." Now everyone is suspicious of one another. Unite the Right caused a rift amongst his associates. Invictus explains that the absence of "Based Stickman" Kyle Chapman caused a problem because afterwards "he threw us under the bus." Fraternal Order of Alt-Knights members who had attended Unite the Right were like "Fuck Chapman" after that.

He shares another important takeaway from Charlottesville. "The lesson is do not trust the police. Do not trust the government. They are an absolute enemy. We cooperated with them. We told them our plans, and they used the information to set us up." Invictus asserts, "They stabbed us in the back so fucking hard. Anyone who trusts the police after that is just plain retarded."

The FOAK pretty much dissolved not long after Unite the Right, says Trace Chiles. He had worked in the music industry with mostly left leaning people who had not been aware of his political views. "People who knew me were quite surprised to see me in Charlottesville." Some former friends turned on him and he was besieged with death threats. Concerned for his children, he relocated from Richmond to another city and has only recently moved back.

Parrot says that the aftermath of Charlottesville "permanently ended public demonstrations... civil liberties are no longer operative for us. We are being spoken about like domestic terrorists. Nationalists have to leave in either an ambulance or a police car. We have to shift to the new reality."

Unite the Right attendee Luke believes the outcome of Unite the Right discredited some of the movement's leaders like Richard Spencer and Mike Enoch, revealing that "the Alt-Right was rotten at the top."

Nathaniel has become disillusioned with the Alt-Right, and is leaning back more towards Libertarianism. He turned against Richard Spencer after the release of an undercover video where Spencer expressed White Supremacist views. Nathaniel says, "I don't think I'm superior to others."

Young Appalachian attendee Chris, who before considered himself a typical Libertarian-leaning Republican, says that his views have moved farther to the right since the event. In part this was because the far-right attendees became his unexpected allies during the fighting that broke out at Unite the Right. "The far right had my back, even though I wasn't one of them. Neo-Nazis came to my rescue multiple times... I started giving their views consideration. I know others that came out very hard core."

Chris' experience touches on an important point. In a state of anarchy, people tend to align along tribal lines. As law and order continue to break down in the United States, it is likely to become more tribal.

Tom laments that the fallout from Unite the Right has been used to push more destruction. "They used this to take the teeth out of nationalists" using lawfare. Tom says that nowadays many people that he invites to rallies are too scared to come. They are afraid the police will not protect them, and that if they protect themselves, they will be arrested or sued. "This is probably what the people who caused the failure envisioned."

When Your Enemies Write Your Story

Asked whether his reputation has improved in the years since Unite the Right, Kessler replies, "Not at all. I mean there's

345

no way anybody could ever get any positive information out. I'm totally censored. I used to be able to go on conservative radio [in Charlottesville]. They won't even mention me, you know? The problem is mainstream conservative circles is that they believe conspiracy theories about me. Stuff that was propagated by people like Alex Jones, and you see a lot of mainstream politicians put weird conspiracy theories out there. So they think that I voted for Hillary Clinton, that I am an Occupy Wall Street activist, and fake bullshit. And I understand why they're doing that. They're trying to shift blame. Because the media came down and said look, this is a bad person. He's associated with this violent event, and he's to blame for it. They want to say, he's not even a conservative. We don't have anything to do with that."

"They're really missing the point, because my personal politics are not the issue. The issue is that they way that the media and the establishment can bring the hammer down on any political dissent and just do this shock-and-awe psyop campaign to make somebody look bad. I'm not a Neo Nazi like Wikipedia says. I'm not an antisemitic conspiracy theorist. I don't even consider myself a White Nationalist. And anybody who saw me in my day-to-day life would think that was absolutely ridiculous what they're saying about me. But that is like the gospel now, and that is how history is going to be told. And history is going to have completely whitewashed the Antifa who were attacking us. It's gonna whitewash the fact that the police stood down and allowed us to be attacked even though we had a permit."

"So the only form of information the Charlottesville community gets about what I'm doing as far as like my legal activism and so forth is through the local newspaper which is the Daily Progress. The Daily Progress writer is like a literal Antifa. He's friends with the people who attacked us. So every article he's writing is a lie or a distortion of the truth that omits crucial details. So I think the lie is by omission. And then those stories get picked up by the AP. That gets picked up by the Huffington Post and everything else that people on the left in particular read."

CHAPTER 28 QUICK LINKS:

The Political Cesspool Radio Show, podcast aired Aug. 12, 2017. Hour 1 URL: qrs.ly/r8cvtl5 ; Hour2 URL: qrs.ly/r8cvtm1 ; Hour 3 URL: qrs.ly/9jcvtm3

CHAPTER 29

AMERICA IN THE AFTERMATH

"It's a dangerous cycle we have entered."

UNITE THE RIGHT ATTENDEE Jim says, "My personal belief is there is a globalist left tied to the CCP [Chinese Communist Party], and that the rise of American nationalism is a threat to that order... The South is the most American of the United States" in that it is pro-God and pro-country, and therefore needs to be destroyed. "Astutely, most on the far left know that the South is the last rock in the way of their Marxist conclusion."

Asked what else he would like the public to know, Jim states, "There was once a country that believed in the freedoms of speech and assembly. You don't have to agree, but we want our country to have those rights. Our country no longer values this. The loss of those freedoms is a loss for everyone, not just conservatives."

Enrique Tarrio chalks up the political fallout to "never let a good disaster go to waste," explaining, "They're using Charlottesville for a fear campaign. I think it's pretty stupid."

Of the disastrous outcome of the rally, Luke concludes, "I think it was a setup. They wanted to blame the violence on Trump and crack down on the dissident right and Confederate imagery. This was meant as political leverage, and the prototype for all the leftist violence we have seen all over the country especially in the Summer of 2020."

Faith Goldy spoke about the new ominous era the events of Charlottesville exemplify. "Several months ago, I predicted a civil war was coming to America. Today, it is without hesitation that I can say, that civil war has begun. No one in their right mind could look at the images that emerged from Charlottesville this weekend and deny it. From mace, shields, and flag poles, to gas masks, kevlar, and firearms, America is experiencing an escalating civil war a la 2017. Sure, neighbor may not be fighting neighbor in the streets without warning, but what we have seen is organized battlegrounds every few weeks, where a right-wing group, be they Alt-Right or alt-light, organizes a rally only to be stormed by the instigating, violent alt-left, let down by the police and then condemned by politicians. It's a dangerous cycle we have entered, one that many of us in the alternative media have been warning everyone about for months. And I'll be damned if a single person out there wishes to label me a sympathizer of violent behavior. I'm one of the very many trying to put a stop to escalating tensions in America's cultural and political civil war. So, sorry guys, just because you label everyone that you disagree with a Nazi, doesn't make it the truth."[1]

In the aftermath of Unite the Right, there has been a chilling effect on political dissent and freedoms that Americans used to take for granted. Kessler explains; "What happened with the Charlottesville Unite the Right rally was a start of a model that they would use which really was the shock and awe campaign to label anybody who is a political dissident engaging in free speech in the public square and turning them into some kind of terrorist or whatever, and the media is brought down to such a powerful psychological weapon, there is no way you can withstand that. The kinds of things they've honed to use against President Trump, they can use against average citizens, and these are tactics that they

---

1 Rebel News "Faith Goldy: Charlottesville, In My Own Words," YouTube video posted Aug. 14, 2017.

probably would have used in a foreign theater against dictators in the Middle East or something."[2]

The self-serving response of many on the right, politicians and citizens alike, allowed the tactics used against Unite the Right attendees to proliferate. Kessler explains: "The Republicans stood down on Charlottesville and allowed the Democrats to run the narrative, and they're paying a big price for that, because they didn't stop with the political dissidents in Charlottesville. They moved on to normal Republicans and Trump supporters." The surge of prosecutions against right-wingers for acts of self-defense is one example of the tactics that are now being used against more mainstream conservatives. "All of these things have an analog in Charlottesville."[3]

---

2 "Jason Kessler," Podcast on DissidentMama.net.

3 "Counter-Currents Radio Podcast No. 292: Jason Kessler," counter-currents. com podcast, Sept. 29, 2020.

CHAPTER 29 QUICK LINKS:

Rebel News "Faith Goldy: Charlottesville, In My Own Words," video, Aug. 14, 2017. URL: qrs.ly/wmcvtqt

"Dissident Mama, episode 27 – Jason Kessler," Jan. 22, 2021. URL: qrs. ly/cycvto9

"Counter-Currents Radio Podcast No. 292: Jason Kessler," podcast, Sept. 29, 2020. URL: qrs.ly/3scvtqz

Part Six:

The Path Forward

CHAPTER 30

THE UNITE THE RIGHT ANNIVERSARY RALLY

"We cannot allow a precedent to be set where they trample on our rights and we take it lying down."

Why Unite The Right Again?

ON NOVEMBER 29, 2017, Kessler announced on his personal website his plan for an anniversary Unite the Right rally, writing:

> I've applied for a new permit at Charlottesville's Lee Park for August 11th and 12th, 2018 on the one year anniversary of Unite the Right. I fully expect the Charlottesville government to try and reject it and I'm ready for that fight.

> First, let me explain why I'm doing this. I simply will not allow these bastards to use the one year anniversary of the Charlottesville government violating a federal judge's order and the U.S. Constitution, in conjunction with violent Antifa groups, to further demonize activists...

[W]e cannot and should not allow our enemies to turn the anniversary of the day they violated our rights into some kind of propaganda victory where they continue to smear us with a distorted version of August 12th, 2017 and hold our attackers up as martyrs and heroes.

In the lengthy post, Kessler went on to detail mistakes that were made at Unite the Right – mistakes such as his having placed too much trust in the authorities and other organizers, having not been prepared for the unexpected legal battles, and having been too lax about messaging that did not translate well from the Alt-Right's edgy internet subculture to the general public.

Finally, without naming him directly, Kessler bemoaned the trust he had placed in Richard Spencer. "I assumed that because one of the Unite the Right speakers was a millionaire and has successfully challenged several universities in court that he would have connections, legal and otherwise, which we could have relied on."

Kessler delineated why the mistakes from the first rally would not happen again, and also called for a commitment to nonviolence. "We should know how to defend ourselves lawfully but we must avoid any violent confrontation at this rally whatsoever... We need to prove to them that we are the good guys... that we are willing to take the abuse and still march forward in furtherance of our cause without becoming the aggressors."

He concluded, "We have 9 months to prepare ourselves. I don't expect the same coalition as in 2017. Undoubtedly there may be hard feelings between different factions or people. . but I hold no hard feelings about anyone who will shake my hand in friendship going forward. We have a duty to our people and our nation to rise above pettiness and become the individuals that history requires us to be. See you in Charlottesville August 11th and 12th, 2018."[1]

However, the second Charlottesville rally was not to be.

---

1 Jason Kessler, "Back to Charlottesville (UTR Anniversary Rally)," JasonKessler.us, Nov. 29, 2017.

As expected, the city denied Kessler's permit application. And as promised, he responded by filing a lawsuit against the city on March 6, 2018, explaining, "I've struggled through enormous personal adversity and financial cost to ensure that we have an opportunity to do this thing over again and do it right... We cannot allow a precedent to be set where a government can trample on our rights, blame us for it and we take it lying down."[2]

With the Charlottesville suit still pending, on May 8, 2018 he filed a new permit for a rally of about 400 people to march to Lafayette Park across from the White House in Washington DC, with the stated purpose of "protesting the civil rights abuse in Charlottesville, VA, White civil rights rally." With an alternative location secured, Kessler's lawsuit for the Charlottesville location was dropped shortly before the scheduled date of the anniversary rally.

Despite the fact that the rally was being held in D.C., Virginia Gov. Ralph Northam and the city of Charlottesville proactively declared a state of emergency for the weekend, allowing for the National Guard to assist with security needs and for two million dollars in state funds to be allocated.[3]

Return To Charlottesville?

The biggest names from the Charlottesville Unite the Right rally did not share Kessler's desire for a second gathering. Some of the former Alt-Right leaders and groups were having legal issues. As previously mentioned, the Traditionalist Workers Party had begun to crumble after a falling out between Matt Parrott and Matt Heimbach led to the arrest of Heimbach in March, 2018. Christopher Cantwell was still mired in defending himself against criminal charges stemming from the first Unite the Right. Others were simply leery because of the calamitous fallout of the first event.

---

2 Jason Kessler, "Lawsuit Filed for Unite the Right Anniversary Rally!," JasonKessler.us, March 7, 2018.

3 Alan Suderman, "Emergency declared ahead of Charlottesville anniversary," AP, Aug. 8, 2018.

"After the unfortunate events and the violent attacks we suffered, I am reluctant to return to Charlottesville. I hope the event, if it happens, is peaceful and that Antifa thugs do not disrupt it with violence as they did the last one," Mike "Enoch" Peinovich told Newsweek.

League of the South President Michael Hill discouraged its members from attending, saying, "We don't have anything to gain by going back to Charlottesville."[4]

League of the South Public Affairs Director Brad Griffin, writing as Hunter Wallace, also discouraged people from attending the rally, but declined to denounce it. "By holding these volatile public events, we're gambling on the police showing up and doing their jobs... I don't think it's worth the risk to walk into a potential trap ... Personally, I think we are better off avoiding these people. I've said that we shouldn't engage with Antifa at all anymore... While I won't be going to Unite The Right 2, I'm not going to condemn those who go."[5]

In an article entitled, "Official Daily Stormer Position: Don't Go to "Unite the Right 2" – We Disavow," Andrew Anglin wrote, "I don't want you to ruin your life by showing your face at a post-Charlottesville rally. Everything is different now... If you show up at this event, and you are identified, your life will be ruined... [at] Charlottesville: I personally thought we would be able to give a few speeches in a park, show that yes, we are a real life movement, then go home. Oh how young I was."[6]

Though much of the Alt-Right decided to stay away, the counter-protesters did plan to attend, and in large numbers. Organizers under the banner of "Shut It Down DC," were arranging for about 1000 people to attend the DC United Against Hate rally and march. Providing a welcome contrast from the stance of law enforcement

---

4 Michael Edison Hayden, "White Nationalist Leaders Don't Want to Return to Charlottesville for Anniversary Rally," Newsweek, May 10, 2018.

5 Hunter Wallace, "Official Position: Unite The Right 2," OccidentalDissent.com, Aug. 7, 2018.

6 Andrew Anglin, "Official Daily Stormer Position: Don't Go to 'Unite the Right 2' – We Disavow," DailyStormer.com, Aug. 5, 2018.

leaders in Charlottesville, D.C. Chief of Police Peter Newsham unequivocally stated his intention for police to do "whatever is necessary" to keep rally attendees and counter-protesters separated.[7]

Rally Day

The rally headliners were protected by police throughout the event, but the day was not without incident. Kessler and other participants got on a bus to be taken to the venue. They were ditched by their driver and left stranded in a Target parking lot. Arrangements were made for them to take a subway train the rest of the way to the venue. Some people who meant to attend were separated from the group, and those who did manage to catch the train arrived quite early, thus the event ended around 5p.m., before it was even supposed to have begun.

Kessler had considered bringing in extreme speakers like Patrick Little and David Duke, but decided on a more moderate approach to be more accommodating of non-White allies who were expected to be in attendance. Ultimately, there were three speakers besides Kessler: Charles Edward Lincoln, Al Stankar, and Jovi Val.

MAGA personality and free speech advocate Jovanni Valle (better known as Jovi Val) had considered going to the first Unite the Right, and regretted allowing himself to be dissuaded from it. He had made a point to meet Jason in the year after the first rally, and though he was working on a campaign in Las Vegas at the time of the anniversary event, he made arrangements to travel to DC to participate. Val was expecting severe backlash for his participation in the event. "I'm going to get excommunicated for this," he told friends.

About two or three dozen rally participants marched with a heavy police escort to Lafayette Park with Kessler, who held an American flag as he walked. When they marched to Lafayette Park, they were escorted by federal agents, including a helicopter above, while throngs

---

7   Mark Segraves and Sophia Barnes, "'Whatever We Need to Do': DC Police Hope to Keep White Supremacists, Counter demonstrators Separate at Rallies," NBCWashington.com, Aug. 8, 2018.

of Antifa followed jeering things like "Nazi!" "Fascist!" and "Kill them!" Val remembers being pelted with wooden pegs. It was impressed upon him, "how far people will go to shut down free speech."

Kessler took the opportunity of the speech to talk about what went wrong at the first Unite the Right and respond to naysayers. He also defended his belief in the need for a White civil rights movement.

> My name is Jason Kessler, for those of you who don't know me. Many of you will be watching this at home rather than here in the park. I organized last year's UTR rally and I organized this year's rally. And I'm going to tell you why I did that.
>
> But first I would like to make a few things clear. I am not doing this to disrespect the memory of people who were hurt or who died last year. My condolences are with the family of Heather Heyer, and with the families of the two VA state troopers who died in the helicopter accident. I thank them for their service.
>
> Second, I would like to thank the law enforcement community of the Washington D.C. area for protecting my free speech rights, and by proxy, the free speech rights of all Americans.
>
> This has been a very weird and imperfect process, and I think hopefully we'll do more demonstrations like this in the DC area in the future, and learn how to work together better. But the main thing is so far, I'm not aware of anybody being hurt. Everybody's safe. That was my number one priority.
>
> My second priority was to uphold free speech because I think a very dangerous precedent was set last year for a number of different reasons. I did not want to allow the tactics of Antifa - using violence to shut down the speech of people they disagree with - to work. That's one of the reasons we don't have more people. There were a lot of people who were at last year's rally that are

very scared this year. They felt like last year they came to express their point of view, they were attacked, and when they fought back, they were overly prosecuted. And the Charlottesville government refused to prosecute the Antifa side of the violence.

He continued, describing the events of the first Unite the Right to the small crowd.

All right. So what happened last year in Charlottesville was that I organized the Unite the Right event. The purpose of the Unite the Right event was to say that White people deserve to be able to stand up for their rights, like other people are able to do. I think the tearing down of that Robert E Lee statue was symbolic of a replacement that is going on in the United States where White people are being guilted for slavery and war and all these things that every racial group has engaged in. But they're saying tear down Robert E Lee, tear down Thomas Jefferson. They're not saying tear down the Great Wall of China that was built with slave labor. They're not saying tear down the Mayan and Aztecan pyramids which were built with slave labor. It's only White people and it's only our countries which have to be flooded with too many people to the point that the host populations don't exist anymore.

Addressing common misconceptions about himself and the White civil rights movement, Kessler continues,

I'm not a White nationalist. I've never claimed to be a White nationalist. I'm okay with sharing this country with people from around the world. But, if you bring in too many people at once, you're not the same country any more. And that's what they're doing and that's why a lot of White people are aggrieved, because they feel like the country they're waking up in, in 2018, is a very, very different country than the one they woke up in, in 1960, 1970, 1980. And so I think therefore the face of White advocacy is very different than it was in the past.

As he has done on other occasions, Kessler calls out the people on the right who engage in counter-productive tactics.

A lot of folks are deliberately misconstruing White identity politics today, as something that's endorsed by the KKK and neo-Nazis, and I think in fact there are a lot of people in the Alt-Right who are encouraging that by trying to be these cartoon Nazis and deliberately stupid and hateful. I've just gotta say, I thank the Alt-Right to some extent for waking me up to the fact that my people had a voice, and had people who were gonna stand up for them. But I've gotta say, a lot of the jokes just aren't funny anymore. Give it a rest. We've gotta be honest. We've gotta be sincere. There is a way forward to help White folks but we cannot be associating with hate or violence or oppression.

Now with Charlottesville last year, I tried to do a demonstration for that Robert E. Lee statue. I invited a lot of people from across the Alt-Right, Alt-Lite, Trump supporters, American heritage supporter. A lot of folks were scared to come and be associated with some of the more extreme speakers like Richard Spencer. So it ended up becoming a more extreme event than I had intended. But nevertheless, even if some of the people had ideas which were offensive at that rally, the vast, vast majority of people on my side were non-violent. And I think even the other side, even though they came prepared to use violence to shut down the first Unite the Right rally, they would have been non-violent too if law enforcement had done what it was supposed to do.

What we were dealing with was a city where the Vice Mayor who was trying to tear down that Robert E Lee statue was pretending to be doing it in the interest of equality or tolerance, but at the same time his tweets were saying "I hate White people," "I hate seeing White people around town," "My favorite thing about being down South was seeing the faces of little White men when they have to look up to a Black man." I mean this was a racist, anti-White bigot and that's why he was going after our heritage.

And I think a lot of people who hate White people are hiding behind this false credo of equality. They are for supremacy. They are marxists, and right now they see the White man as being on top. But not all White people are on top. I'm a White man. I'm not rich. I'm not privileged. I've had a hard time just as other people have had. I have an army of people trying to stop me from being able to speak.

There was an independent review done of the Charlottesville government's conduct last year by former Federal prosecutor Tim Heaphy. Tim Heaphy said that the cause for the violence was the Charlottesville government. As the first fights broke out last year, the police chief, Al Thomas, said "Let them fight. It will make it easier to declare an unlawful assembly." That's why I wanted to speak to President Trump at the White House. I think that is was criminal misconduct by the Charlottesville government. They shut down that event by allowing violence. They promised eight squadrons of police officers to keep the peace. They didn't show up. They promised 200 cops in the back of the park. They didn't show up. They promised cops at the front of the park. They didn't show up. And in fact when the violence started, they were allowing people to riot in the streets, point rifles at people in cars, attack cars, and I think that's part of why people lost their lives last year.[8]

When Val took the stage, he used the opportunity to talk about how there is diversity within groups of White people, and how White Nationalism differs from White Supremacy.

I came out here to stand for free speech. I will always stand for free speech. Not only will I stand for it but I will fight for it. I don't care what race or religion you are. You have every right to speak in this country. But Jason made a valid point. There is a problem going on right now in America when people like him are being attacked when he wants to peacefully assemble in this country. Why? People are afraid of a country being predominately White. I am here today, but I said to myself, if every speaker on this stage was White, why should that bother me? Why should it bother you? I don't need to tell you what race I am. I don't need to tell you what gender I am there's only two of course. I don't need to tell you what religion I am.

I'll tell you one thing though. I am an American. Are you an American? Do you love this country? Then you sir, you ma'am, you are a nationalist. And if you're White and you love this country, you're a White nationalist. There's a big difference between White supremacy and White nationalism, okay. You have to stop using that word to describe someone who you believe is a Nazi... Whether you like it or not, whether you agree or disagree, it's not fair that my family can go back to the island, and wave their flag, and say that they're from this country, and they're proud, but if somebody from here says they're proud to be an American and they're White you label them a Nazi. That is BS.

---

8 News2Share, "Jason Kessler's Full Speech at 'Unite the Right 2,'" YouTube video posted Aug. 13, 2018.

I'm gonna tell you this right now, okay? I don't care what race you are. You have every right to get on this stage and speak your peace. If you are hosting free speech rallies - and this goes for the Trump supporters - there should be no reason why you excommunicate people because you don't agree with their message... I don't care how many people told me not to come. I came today for a reason.[9]

More Deplatforming

Around the time of the anniversary rally, there was another flurry of bans from social media and other services for would-be participants.

A Washington Restaurant Association sent information to its members giving them legal guidance for refusing service to White nationalists. Airbnb announced that like the previous year, they may remove people associated with the event from their platform.

The social media and payment processor purge that began after the first rally gathered steam once again around the time of the anniversary rally. In July 2018, an article in Guardian happily reported that Facebook accounts for Kessler, who had been using its Messenger feature to plan Unite the Right 2, and several local League of the South chapters, as well as an Instagram account for the Patriot Front were deleted after their "journalists" brought them to the company's attention. Guardian "journalists" also reported to YouTube that some Unite the Right-affiliated people and groups still had functional channels, resulting in a ban for Christopher Cantwell and limitation of features for AltRight.com, Duke, Kessler, Patriot Front, the Rise Above Movement and the Traditionalist Workers Party.[10]

---

9 News2Share, "Jovi Val Speaks out at 'Unite the Right 2,'" YouTube video published Aug. 13, 2018.

10 Julia Carrie Wong, "A year after Charlottesville, why can't big tech delete White supremacists?," *Guardian*, July 25, 2018.

A PayPal account to collect money for Kessler and Cantwell's legal expenses through the California-based Zyniker Law Firm was closed after reports that the funds were being used for other purposes.[11] The Red Ice Channel (run by Lana Lokteff and Henrik Palmgren) and Faith Goldy had their accounts closed by PayPal around the same time.[12]

Val lost his job for his attendance at the rally, and knows others that were doxed and forced to move from their homes. "We lost everything after that... It showed the teeth of this Marxist movement. I'm disgusted by it all. People that claimed to be for free speech denounced us. Nobody deserved what happened to them. Disgruntled Americans can't have a voice without you trying to take everything away from them."

The Reaction

The Unite the Right 2 rally, with its sparse showing against a deluge of protesters, was derided by the mainstream media. "Unite the Right 2018 was a pathetic failure," declared one Vox headline. Citing a counter-protester who left the rally early because "it was kind of boring," the article's author deduced that lawsuits, prosecutions, and doxing stemming from Charlottesville had caused the Alt-Right's leaders to crumble and its supporters to scatter.[13]

Richard Spencer offered his explanation for the anemic attendance to the New York Times. "We [Alt-Righters] are facing so much pushback that people are not in the mood to celebrate." [14]

Afterwards, Wallace summarized the impact of the event.

UTR 2 is officially in the books.

---

11 Luke Barnes, "Struggling White nationalist running out of fundraising options for second 'Unite the Right' rally," ThinkProgress.com, July 28, 2018.

12 Luke Barnes, "3 more prominent far-right accounts get de-platformed by PayPal," ThinkProgress.com, July 23, 2018.

13 German Lopez, "Unite the Right 2018 was a pathetic failure," Vox.com, Aug. 12, 2018.

14 Richard Fausset, "Rally by White Nationalists Was Over Almost Before It Began," New York Times, Aug. 12, 2018.

It went much like I expected it would too... Jason Kessler held what was essentially a small Alt-Lite free speech rally in Washington, DC which was protected by a massive police presence. No one got hurt. There won't be any fallout from this event for the movement.

We knew beforehand that no one was going to UTR 2. The question was whether the DC police would stand down, allow Kessler & Co. to be lynched and we would all be blamed for the violence. There has been a black cloud hanging over the movement since Charlottesville. No one wants to walk into another trap and have their lives ruined because police are prevented from doing their jobs by politicians. The country saw in DC the difference it makes when police are allowed to do their jobs.

I thought Jason Kessler did a great job today explaining why there was violence in Charlottesville. I don't think he could have done a better job given the level of support he got in DC.

Kessler was a Boy Scout compared to his enemies.[15]

Unite the Right 2 was a "triumph" according to Greg Johnson of Counter-Currents. He had tried to dissuade Kessler from holding the event, but to no avail, describing Kessler as "a principled and stubborn guy." However, after the rally took place, Johnson declared it a success. "Unite the Right was a disaster. So repeating Unite the Right was obviously a bad idea. But when the Alt-Right did not show, Unite the Right 2 was no longer a repeat of a bad protest. It became something entirely different. It actually became something good."

Johnson pointed out that the marchers' behavior and arguments appeared quite reasonable compared to those of their leftist opponents, whose violent antics were the focus of most of the media

---

15 Hunter Wallace, "Review: Unite The Right 2," OccidentalDissent.com, Aug. 12, 2018.

coverage. He also explained that the small turnout worked for good, reasoning, "At Unite the Right 2, the police did their jobs, and the vast disparity of numbers made it clear that the purpose of the police was to protect Unite the Right from a raving Leftist mob."[16]

---

16 Greg Johnson, "Unite the Right 2 Couldn't Have Been Better," Counter-Currents.com, Aug. 13, 2018.

CHAPTER 30 QUICK LINKS:

News2Share, "Jason Kessler's Full Speech at 'Unite the Right 2,'" video, Aug. 13, 2018. URL: qrs.ly/chcvtpq

News2Share, "Jovi Val Speaks out at 'Unite the Right 2,'" video, Aug. 13, 2018. URL: qrs.ly/vocvtr4

CHAPTER 31

HINDSIGHT

"I was so naive"

Kessler Reflects On Mistakes

"I THINK THAT I WAS VERY NAIVE about some of the people that I associated with. The event was perceived by the public as totally different from what I was intending. What I was intending was - and I was so naive - was I said that we were gonna have some kind of White civil rights event that was standing up for European American history, standing up for American history, people like Thomas Jefferson and Robert E Lee. And the only people at the time that I felt like were really unapologetically saying it was okay to be White, basically, were these people like Mike Enoch and Richard Spencer, the people that I invited essentially. I didn't take seriously enough the anti-Jewish rhetoric. I felt that stuff was going to go away, that it was more shock, that they were trying to make a point about how the treatment of White people - saying well White people are overrepresented in this category - well what about this group of people? I was totally misguided."

"I tried again and again to tell folks that it's important to focus on being pro-White and not anti-anybody else. And I've seen from that event and from other following events that it's impossible. That you're never going to be able to do it that way, because that tendency is always gonna come out from these folks."[1]

"It was supposed to be about saving American history, you know. On August 11th, we marched to a statue of Thomas Jefferson, and on August 12th we held our rally, or were planning to hold it, at a statue of Robert E. Lee. To advocate for our history, American history but also European American history. And for the ability for White people to define themselves and advocate for themselves. And my vision of it was to have it not be about hating any other group of people but purely to be standing up for ourselves."

"Now I think that obviously the way the rally is portrayed is like totally different from that. And some of that is the problems with some of the people who attended, but it's also there's no way you could ever hold an event like what I'm describing, where the media is gonna say "well these are supporters of American history," or "these are White civil rights people." They're never gonna say that. They're always going to call you a White Nationalist, a Neo-Nazi, a Neo-Confederate, whatever label it is that they're trying to use to demonize you."

"That rally went so differently than what I was expecting. I was expecting to have a "good optics" rally. I was telling people to stay clean, to only be pro-White, to be pro-American history, and yet whatever trolls that were there that strayed off the reservation and were saying things that were more controversial, those were the people that had cameras in their faces. And it all became about that."

"And the violence, which was a result of the police stand down, I mean there's no way. The media just bashes you over the head with that violence stuff, whether or not you were actually to blame for it."[2]

---

1 Kessler Interview, LukeFord.net, Jan. 14, 2021.

2 "Jason Kessler," Podcast on DissidentMama.net.

Kessler believes that with time, the public perception of Unite the Right has somewhat changed for the better. "I think a lot of people's understanding of the event and the context changed after this summer [of 2020]. I think we were vindicated a bit because of how people were gaslighting us over what happened at Unite the Right and the unfortunate violence, but blaming us. And then you saw the Antifa and BLM just like take the level of violence and the length of time that that violence was going on, and the body count to like a new level that it was just epic and historic in proportions, and yet they weren't getting condemned. They weren't facing any consequences. They were having their demands met... And they had the same targets as we warned about at Unite the Right. We were trying to stand up for history, for Robert E Lee and Thomas Jefferson and that was exactly what they were attacking. Basically they started with the Confederacy, they went on to the American founders and they went on to every prominent American or White person throughout history. Even Abe Lincoln, Ulysses Grant, people associated with the Union. It was a horrible thing. And I think a lot of people understood a little bit better the context of what we were trying to do in that event, and how timely it ended up becoming to the national conversation."[3]

Activism Now

Kessler considers himself retired from activism, but much of what he has learned is useful for people who still want to be involved.

"So I think the civil rights approach is right and I think that if we live in a society where all these different identity groups are able to advocate for themselves, then we have to find a healthy way for White people to advocate for ourselves. You're not talking about White supremacy; you're talking about the supremacy of other groups that just dominate White people so that they don't have a voice in the conversation."

"The Unite the Right rally for me was supposed to be an event to help address some of those issues. It was supposed to be a pro-White civil rights event that incorporated different elements of

3 Kessler Interview, LukeFord.net, Jan. 14, 2021.

the right as I saw it right after the Trump election. It was supposed to have MAGA people, Alt-Lite people, and Alt-Right people. And the reason that I wanted to include all of those groups was because I think that they all saw a changing America, the fact that our history was being attacked. At that time, in Charlottesville was the Confederate statues, Stonewall Jackson and Robert E Lee, but also we were clearly anticipating that that was gonna happen to other European American figures like the Founding Fathers."

"So I saw a lot of promise in MAGA to be able to address these issues, but they still weren't comfortable saying 'White,' you know, so Trump would come out and say, "the lowest Black unemployment, and we have this many Hispanic supporters, but he wouldn't say White, and I thought that that was really holding us back, and something that we really needed to evolve our mindset on. So, the Alt-Right were comfortable with that, and that was why I invited them."[4]

"I think with regards to like dealing with the potential for Antifa violence, at the time I think folks were looking at it like self-defense is the operative term. Because people, I mean look - no one wanted to strike first, but there were a lot of fights going around places like Berkeley or wherever, and people got attacked by Antifa and they're ready to fight back if you give them a lawful reason to do so. But I think that that's always going to be taken out of context. You're never going to be seen as the righteous person if you're a right-wing dissident, if you express pro-White views in any way. I think that total nonviolence is the only approach. That's something that not everybody is going to be able to commit to. People who are unable to commit to total nonviolence, I would advise to not even do these things, because it will turn into a trap for you. It will turn into a legal trap, and folks are seeing that in DC right now. Even people who are non-violent, you know, are being sucked into this thing because of the small minority of people who were... Also if you're doing anything, go with people you trust, who know you better. Because in this political stuff, everybody is such a treacherous asshole, a backstabber... And you've gotta have solidarity among

---

4 "Jason Kessler," Podcast on DissidentMama.net.

people. You've gotta have people to have your back. Because if it goes wrong you don't want everybody turning on each other." [5]

"So I think from a certain perspective, everything's a honeypot, everything is a psyop when it comes to right-wing activism. If you're on social media group there are people who are watching you, the Antifa are there, the tattletales who are sending info to the Feds, and they work hand in hand with one another. And not just illegal activity which is a different thing. We're talking about disrupting political organizing which is protected by the First Amendment. And every event that you could possibly go to, if the left decides that they want to turn it into an op, they want their media people to come in and really destroy the people involved with it, they're gonna do that. And they can take any set of facts to bolster that narrative. It could've been somebody getting shoved or something and turn it into domestic terrorism. There could have been no fatalities, they could've called it domestic terrorism on Jan 6."

"Personally I think people should still do activism for the thing that they believe in but that should always be a part of the calculus when you're deciding your event - that this is going to be set up by the media and there's nothing you can do about that. And a big problem with the American right is that they 're terrible at dealing with that. What they do is point fingers at each other... They're terrible at supporting one another. It really is going to take divine intervention or deus ex machina to deal with this situation. It's really bad... It's really counterproductive and you have to let go of that stuff. I think the key is to be totally lawful, to embrace non-violence and to love one another. That might be where the Christian aspect comes into it because I think having some kind of godly principle is going to make it easier to love your brothers and sisters. I think that's really what's missing."[6]

Asked how his views have changed since Unite the Right, Kessler says, "I think I'm more disaffected, more disillusioned. I feel like I was totally conned by Trump. And I don't support any politicians anymore. In fact I don't think democracy is working out

5 Kessler Interview, LukeFord.net, Jan. 14, 2021.

6 "Jason Kessler," Podcast on DissidentMama.net.

for us right now. Not that it's not a noble idea, but I think it requires a unified culture... I'm really disaffected with the whole White identity political scene. Not that I don't feel that White people are being poorly treated. I'm desperate to find a movement that will be able to stand up for White people without scapegoating others. I just don't see that right now."

"In my daily life, I'm ready to move on. This whole political thing, this social media thing, is poisonous in a lot of ways."[7]

---

7   Kessler Interview, LukeFord.net, Jan. 14, 2021.

CHAPTER 31 QUICK LINKS:

 "Were the Capitol Hill Riots Charlottesville II? A Jason Kessler Interview," LukeFord.net, Jan. 14, 2021. URL: qrs.ly/e1cvtdi

 "Dissident Mama, episode 27 – Jason Kessler," Jan. 22, 2021. URL: qrs. ly/cycvto9

CHAPTER 32

THE ROAD AHEAD

"I'm ready to fight this thing"

REFLECTING UPON HIS ROLE in Unite the Right, Kessler replies, "Mostly it makes me angry. There are times when I feel both love and hate. I feel like I'm innocent and I'm driven, I'm very passionate to exonerate myself. I think initially I was more hesitant about expending the resources to vindicate myself, and now I see how important this is, not only for myself, but for the historical context. And I think that this is a worthy cause because, even though it's got this private dimension for me personally, it is having enormous ramifications on our national conversation, on free speech and civil liberties, and I think a lot of times I have more a Zen approach to it. So much time has gone on [with regards to the lawsuit], you don't think, you just do it. And that's where I'm at. I come up with ideas ... I'm ready to fight this thing and I'm looking forward to having my day in court."

Asked what he has learned about himself, Kessler replies, "I'm becoming more of a man than I ever was before. I see a lot more of my grandfather in me. I've learned to work a lot harder because I'm the underdog, but I believe I'm in the right, so I've embraced more of my working class spirit and I've tried to be humble and fight for every inch. I've just become a more responsible, well-rounded person. I think I've been humbled. Maybe I took on some of the negative elements of the Trump era in 2017, being over the top, too full of myself, and I've been appropriately humbled since then.

Kessler reflects on how he's changed spiritually since the events of August 2017. "I think I've become more spiritual. I pray more now. And I do believe in Divine Intervention in things. I think God will have a plan. I think that it was right for me to be humbled. I don't think I need to be the champion or the victor in everything, but I think that in the end, God has an interest in vindicating falsely accused people. And for the truth to come out. I'm praying that's the case."[1]

Whether in this life or the next, the truth will certainly come out and the innocent parties will be vindicated.

Deo Vindice.

---

1   Kessler Interview, LukeFord.net, Jan. 14, 2021.

CHAPTER 32 SOURCE LINKS:

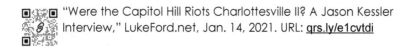 "Were the Capitol Hill Riots Charlottesville II? A Jason Kessler Interview," LukeFord.net, Jan. 14, 2021. URL: qrs.ly/e1cvtdi

ABOUT THE AUTHOR

ANNE WILSON SMITH is the author of *Robert E. Lee: A Biography for Kids*, published by Shotwell.

CPSIA information can be obtained
at www.ICGtesting.com
Printed in the USA
BVHW041433141021
618951BV00015B/497

9 781947 660588